BIOTERRORISM
Disguisting Face of Future

BIOTERRORISM
Disguisting Face of Future

Dr. Abhay Kumar Shrivastava

MD Publications Pvt Ltd
New Delhi
www.mdppl.com

Published by :

MD Publications Pvt Ltd
"MD House", 11, Darya Ganj,
New Delhi - 110 002
Phone : +91-11-41563325 (Customer Service)
+91-11-41562846 (Editorial)
E-mail (orders): order@mdppl.com
Website: www.mdppl.com

ISBN: 978-81-7533-218-8

Published and Printed by Mr. Pranav Gupta on behalf of **MD Publications Pvt Ltd** at Mohit Enterprises, Delhi.

PREFACE

With the end of the Cold War, the proliferation of weapons of mass destruction (nuclear, biological, and chemical) replaced the U.S.-Soviet nuclear standoff as the dominant U.S. security concern. Chemical and biological weapons (CBW) proliferation and the potential use of these weapons by terrorists deserve particular attention, as CBW capabilities have been confirmed or suspected in some 20 nations.

Biological weapons include any organism (such as bacteria, viruses, or fungi) or toxin found in nature that can be used to kill or injure people.The act of bioterrorism can range from a simple hoax to the actual use of these biological weapons, also referred to as agents. A number of nations have or are seeking to acquire biological warfare agents, and there are concerns that terrorist groups or individuals may acquire the technologies and expertise to use these destructive agents. Biological agents may be used for an isolated assassination, as well as to cause incapacitation or death to thousands. If the environment is contaminated, a long-term threat to the population could be created.

The anthrax mailings to journalists and members of Congress in 2001 drove home the reality of the bioterrorist threat to U.S. citizens, though evidence of global CBW threats had been mounting for several years. Revelations about the size and sophistication of Iraq's CBW programs in the summer of 1995 provided a disturbing reminder of how advanced such programs can become while avoiding international attention. Iraq's use of chemical weapons in the Iran-Iraq War (1980-88) and Aum Shinrikyo's use of sarin gas in the Tokyo subway on March 20, 1995 suggest that inhibitions on CBW use are not as strong as one might like.

I am very grateful to Mr. Pranav Gupta, Director of MD Publications Pvt Ltd, New Delhi, for his cooperation and support for this book.

Dr. Abhay Kumar Shrivastava

Contents

1

Bioterrorism

An Introduction

Biological pathogens (for example, anthrax bacteria or the smallpox virus) or toxins produced by biological organisms (for example, botulinus toxin or staphenterotoxin) that are released intentionally or accidentally—or that occur naturally—can result in disease, fear, disruption to society, economic harm, diminished confidence in public and private institutions, and large-scale loss of life. People or livestock can be exposed to these agents from inhalation, through the skin, or by the ingestion of contaminated food, feed, or water.

After exposure to a pathogen or toxin used as a biological weapon, physical symptoms can be delayed and prove difficult to distinguish from naturally occurring illnesses. Similarly, crops can be exposed to biological weapons in several ways—at the seed stage, in the field, or after harvest.

The deciphering of the human genome sequence and elucidation of the complete genomes of many pathogens, the rapidly increasing knowledge of the molecular mechanisms of pathogenesis and of immune responses, and the development of new strategies for designing drugs and vaccines offer unprecedented opportunities for using science to counter bioterrorist threats. But these advances also allow science to be misused to create new agents of mass destruction. Two kinds of biological terrorist threats must be envisioned. The first is the release of communicable infectious agents—like smallpox, Ebola, or foot-and-mouth disease—that can spread rapidly within communities and farmland through contact and have the potential, as does influenza, to spread around the world and cause epidemics.

The second kind of threat consists of biological agents that may cause disease or death in individuals but generally may not be transmitted between individuals—the most familiar example being anthrax. In either case, some agents may persist in the environment, as do anthrax spores, and continue to cause problems long after their release. In addition to naturally occurring pathogens, biological agents used offensively can be genetically engineered to resist current therapies and evade vaccine-induced immunity. Though it is vital that the molecular mechanisms by which classes of organisms cause disease (pathogenesis) be elucidated in order to understand and counter their effects, this is no simple matter. Preparedness for a biological attack against people, crops, or livestock is complicated by the large number of potential agents, the long incubation periods of some agents, and their potential for secondary transmission. Biological agents do not need to be weaponized for effective dissemination.

Deliberate contamination of food looms as perhaps the easiest method, despite the recent focus on release of these agents as small-particle aerosols or volatile liquids. Moreover, because of its size and complexity, the U.S. food and agriculture system is vulnerable to deliberate attacks, particularly with foreign diseases that do not now occur domestically. Even without actual attack, plausible threats to infect populations or poison the food supply could, in and of themselves, damage the U.S. economy and reduce public confidence in the government's ability to safeguard health and security. Recent experiences with the West Nile virus and anthrax spores in the United States, and with foot-and-mouth disease in the United Kingdom, offer practical lessons in human and agricultural outbreak detection, laboratory diagnosis, investigation, and response that might be useful in planning for future attacks involving biological terrorism.

The experience with the West Nile virus outbreak highlighted the importance of communication and coordination between responding agencies. The GAO study noted that although the system worked, there were several obvious places for improvement. A single alert physician at a local hospital initiated the investigation early enough that an effective intervention was possible before the outbreak became widespread, but the investigation subsequently found many other cases, which were either not properly diagnosed or not reported to the health department. The GAO report concluded that much more systematic surveillance and reporting at the local level are needed. Similarly, improved communication among public health agencies, including those dealing with animal health, is needed. Increased laboratory capacity will also be important to an efficient and effective response to disease outbreaks (at first only one public health laboratory in the country was equipped to diagnose West Nile virus) (IOM, 2002). Moreover, these Events raise vexing concerns about how many outbreaks could be managed at one time. The attacks of September 11, 2001, and the intentional release of anthrax spores shortly afterward also revealed vulnerabilities that are the results of long-term declines in the nation's public health and agricultural infrastructures.

The decline in the U.S. public health system is the result of its systematic dismantling over time by Congress and the executive branch. In fact, the response of the Centers for Disease Control and Prevention (CDC) to the anthrax attacks was admirable given its limited resources and outdated communications system. CDC, together with state and local health departments, has provided this nation with an outstanding cadre of people who understand how to perform surveillance, prevention, and detection of infectious agents, whether they are endemic, emerging, or a result of bioterrorism. These agencies must be supplied with the tools and resources taken away from them in the past. Restoring the public health system of the United States should be the first order of business in the efforts to defend the nation against bioterrorism.

Approaches with Multiple Benefits

Bioterrorism poses a unique challenge to the security of the U.S. population. A state-sponsored enterprise, or just a few individuals with specialized scientific skills and access to a laboratory, could easily and inexpensively produce panoply of lethal biological weapons, although it is no trivial matter to disseminate or disperse such agents across large populations. Such operations may be difficult to detect because, in contrast to nuclear weapons, biological agents can be manufactured with ordinary pieces of equipment that are listed in commercial catalogues and are legitimately purchased for producing such things as chemicals, pharmaceuticals, or even beer.

Fortunately, investments made to protect the country against bioterrorism will help protect the public's health and the U.S. food supply from naturally occurring threats as well. Although it may be difficult to distinguish an introduced infectious disease from a naturally occurring one, the strategies to protect against either—requiring preparation and new scientific and technological approaches to surveillance, prevention, response, recovery, decontamination, and forensics—must be the same.

Similarly, investments made to protect the country's food supply against bioterrorism have the potential, and are even necessary, to protect it from more routine threats as well. Because the most likely breakthroughs will come from the study of both pathogenic and nonpathogenic bacteria and viruses, they should be studied together—indeed, the study of bioterrorism agents alone is likely to give a low return on investment. There are also indirect benefits associated with investments in protecting ourselves from bioterrorism. Money spent on research to develop new types of sensitive detectors and related monitors for biowarfare agents will almost certainly carry over to the public health sector in the form of rapid, improved diagnostics for disease. Money spent on coordinating and developing emergency response teams at the federal, state, and local levels will also bring better mechanisms for dealing with natural outbreaks of emerging diseases. Money spent on vaccine research and delivery may help to buttress our limited capacity to protect civilian and military populations.

Changing Research Paradigm

While this report was being prepared, the National Institute for Allergy and Infectious Diseases (NIAID) released a bioterrorism research agenda for rapidly addressing the most threatening biological agents (NIAID, 2002). Though important and commendable, this agenda lacks several major components—such as surveillance strategies, epidemiology of transmission, and the entire range of agricultural threats—needed for a comprehensive plan to counter bioterrorism. Consideration must also be given to preparing for still-uncharacterized threats and to assuring investment in long-term, broad-range strategies. These gaps must be filled, where not appropriate for NIAID action, by other federal agencies.

CDC is the logical place for surveillance efforts, given its expertise, and therefore it will require additional resources. NIAID's expanded role in bioterrorism research demands a focused effort to coordinate activities with other agencies—CDC, the Department of Defense (DOD), the Department of Energy (DOE), the Environmental Protection Agency (EPA), the U.S. Department of

Agriculture (USDA), and the very recently proposed new Department of Homeland Security, for example.

All of the governmental entities must seek expertise from private organizations, such as industry and professional societies with relevant expertise, for example, the Infectious Diseases Society of America and the American Society for Microbiology. It also demands that NIAID's parent, the National Institutes of Health (NIH), find new mechanisms to fund research in this area, particularly for taking on long-range, highly managed, higher-risk projects and for moving the research at a faster pace. Likewise, CDC's role is critical to the nation's preparedness, but it must have the resources to improve its focus, strengthen its extramural capacity, and extend its international collaborations. National security also depends on public-private sector cooperation and communication and on an increased willingness to collaborate.

This is organized into three chapters:

- Intelligence, surveillance,
- Prevention, response, and recovery; and
- Policy and implementation followed by concluding remarks. Each chapter describes the desired capabilities that could soon exist through better application of existing science and technology (and that might therefore have a near-term payoff) as well as desired capabilities that cannot now be provided through existing science and technology (S&T) but might be available in the future, given longer-term research and possibly more innovative funding and organizational approaches. The report focuses on research needs related to both human and agricultural health. Many of the recommendations apply equally to both areas while others are specific to one area or the other. In general, recommendations focus on R&D goals or organizational goals. The report concludes with

recommendations about education and information dissemination, strengthening the public health and agriculture infrastructures, and organizing the research and development effort through improved policies, new funding models, and public–private partnerships.

Art or Bioterrorism

One spring morning, Professor Steven Kurtz of the State University of New York (SUNY), Buffalo campus, woke to the horrid discovery that his wife of 20 years had died overnight from a cardiac arrest. He called 9-1-1. Paramedics arriving at the Kurtz home noticed technical equipment that would normally only be found in a laboratory. If the emergency responders had not been suspicious and reacted, it would have been worrisome, particularly given the unexpected death. What happened later - the investigation of Kurtz and colleagues by the Department of Justice and the Federal Bureau of Investigation's (FBI's) Joint Task Force on Terrorism under bioterrorism statues - may have more worrisome implications.

Professor Kurtz is a founding member of the Critical Arts Ensemble (CAE). CAE is a multi-media, artist collective exploring the political and social implications of science, particularly biotechnology, on people and for people who aren't scientists. Many of the CAE productions are theatrical in nature. One current project is intended to evoke dialogue regarding the historical and modern roles of the United States in biological warfare (BW). As part of a mock "anthrax" attack, the CAE uses BW simulants - some of the same microbes that the U.S. military used for testing the dispersal and spread of BW agents. Some of these simulations were done over civilian areas. Among the materials seized from Kurtz's home were unspecified books on BW, books which had been incorporated in the CAE's "The Marching Plague" project.

Neither Kurtz nor the CAE is the first to incorporate biotechnology or even transgenics into art. Chicago-artist Eduardo Kac caused something of a stir in 2000 when he announced the creation of Alba - a green fluorescent bunny. Kac's transgenic artwork involved the insertion of a gene isolated from jellyfish, for the green fluorescent protein (GFP), into the rabbit's DNA. MIT's Joe Davis actually preceded Kurtz and Kac in pursuing the interplay between genetic engineering and art. But his work, like *E. coli* engineered with an iconic image encoded into the bacteria's DNA, is considerably less tactile. Other artists to explore biotechnology include Lauri Cinto, who has claimed to create a cactus that grows human hair, and Marta de Meneze, artist-in-residence at Imperial College in London, who uses modern biology techniques to manipulate developing butterflies that display unnatural "artistic" wing patterns.

The Agents

The three agents found in Kurtz's home, *Bacillus atrophaeus, Serratia marcescens* and a nonpathogenic variant of endogenous *E. coli,* do not appear on any select agent list. All of the microbes are considered suitable for manipulation under the lowest level Biosafety standards. These microbes are the types found in high school and freshman college biology laboratories, even some middle school laboratories. The New York State Health Department acknowledged that the microbes found at the Kurtz home "posed no health risk in or around the house."

One of the agents, *S. marcescens,* is a classic BW simulant. Used as model organisms in place of more lethal biological agents, simulants are non-pathogenic microbes or biological substitutes. Between September 1950 and February 1951, aerosolized *S. marcescens* ("SM" in U.S. military code) was intentionally released from offshore U.S. Navy vessels in the San Francisco Bay and spread over the inland San Francisco area to test the effectiveness of novel dispersal methods. The simulant was successfully disseminated and tracked. It later was implicated in the death of one man and the hospitalization of 10 men and woman.

Though the cause of this particular outbreak has never been conclusively linked to the BW simulations, *S. marcescens* is now known to be a human pathogen responsible for a significant percentage of nosocomial (i.e., hospital-acquired) infections. Kurtz wanted to use *S. marcescens* for the same reason that the former U.S. offensive biological weapons program did - it has a bright red-pink color that is easy to track making the determination of its successful spread simple and straightforward, whether used as a true BW dispersal simulation or part of a performance art project. Kurtz received the samples from Professor Robert Ferrell, chair of the University of Pittsburgh's Human Genetics Department within the Graduate School of Public Health.

When Kurtz became aware that *S. marcescens* has been rarely associated with pneumonia and urinary tract infections, he wrote to Ferrell asking for "any other ideas on another bacterium [sic] that can travel by air and be easily identified on a pertri [sic] dish, and-most importantly, is unequivocally classified as nonpathogenic?" Kurtz was clearly concerned with using bacteria that would not harm himself or anyone in a CAE project audience. The non-pathogenic *E. coli* recovered from Kurtz's home was part of a two-year-old performance art project that toured across the nation. There was no subterfuge or attempt to conceal what was being attempted by any of the CAE members.

Concern for public safety was cited as a major factor prompting investigation. This is a legitimate reaction. Supporters of Kurtz recognize and accept this public health need. Even the CAE Legal Defense Fund spokesman, Greg

Bardowitz, has acknowledged that the initial circumstances "were enough to warrant a full investigation." Claire Pentecost of the School of the Art Institute of Chicago and past collaborator on CAE projects agreed. "I think it was reasonable for them to look into it when they first saw the equipment in someone's house."

The Legal Case

The original search warrant and subpoenas issued to Kurtz and eight art colleagues by the FBI's Joint Terrorism Task Force referred to the portion of the U.S. Biological Weapons Anti-Terrorism Act of 1989 dealing with prohibitions on possessing "any biological agent, toxin, or delivery system of a type or in a quantity that, under circumstances, is not reasonably justified by a prophylactic, protective, bona fide research, or other peaceful purpose." It is that last part - for other peaceful purpose - that CAE supporters from art and science see covering Kurtz's activities. Richard Mears, University of Maine professor of criminal justice commented that "the real issue is what his intent was."

Eventually, Kurtz was not charged under bioterrorism laws but was indicted on two counts of mail fraud and two counts of wire fraud for each of two bacterial cultures found in his home, *S. marcescens* and *B. atrophaeus*, which had been obtained from the American Type Culture Collection (ATCC). His wife's death was determined to be from natural causes, nothing related to the bacteria found in their home. Indicted along with Kurtz was Professor Robert Ferrell, who gave Kurtz the ATCC samples. Recipients of ATCC products are prohibited, by contract, from redistributing any microbiological samples purchased.

According to the indictment basically Kurtz is charged with not being a properly registered customer with the ATCC - which he wasn't. He did apparently submit an application to become a registered customer, but it was denied due to his improvised facilities and lack of established biosafety protocols. Ferrell is charged with ordering with intent to transfer material to Kurtz and with the transfer of the ATCC-supplied material in violation of the letter of the contract he signed - which he did. At this writing, the case has not gone to trial. Questions about the after-effects of the investigation and indictment are already surfacing.

The main issue is whether this case will discourage those contemplating work that might bring similar scrutiny. The question of a "chilling effect" is probably less critical for iconoclastic artists than researchers seeking tenure track positions or National Institutes of Health grant renewals. In direct response to the Kurtz case and after questioning by the FBI, Professor Adele Henderson, chair of the SUNY-Buffalo art department, commented "this is a free speech issue, and some people at the university remember a time during the McCarthy period when some university professors were harassed quite badly." This cooling enthusiasm, however, can be read in the skeptical words of Steven Teitelbaum, President of the Federation of American Societies for Experimental Biology: "Bureaucracies want to justify their existence. They tend to be overzealous."Teitelbaum speculated that scientists will not pursue research that attracts "such negative scrutiny."

The Kurtz investigation follows two other academic cases with bioterrorism overtones. University of Connecticut graduate student Tomas Foral was convicted of possession of anthrax-containing tissue. Texas Tech University Health Sciences Center Professor Thomas Butler, like Kurtz and Ferrell was charged with mail and wire fraud along with more serious accusations relating to illegal payments from major pharmaceutical firms; he was convicted. These cases further illustrate the tough stance that the Justice Department is taking toward allegations that even hint at bioterrorism or the involvement of select agents. These two legal actions involved practicing academic researchers - one just starting a technical career and the other a highly respected expert on *Yersinia pestis* (the causative agent of the plague and high on the select agent list).

The Kurtz case pulled in a bioscientist, University of Pittsburgh's Ferrell. Before moving to SUNY-Buffalo, Kurtz had taught at Carnegie Mellon University, also located in Pittsburgh. Allegedly Ferrell obtained microbes from the ATCC then transferred them - apparently as a collegial gift - to Kurtz. Rarely have academics been charged for exchange of samples. Small samples are regularly shared domestically and internationally by life and physical scientists. Much such collaboration has existed for a decade or more. Some of these may be formalized in grant proposals or coauthorships in technical papers, but more often the exchange is noted in acknowledging footnotes to a manuscript. Typically it is considered part of the academic culture or, more realistically, done with the expectation that in the future there will be a return of assistance in some manner.

On the bench-side, researchers with historical access to agents for legitimate purposes cannot return to the old way of thinking or behaving. The research culture is struggling to catch-up to the legal culture. Attitudes and boundaries on biotechnical research have changed. Scientists need to understand and internalize the reality that there are no longer *pro forma*-style regulations that can just be checked off or initialed without considerable fore- and after-thought. This applies to both the choice of research - what agents might be involved and repercussions for terrorist use - and how research and sharing of samples will be done. Casual exchange of materials for legitimate research endeavors among colleagues who have known each other for years or decades - from cell lines to mutants (transgenic organisms) to DNA sequences - cannot be done without considering implications regarding bioterrorism and the associated U.S. statutes. The scientific culture has to change to keep up with the Justice Department's shift in focus.

Reactive prosecution is one route that can be taken to accomplish this culture change. Another, path is via pro-active education of the scientific community on the risks and new responsibilities of biotechnology research in an age of terrorism. The Federation of Atomic Scientists (FAS) recently launched a pilot program, "Biosecurity for Biologists," to promote awareness of security issues among undergraduate- and graduate-level biologists at Research institutions. Academics need to participate in meaningful dialogue to implement policies and protocols from within their ranks. If scientists ignore the ways research culture might need to be systematically altered or react purely defensively to an enjoinder to their scientific or proprietary territory, a regulatory policy will develop and be implemented from outside the scientific and technical community.

Alternatively, federal investigations of scientists might proliferate. More bridges need to be built and fortified between technically trained individuals, especially those with recent experience in the modern research setting, and those instrumental in policy development and implementation, on the national and international stage. It is notable that all three of these cases - Kurtz, Butler, and Foral - have focused on individuals engaged in academics, from art to molecular biology. We haven't seen any publicized investigations of behaviour in violation of bioterrorism prevention statutes directed toward private industry.

There is another "chilling effect" to be considered in the fallout from the Kurtz case. The seriousness devoted to bioterrorism investigations risks being diluted to the level of white powder "anthrax" scares. While law enforcement must react to every case, the greater public's response is quickly numbed. As an *LA Times* editorialist wrote "the effort to paint Kurtz as a bioterrorist in the making would be funny if it wasn't so frightening." It is a legitimate question to ask how this case contributes to securing the nation from a bioterrorist attack. In the end, Kurtz and Ferrell have been charged with mail fraud. The individual or individuals responsible for the fall 2001 anthrax deaths have not been identified or caught to be charged with anything. Preventing another bioterrorist attack is a very serious matter. By comparison mail fraud is not.

The Kurtz case may also be valuable in terms of assessing the capability of non-technically trained individuals to generate an air-dispersed microbiological. How good of a job did the CAE artists do in making their anthrax simulants? Much of the argument surrounding the fall 2001 mailings of anthrax-spore containing envelopes has revolved around the question of expertise required to produce the weaponized agents that resulted in five deaths. How successful was the CAE at creating a free-flowing, micron-sized powder? What did they try? And what resources did they find that led them to pursue those choices? These are all legitimate questions that can provide information for construction of empirical models of behaviour as part of threat anticipation and reduction. From a technical security studies perspective, there is an edifying aspect regarding how successful a group of non-technically-inclined individuals can be without any malicious intent.

In the late 1990s, the Defense Threat Reduction Agency (DTRA) sponsored a project that attempted to assemble a make-shift laboratory to produce weaponized *Bacillus anthracis* (the causative agent of anthrax) in Nevada. It was called Project Bacchus. How does CAE compare to Project Bacchus? The comparison should provide useful information in distinguishing a makeshift BW production facility from improvised biotechnology for peaceful purposes. What critical differences distinguish the two experimental set-ups? Most of these answers can only be evaluated by someone with access to both the DTRA exercise and the FBI investigation. This is a further example of the need for interaction across traditional boundaries in the fight against bioterrorism, against co-option of legitimate research for malicious purposes and in protection of the civil liberties that underlie America's freedom.

A June editorial in the pre-eminent British science journal, *Nature,* encouraged scientists to support Kurtz, noting that "art and science are forms of human enquiry that can be illuminating and controversial, and the freedoms of both must be preserved as part of a healthy democracy - as must a sense of proportion." In the war against terrorism, neither art or science, nor democracy should be an unintended casualty.

2

Terrorist Motivations for Chemical and Biological Weapons Use

Current popular attention being paid to the threat of chemical and biological weapons (CBW) use by terrorists may give the impression that this is a new phenomenon, but it is not. Most chemical and biological weapons themselves have a long history; the first chemical weapons were used in ancient Greece; biological weapons have been used in a wartime context since at least the middle Ages.

Employed extensively in the First World War, notably in the use of mustard gas, chemical weapons have evolved very little in their technology since the mid-twentieth century. Although recent technological advances in biological weapons have been made, the vaccines and treatments available to deal with some of them have also advanced. Historically, most terrorist groups have avoided using CBW, in part because they do not want to alienate their own constituencies, and in part because they have not had the technical expertise to turn them into effective weapons.

Those CBWattacks that have occurred represent a small proportion of the total number of international terrorist incidents. CBW weapons have rarely been used by subnational groups but there is growing concern that past patterns of use could be about to change. Many experts worry about the increasing availability of CBW in the last decade or so, combined with the serious psychological impact that their use would have. This concern was heightened after 1995, when the Japanese terrorist organization Aum Shinrikyo used the chemical nerve agent sarin on the Tokyo subway, killing 12 people and injuring up to 6,000. The group's efforts, which fell far short of its goals, attracted widespread attention and helped increase focus on the so-called weapons of mass destruction (WMD) terrorist threat. While there is considerable information about state acquisition and/or use of CBW, evidence regarding non state acquisition and/or use is contradictory and often sketchy.

Although hard evidence is limited, a sampling of terrorist groups or individuals that are reported to have shown an interest in or used chem-bio agents (usually in very limited ways) includes the PKK (Kurdistan Worker's Party), believed to have weaponized the nerve gas sarin; HAMAS (Islamic Resistance Movement), which has reportedly coated shrapnel with poisons and pesticides; numerous U.S. domestic individuals and groups without foreign connections (including the Minnesota Patriots Council, the so-called "Alphabet Bomber," R.I.S.E., Larry Wayne Harris, and others) who have used or intended to use ricin, plague, anthrax, hydrogen cyanide, sarin, and other agents; and of course Al Qaeda and its associated groups. But the efforts of Aum Shinrikyo represented a watershed, with its bizarre and seemingly irrational agenda, its systematic pursuit of technical competency, and its repeated attempts to kill a large number of Japanese civilians.

Even with its multiple technical failures, Aum Shinrikyo led to heightened anxiety about the attractiveness and feasibility of future mass casualty terrorist use of CBW.

Still, numerical trends for CBW attacks have not increased. According to the Monterey Institute of International Studies' terrorism chronology, between 2000 and 2001 (the last year for which published data are available), the number of hoaxes went up (from 25 to 603) but the number of CBW incidents actually decreased (from 48 to 25). Thus it would appear that the fall 2001 anthrax attacks in the United States resulted in numerous copy-cat hoaxes, but they did not reflect an overall increase in bio terrorism events. However, terrorism experts continue to worry about the use of chemical and biological agents.

Possible Reasons for Increased Terrorist

The reasons for increased potential use can be grouped into four major categories: the growth of militant religious groups with political agendas as a percentage of all terrorist groups, the increasing global availability of CBW information and stockpiles, the internationalization of the threat of terrorism, and the clear evidence of terrorist interest and capabilities. First, there has been a sharp increase in militant religious groups internationally as a percentage of all terrorist groups. Over the last years of the twentieth century, such groups went from being just over three percent of all identified terrorist groups in 1980 to forty-three percent by 1995. Militant religious terrorists, experts note, may label their victims as heretics or infidels and thus unfit to live.

The incentives for such groups to kill large numbers of people may thus be unconstrained by the scruples of earthly constituencies. In combination with this worrisome development, the lethality per terrorist attack went up over the course of the past decade. While there were fewer attacks overall in the 1990s, the number of people killed and maimed per attack increased. This confirmed the fear of many experts that terrorism based on extreme religious beliefs, in association with other developments discussed below, might beeven more dangerous than were the left wing, right wing, and ethno nationalist/separatist groups that predominated in earlier years.

A larger proportion of the attacks that did occur were executed by persons with religion-based animus. The tragedies of September 11th seemed to bear out both of these trends. Second, there is a growing concern about the increasing availability of information and resources for the building of weapons by sub national groups that in former years had been feasible only with the resources of a state. Like the rest of the world, terrorist groups have access to the vast amount of technical data disseminated through the Internet. More and more information that might previously have been difficult to collect is becoming easily accessible.

Among the groups that have reportedly demonstrated interest in acquiring unconventional weapons (besides Al Qaeda) are the PLO, the Red Army Faction, Hezbollah, the Kurdistan Workers' Party, German neo-Nazis, and the Chechens. At the same time, the breakup of the Soviet Union increased potential access to a vast, highly advanced arsenal of not only nuclear but also chemical and biological weapons and expertise. The combination of greater movement of people, knowledge and products across borders in a globalized world, and greater availability of materials and expertise in the post-Soviet era, have together led to a potentially serious erosion in state control over chemical and biological weapons (or their ingredients). Third, the nature of international terrorism has evolved in dangerous ways in recent years.

Although many traditional groups carryon in their struggles, the growth of religiously-oriented groups has led to an increased commonality of interests between populations in disparate geographical areas. In part in reaction to American global policies and cultural as well as political global reach, groups are developing ties across formerly divisive ideological, ethnic, and national lines. The area of potential recruits is thus broader than it might have been for a traditional ethno nationalist/separatist group supported only by its local constituency, for example. Also, this internationalization of the threat has often led to a greater distance between groups and targets.

The result is not only a removal of moral constraints but also political constraints, with less worry about potentially sullying a homeland or killing potential constituents. Thus, the internationalization of terrorism may unfortunately imply an increase in just the sorts of incentives that lead groups to consider unconventional weapons. Fourth, and perhaps most important, there are clear indications of interest in CBW on the part of contemporary terrorist groups, as well as some evidence of actual capabilities. With a long-standing expressed desire to acquire them and a demonstrated willingness to kill Americans, Al Qaeda (and its associates) is the group that most worries U.S. experts. Osama bin Laden has reportedly pursued the development of chemical and biological weapons since the early 1990s.

In 1998, he spoke of acquiring weapons of mass destruction being a "religious duty," and the eleventh volume of Al Qaeda's 5,000-page "Encyclopedia of Jihad" is devoted to explaining how to construct CBW. There are many substantiated examples in the open press of efforts by Al Qaeda and its allies to develop these weapons.

During operations in Afghanistan, coalition forces found trace amounts of ricin and anthrax at five or six sites, as well as evidence of an interest in plague, cyanide, and botulinum toxin. In December 2001, CNN obtained a cache of 64 Al Qaeda video tapes containing gruesome evidence of experiments using an apparent nerve gas against dogs. Further afield, in 2002 a reported plot by nine Moroccans to use a cyanide compound to poison the water supply of the U.S. Embassy in Rome was disrupted; several of the men involved had ties to Al Qaeda. In January 2003, a reported plot by six Algerians to use ricin was uncovered in a London apartment. One of the six arrested had attended Al Qaeda training camps, whereas the others had received training in Chechnya and the Pankisi Gorge region of Georgia. Most recently, evidence seized in March 2003 with the arrest of operations chief Khalid Shaikh Mohammed demonstrated surprising technical sophistication, with production timetables and manufacturing specifications for bio-chemical agents, especially weaponized anthrax. In addition to these highly publicized examples, there are many other press reports of varying reliability.

It is hard to know with confidence what the logic of this apparently growing interest in CBW is. If high casualties are the intended end, these agents are not the most effective means: chem-bio agents are generally more useful for increasing anxiety and panic than causing high numbers of casualties. Projections of tens of thousands of casualties are theoretically possible, but many such estimates are worst-case scenarios likely to occur in hard-to-achieve circumstances, with ideal weather conditions, temperature controls, dispersion rates, concentrations of agent, and so on. Still, terrorism is a psychological weapon, intended for political effect. The goal might instead be to cause economic damage, or to show strength and increase political support or leverage, or to copy other terrorist groups, or to emulate the technological capabilities of states–or some combination of these. While this is a fine line to draw, there is a danger that Western governments might overstate and hype the threat, leading to some of the same outcomes by heightening anxieties.

Possible Reasons against Terrorist Use

There are at least four reasons why terrorist groups like Al Qaeda might avoid using chem-bio agents in attacks against the United States and its interests. First and most important, the technical difficulties in carrying out such attacks continue to be significant. Aum Shinrikyo is a good example of a group that had unusually favorable circumstances for producing chemical and biological weapons, including money, facilities, time and expertise, yet they were unable to do so effectively. Some experts argue that Aum Shinrikyo's experience, which included problems ranging from obtaining biological seed cultures to effectively disseminating them to chemical leaks and accidents, is as easily a warning of the technical challenges involved as it is an example for future groups.

For most non state actors, difficulties with acquiring materials, maintaining them, transforming them into weapons, and disseminating them effectively are numerous. While many technical advances have occurred in recent years, arguably reducing the barriers somewhat, there are still considerable obstacles to terrorist development of chemical and biological weapons. Second, as mentioned above, there are far easier and potentially more "effective" (at least in terms of casualty numbers) alternatives to chemical and biological weapons. On the rare occasions when they have been used, CBW have not resulted in large death tolls, especially compared to conventional weapons such as truck bombs and individual explosive devices. It is worth bearing in mind that the attacks of September 11h accomplished mass destruction without any unconventional weaponry. If measured strictly in terms of their proven capacity to kill people or the frequency of terrorist use in the past, CBW weapons are not the most worrisome threat.

Third, the incentives and disincentives for individual terrorists to use chemical and biological weapons are complex and may not be exactly the same as those that guide the use of more conventional weapons. Recent suicide attacks indicate, among other things, an, apparently growing willingness on the part of terrorist organizations to plan and condone the death of their own operatives in the service of the cause. It is difficult to handle many chemical and biological agents without putting the handler at risk, especially in the absence of the kind of top-quality equipment that is more commonly available to states. But instantaneous death in a dramatic explosion is a far cry from the agony of a slow death from smallpox or exposure to a nerve agent.

Of course, there are many unknowns; but from an individual perspective, the incentives and disincentives for dying in a CBW attack should not be assumed to be the same as those that factor into other types of attacks. Indeed, the existence of larger numbers of religious terrorists could actually imply a *decreased* likelihood of the use of chemical and biological weapons. Although this point should not be overstated, violence whose primary aim is to kill as many perceived enemies as possible may not be likely to employ these agents. It is difficult in most scenarios to execute an attack with chem-bio weapons that kill a large number of people.

Finally, groups tend to mimic previous successes. Although terrorists do innovate in various ways, groups have most often preferred to use weapons that have a proven track record. There are no guarantees, but going strictly on the odds and the historical patterns of terrorist behaviour, most experts posit that there is a higher likelihood that the next major attack will use conventional not unconventional means. But, again, the caveat is that terrorism seeks to shock.

If a chemical or biological terrorist attack were to occur, it is most likely that the event would be on a small scale physically, with much larger effects on the population psychologically.

For this reason, targets of terrorism are forced to seek a fine balance: On one hand, it is important to prepare the public for the possibility of an attack. Among other things, since one of the incentives for using these weapons is to induce panic, preparations lower the likelihood of their occurrence in the first place. On the other hand, hyping and publicizing the threat potentially distorts its probable magnitude and likelihood. This could arguably add to the incentives for a terrorist organization to attempt an attack.

Additional measures to counter both state and especially non-state means of proliferation of chemical and biological weapons are crucial to reducing the threat in the future, both domestically and internationally. This is a difficult technical challenge in an age of globalization, when the expertise and means to carry out attacks are becoming much harder to control through traditional state measures like border controls, export controls, treaties and sanctions. Defensive measures and consequence management to reduce both the effects of an attack and the incentives to carry one out will be increasingly important. Within the United States, some measures enhancing the security of laboratories/facilities have already been enacted. Some believe that existing measures are adequate, and others disagree.

With respect to the increasing global availability of information and materials related to chemical and biological weapons, an important issue could be the fate of the people who have worked in the Iraqi weapons programs. At this writing, the full nature of those programs is not publicly known; however, as the United States forcibly disarms Iraq, it could become critical to ensure that CBW materials and expertise are not disseminated during and after military operations. This is a potential danger not only with respect to keeping track of the whereabouts and behaviour of the scientists who have been in charge (and may have already been identified by UNMOVIC and/or U.S. intelligence) but also the production-level technicians and others who may have access or some degree of knowledge.

At least in the short term, the nightmarish scenario of loss of control of Iraqi CBW, including potential sale or transfer to terrorist organizations, could arguably be more likely in an atmosphere of political or economic instability. There might be incentives for new links to develop between Iraqis who might have benefitted from the previous regime, and well-heeled groups like Al Qaeda (and its associates). Osama bin Laden's expression of support for the Iraqi people (if not the Ba'athist regime), as well as evidence of Al Qaeda's existing interest and capabilities, argue for scrupulous caution along these lines.

There have been extensive measures under the Nunn-Lugar Comprehensive Threat Reduction program oriented toward the arsenal of the former Soviet Union, but a post-conflict Iraq could present important new proliferation risks. Existing legislation, including the Iraq Sanctions Act of 1990 and existing provisions under the Chemical Weapons Convention and the Biological and Toxin Weapons Convention, may not adequately address this new concern, and additional measures targeting this emerging danger may be worth considering.

Reducing the Risk of Nuclear Terrorism

On April 25, the United Nations Security Council reaffirmed the danger of nuclear terrorism, expressing its "'grave concern' at the risks posed by non-State actors who attempt to develop, acquire, manufacture, possess, transport, transfer or use nuclear, chemical and biological weapons and their means of delivery." On May 2, at the opening of the Nuclear Non-Proliferation Treaty (NPT) Review Conference in New York, International Atomic Energy Agency (IAEA) Director-General Mohamed ElBaradei called on the conference to support initiatives "to minimize, and eventually eliminate, the use of high enriched uranium in peaceful nuclear applications." This echoes a statement made by U.S. National Nuclear Security

Administration head Linton Brooks to the IAEA Conference on Nuclear Security in London on March 16, where he stated that "efforts to secure high-risk materials must be expanded," and part of the strategy to ensure this security was "to the extent possible, ending the use of [highly enriched uranium] in civil nuclear applications."

Other countries have added their voices to these calls. On May 3 the Kyrgyz delegation to the NPT pointed out that "creative efforts must be undertaken to reduce the possibility that terrorists could gain access to fissile material, and especially highly-enriched uranium, which might be used to fabricate crude nuclear weapons," adding that "the Kyrgyz Republic believes this Review Conference should consider means to enhance the security of existing stockpiles of highly-enriched uranium, while consolidating them, reducing their size, and moving toward the elimination of the use of highly-enriched uranium in the civilian nuclear sector." Two days later, on May 5, Norway issued a Position Paper encouraging the Conference to adopt "a moratorium on the production and use of highly enriched uranium (HEU), like the moratorium on the production of weapons grade material declared by certain [nuclear weapons states]. The long-term objective should be the establishment of a total ban."

Moving towards the elimination of the civilian use of this material is an important part of the fight against WMD terrorism, since HEU is the terrorist's fissile material of choice for constructing a nuclear device. Current efforts to reduce this risk are inadequate. Additional steps need to be taken as soon as possible—adopting the principal that HEU should not be used for civilian purposes would be a good first step, facilitating further practical action.

The most difficult challenge for a terrorist organization seeking to build a nuclear weapon or improvised nuclear device is obtaining the fissile material needed either plutonium or HEU. HEU, or uranium that has been processed to increase the proportion of the U-235 isotope from the naturally occurring level of 0.7% to 20% or more, is required for the construction of a gun-type nuclear device, the simplest type of nuclear weapon. The greater the proportion of U-235 (i.e. the higher the enrichment level), the easier it is to cause a nuclear detonation. "Weapons-grade" uranium generally refers to uranium enriched to at least 90%, but material of far lower enrichment levels, found in both fresh and spent nuclear fuel, can be used to create a nuclear explosive device.

In 2002, the U.S. National Research Council warned that "Crude HEU weapons could be fabricated without state assistance," noting that "the primary impediment that prevents countries or technically competent terrorist groups from developing nuclear weapons is the availability of [nuclear material], especially HEU." Creating a nuclear weapon from plutonium requires the construction of an implosion-type device, which is a more technically difficult proposition (plutonium cannot be used in a gun-type weapon). Therefore, securing and eliminating stocks of HEU is the surest way to decrease the risk that terrorist groups use this material to create a nuclear explosion. As of the end of 2003, there were some 1,900 tons of HEU in global stockpiles. These stocks, spread over hundreds of sites, continue to grow each year. Yet as little as 25 kg needed to produce a nuclear weapon.

The dangers posed by HEU have been recognized since the 1940s. The most obvious way to deal with the threat of HEU would be simply to ban its production and use entirely. However, efforts to achieve a production ban have proven unsuccessful thus far, while there have only been partial successes to date in restricting the use of HEU. Most endeavors to ban production have focused on all fissile materials, both plutonium and HEU, although the latter is the greater terrorist threat. Further, the focus has been on HEU for military, not civilian, uses, though some countries, like Mexico and Egypt, have argued that a comprehensive fissile material ban is needed as fissile materials could be clandestinely diverted from civilian programs for weapons purposes. The United Nations General Assembly finally adopted a resolution recommending that a multilateral treaty be negotiated to ban the production of all fissile material for nuclear weapons or other nuclear explosive devices in 1993.

Last year there was some progress towards re-starting negotiations on such a treaty, after a six-year deadlock, but an actual agreement remains a long way off (for an overview of the Fissile Material Treaty negotiations to date, see Jean duPreez, "The Future of a Treaty Banning Fissile Material for Weapons Purposes: is it Still Relevant?" While it is important to continue efforts towards a ban on military production of fissile materials, restricting and eventually eliminating the civilian use of HEU (not plutonium) is both relatively realizable and important to achieve in the near-term in order to reduce the terrorist threat.

The overwhelming majority of HEU stocks are held by the United States and Russia, a legacy of the Cold War. Bilateral efforts to reduce these military fissile materials stocks have been moderately successful. In February 1993, the United States and Russia signed the HEU Purchase Agreement, whereby 500 metric tons of HEU from dismantled nuclear warheads are being converted into low enriched uranium (LEU) and sold for use in US commercial reactors. As of March 31, 2005, 237 metric tons of weapons-grade HEU had been recycled, eliminating the material derived from 9,482 nuclear warheads. This still leaves more than half of the original amount of HEU destined for recycling untouched, and at the current rate of some 30 tons per year, the downblending process cannot be completed by the expiration of the current contract, in 2013.

In addition, Russia has large military stockpiles that it has not declared excess, by some estimates as much as 500 additional metric tons of HEU, of which only some 150 tons are needed for Russian weapons. The United States, too, has been estimated to have some 385 tons of HEU in excess of its weapons needs, which it is holding in reserve for possible future use in naval fuel. Since 9/11 it has become clear that the timeline envisioned by the HEU Purchase Agreement is dangerously lengthy, additional military HEU stocks should be eliminated, and civilian HEU stocks, in Russia and across the globe, pose as much or greater risk than military HEU—civilian HEU tends to be less well-guarded than military holdings, and often is enriched to the very high levels that make construction of an improvised nuclear device relatively easy.

The U.S. Department of Energy has a program to address this problem within Russia: the Materials Consolidation and Conversion effort removes HEU from potentially vulnerable facilities and blends them down to 19% U-235. The program hopes to address 29 tons of HEU in this manner. Although concern over insecure civilian HEU was voiced before 9/11, efforts to recover this material were greatly accelerated after the terrorist attacks.

HEU is currently used to fuel research reactors, critical facilities, pulsed reactors, and a few icebreakers. Globally, 672 research reactors have been built, of which some 272 are operational in 56 countries (85 in 40 developing countries), 214 are shut down, and 168 have been decommissioned. Quite a few of these facilities use HEU fuels. The table only covers research reactors, however: there is no comprehensive, authoritative inventory of civil HEU globally, another obstacle to progress in this area.) Many of the reactors that have been shut down, but not decommissioned, have spent HEU fuel on site—and spent fuel, like fresh HEU fuel, can be used in the construction of a nuclear explosive device. There are also four research reactors under construction in developed countries, five under construction in developing nations, and eight more planned for the future (three in developed nations)—all but one of these new reactors are to use LEU fuels.

The United States and Russia supplied much of the HEU fuel used in research reactors world-wide; other producers include China (which sent HEU fuel for research reactors to Nigeria, Ghana, Iran, Pakistan, and Syria, as well as enriched uranium to South Africa, and Argentina), France (to Chile and India), the United Kingdom (to Australia, India, and Japan) and South Africa (which did not export this fuel). Most of the fuel supplied by the United States (the bulk of which went to North American and the Asia-Pacific) was of very high enrichment levels (90% and above), while most of the Soviet-supplied fuel was 36% enriched (this fuel was chiefly send to Eastern Europe). At present, there is more HEU than LEU in North America, while LEU now outweighs HEU in Western Europe (more European reactors have already been converted to LEU).

Many of these reactors are underutilized, and should be shut down. Others, as explained below, should be converted to LEU fuels (either immediately, or as appropriate technology is developed). Other civilian uses of HEU are similarly unnecessary in the long run. Reactors that use HEU as targets, for the creation of medical isotopes, can be converted, though current production capacities for appropriate LEU fuels are limited. Studies on the conversion of naval reactors that use HEU fuels, too, are being conducted. Since 1996, the U.S. Foreign Research Reactor Spent Nuclear Fuel Acceptance Program has facilitated the return of spent nuclear fuel of U.S. origin from countries around the world. Most of this fuel was enriched to 90% and above.

As of October 2003, there were 12,850 spent fuel assemblies of U.S. origin at research reactors abroad; most of them are eligible to be returned under the U.S. acceptance program, as long as they are discharged before

13 May 2006. The U.S. program also seeks to assist in the conversion of research reactors to LEU fuel, in both the United States and abroad. A related program, the Reduced Enrichment for Research and Test Reactors (RERTR) Program, was launched in 1978 to develop the technical means to convert these reactors through the development of new LEU fuels. The IAEA has been involved with this program since its inception. To date, 39 research reactors in 22 countries (including 11 in the United States) have been fully or partially converted to LEU fuel. A similar number of Western-supplied reactors remain to be converted.

In addition to the United States, Argentina, Canada, China, France and Indonesia produce LEU fuels for export, and Brazil, Chile, and South Korea are developing this capacity. Argentina and China have supplied LEU fuel to converted research reactors in Iran and Pakistan, respectively. To give reactor operators a strong incentive to convert to LEU, in 1992 the U.S. Congress adopted the Schumer Amendment to the Atomic Energy Act, whereby the export of HEU as fuel or targets for use in foreign research reactors was prohibited unless 1) there is no suitable fuel or target of lesser enrichment than the proposed export that can be used in the reactor, 2) the reactor operator agrees to convert the reactor to LEU as soon as an appropriate fuel or target is available, and 3) the United States has an active program to develop an LEU fuel or target suitable for the reactor in question.

Funding for the RERTR program was increased after 9/11, and much scientific progress has been made in reactor conversion. As of 2003, the program scientists indicated that conversion of all U.S. and Russian-supplied research reactors should be possible within nine years. Nevertheless, there continue to be difficulties persuading some companies to live up to their conversion commitments. For instance, Canada's MDS Nordion, the largest provider of medical isotopes to the United States, has been accused by analysts at the Nuclear Control Institute, a nonpartisan NGO, of "deliberately [taking] actions that increased the cost of converting its facility to LEU [targets]" and subsequently trying to claim an exemption from conversion because the costs are too high. The U.S. Nuclear Regulatory Commission continues to investigate the situation.

In 1978, Moscow initiated a program to reduce the enrichment of research reactors outside of the Soviet Union and changed its HEU export policies, supplying these reactors with 36% HEU in lieu of 90% HEU. However, Russia's economic difficulties in the 1980s hampered the conclusion of the conversion program. In 1994, the US Department of Energy and Russian Ministry of Atomic Energy signed a protocol of intent to reduce fuel enrichment in civilian research and test reactors. This program has focused on the development of higher-density 19.75% enriched uranium fuels and has demonstrated the feasibility of converting specific reactors to LEU fuel. As of October 2003, there were 24,803 fuel assemblies originally enriched in the former Soviet Union at research reactors abroad, however, the total amount of HEU in these assemblies is significantly less than in the U.S.-origin inventory. Russian work on developing LEU fuels for reactor conversion continues. Russia, however, continues to supply small quantities of HEU fuel abroad (it has no legislation like the U.S. Schumer Amendment), and has supplied European reactors that can no longer import U.S. HEU fuel.

Along with converting research reactors, the removal of Soviet-supplied HEU from vulnerable facilities has continued off and on for over a decade. The earliest transfers were from facilities in former Soviet states: the removal of 581 kg of HEU from the Ulba Metallurgy Plant in northern Kazakhstan in November 1994 (under "Project Sapphire," the material was taken to the Oak Ridge National Laboratory in Tennessee), and the April 1998 removal of fresh and spent

HEU- and LEU-based nuclear fuel from the IRT-M research reactor in Mtskheta, Georgia to the Dounreay Nuclear Complex in Scotland (through a joint U.K.-U.S.-Georgian endeavor).

However, removing HEU from other vulnerable locations was not a priority at the time. The first project to remove civilian HEU from an insecure site outside the former USSR, the Vinca Institute of Nuclear Sciences near Belgrade, Serbia, did not occur until August 2002. Since that time the repatriation of HEU fuel to supplier states (the United States and Russia) has accelerated, as have efforts to convert HEU reactors to LEU fuel.

Since Vinca, HEU fuel has been repatriated to Russia from Bulgaria, Romania, Uzbekistan, and the Czech Republic; on April 25, Latvia signed an agreement with the U.S. Department of Energy on cooperation in the return of HEU fuel from the Salaspils reactor to Russia. Russia, the United States, and the International Atomic Energy Agency (IAEA) have formalized their cooperation in this sphere under the so-called Tripartite Initiative, which was brought under the framework of the new Global Threat Reduction Initiative (GTRI), announced in May 2004. However, much remains to be done on both conversion and HEU repatriation.

One essential problem that besets both efforts is the lack of a commitment by the global community to halt the use of HEU in civilian reactors, and the concomitant reluctance of individual facilities and countries to give up their holdings of this material.

China too, though not part of the U.S. RERTR program, has been working toward the conversion of research reactors to LEU fuels, and designed its new 60 MWt China Advanced Research Reactor to use LEU fuel. France has led the way in the military sphere by converting its nuclear navy to LEU fuels. This can also be done for civilian naval propulsion plants. Further, France will shut down one of its two HEU-fueled research reactors and has pledged to convert the other. In tandem with the U.S. RERTR program, France has been working since 1999 to develop, qualify and license a high density fuel for reactor conversion (involving France's CEA, CERCA, COGEMA, Framatome-ANP and Technicatome). The Argentine Atomic Energy Commission (CNEA) has had a similar program since 2000.

Unfortunately, not all countries have committed to converting every research reactor to LEU fuels. Germany, for instance, has only promised to convert its new FRM-2 research reactor, which began operation in early 2004, to what it refers to as "medium" enriched uranium (less than 50% enriched) before the end of 2010. However, this level of enrichment is far above that of much of the HEU fuel the GTRI program is removing as a security hazard from research reactors worldwide. The only other HEU-fueled reactor under construction since 1978, the Jules Horowitz Reactor in Cadarache, France, will likely be started up on 35% HEU fuel but converted to LEU fuel as soon as that fuel becomes available.

Continuing Problems

Despite the efforts outlined above, much more will be required if the risk of HEU falling into terrorist hands is to be eliminated. While the United States and Russia have agreed that all research reactors should be converted, many states have yet to agree to conversion, and the conversion of research reactors in Russia itself is likely to be contentious. Similarly, not all states are willing to give up HEU stocks, either because they argue that it is necessary for scientific work or, as is more typically the case, because of a political view that holding on to the HEU is in some way prestigious. Still other countries may be willing to give up HEU, but not return it to particular countries—diversifying material destinations could solve this problem.

While some technical issues remain in a few cases, it is critical that the principle of eliminating the use of HEU from civilian use be set, so that countries are willing to undertake the scientific and financial costs of conversion. Further, eliminating HEU stocks through downblending is also an important part of the puzzle—while Russian and U.S. HEU stocks are arguably better secured than HEU at most research reactors, it remains difficult to persuade states that they should give up their last holding of HEU if Russia and the United States do not continue to make strong efforts to eliminate all excess HEU stockpiles as quickly as possible.

Furthermore, additional civilian uses of HEU should be reconsidered, as they are security risks, like research reactors, and provide disincentives for states considering whether to eliminate the use of HEU in research reactors. The RERTR program has already tackled the problem of converting reactors that use HEU targets in the production of medical isotopes. A greater problem is the use of HEU in other civilian applications: fast breeder reactors, icebreakers, and, possibly, floating nuclear power plants. New initiatives to eliminate these uses are essential partners to an overall effort to abolish the use of HEU.

There have recently been quite a few ideas mooted on how to accelerate the elimination of HEU, both in the civilian and the military sphere. Several deal with the acceleration of excess Russian uranium blenddown. One proposal involves the funding of accelerated blenddown by European nations, and the eventual sale of the resulting LEU on the commercial nuclear power market. In addition, there are purely commercial efforts that result in HEU blenddown: at present, one ton of HEU is being blended down with European uranium each year at Russia's Elektrostal, under license from France's Framatome. TVEL, the Russian nuclear fuel producer, and Framatome are currently exploring blending down additional quantities of HEU to produce LEU for sale on the U.S. market; however, such sales would require a U.S. Commerce Department finding that they do not violate U.S. uranium antidumping legislation.

While the amounts of HEU to be blended down under such a plan are unlikely to be large, Washington should be encouraged to allow such imports. Another effort, spearheaded by the Nuclear Threat Initiative (NTI), involves a detailed study by Russian scientists, with the cooperation of the Russian Federal Atomic Energy Agency (Rosatom), of the options for accelerating HEU blenddown at Russian facilities. The study examines various options for increasing the amount of HEU blended down each year from 30 metric tons to 35, 40, 50, or 60 tons per year, and considers different possible enrichment levels for the final product—4.5%, 12%, and 19% U-235, taking into account technological, proliferation, and financial considerations.

Results of the study are expected within the next few months, and will be presented at the Institute of Nuclear Materials Management's annual meeting this July. If it were possible to double the rate of HEU blenddown, significant reductions in the risk that this material might fall into terrorist hands would be made. Further, such facilities might subsequently be available to blend down additional military and civilian HEU stocks, which are considerable. Only by eliminating these materials, can we truly ensure that they cannot be used to construct a nuclear device.

NTI is also funding a preliminary study on the conversion of Russian icebreaker reactors to LEU fuel. Russia's nuclear icebreakers, which typically use 36% HEU but can use enrichment levels as high as 90%, operate along Russia's Northern Sea Route, which runs from near the Norwegian border to Kamchatka. Based in Murmansk, on the Kola Peninsula, fresh and spent HEU fuel for these vessels is stored in the center of this regional capital. While the storage facilities have received security upgrades, with U.K. and Swedish assistance, the fuel continues to be transported to and from these facilities, increasing the vulnerability to theft and the consequences of an accident. Further, the use of HEU fuel maintains a civilian market for this material.

Finally, the icebreakers themselves, though they too have upgraded security measures to some degree, pose risks. Furthermore, if the conversion of icebreaker reactors is technically and financially feasible, then it should also be possible to construct floating power plants fueled by LEU. Rosatom has plans to construct such floating plants for sale or lease world-wide, including China, Indonesia, Brazil, and India. If the floating reactor program does indeed get off the ground, it is of critical importance in the fight against terrorism that these power plants are do not use HEU fuel. There are currently some 1,900 tons of HEU stockpiled around the globe, while more is produced every year.

As the material of choice for would-be nuclear terrorists, it is critical that everything that can be done to secure, consolidate, reduce, and ultimately eliminate this material is done as quickly as possible. Accelerating the downblending of military HEU stocks, through both commercial means and with foreign assistance, is necessary if we are to really reduce the risks of theft. Downblending must also come to include additional military stocks and civilian stocks too. Accelerated downblending not only makes the downblended material safe; it also makes arguments for repatriation more palatable for all involved (the argument that one nation is turning over a "valuable commodity" to another country is invalidated if the recipient nation is eliminating the material as quickly as possible). In tandem, removing HEU from vulnerable facilities too should be accelerated.

As long as there is commercial demand for this material, however, it will be extremely difficult to eliminate from civilian sites - generally the most vulnerable locations. The successes of the RERTR program suggest that there may be some momentum to make the elimination of the use of HEU in research reactors possible, though the start-up of two European research reactors with HEU in the past decade make such an effort far more difficult (though not impossible, as these reactors too as slated for eventual conversion to LEU). But all civilian uses of HEU, including HEU icebreaker fuel and floating power plant fuel, must be stopped for a ban to hold. Only agreement on a future total ban will put further pressure on all countries to agree to HEU removal.

This report focuses on civilian use as civilian sites are the most vulnerable, and the minimization and eventual elimination of civilian HEU use is most achievable. In future, however, nations with nuclear-powered navies should also consider following the French Navy's example, and convert their nuclear-powered ships and submarines to LEU fuels. Currently, some 175 tons of HEU is stockpiled for naval fuel worldwide. But nuclear submarines could be converted to LEU without significantly increasing their size or reducing performance characteristics. Efforts to convert naval vessels and the negotiation of a Fissile Material Treaty are needed, but will take some time. In order to reduce risks today, the world should focus its attention on the greatest risks, especially where there are clear ways to reduce those risks.

Consolidating and blending down stockpiles are mutually reinforcing policies, doubly so if all nations agree to the principle that the civilian use of HEU should ultimately be eliminated worldwide. Given the vulnerabilities posed by the presence of HEU in the civilian nuclear sector globally, and the on-going programs to convert research reactors to LEU, it would be timely for States Parties at the 2005 NPT Review Conference to recognize that the wide distribution of and international commerce in HEU for peaceful purposes poses serious security risks in the age of global terror. The Parties, therefore, should agree that minimizing HEU commerce and use of HEU in civilian nuclear activities is desirable, as is the goal of total elimination of HEU is the civilian nuclear sector as soon as technically feasible. In this regard, States Parties should call on the IAEA to undertake further study, and to promote activities in pursuit of this goal.

3

Game of Nuclear Poker

In what many consider to be Iran's final chance, the International Atomic Energy Agency (IAEA) Board of Governors, during an emergency meeting on August 11, called Iran's bluff by adopting yet another resolution on the implementation of the country's Nuclear Non-Proliferation Treaty (NPT) Safeguards Agreement. While the Board's resolution noted that the Agency has accounted for all declared nuclear materials in Iran, it also stated that it has not yet been able to verify that there are no undeclared nuclear materials in the country.

The Board urged Iran to allow the IAEA to reinstate seals and urged Iran to re-establish a full suspension of enrichment activities as a confidence-building measure. Although not evident from its decision, the request for the Director-General to issue a "comprehensive report on the implementation of Iran's NPT Safeguards Agreement and this resolution" by September 3, 2005 may be a final ultimatum to Iran to continue with full suspension.

Potentially improving Iran's hand dramatically, the IAEA released a report this week prepared in secret by a group of scientists from the United States, France, Japan, the United Kingdom and Russia over the past nine months that confirmed Iran's claims that the traces of weapons-grade uranium found at Iran's Natanz site were, in fact, a result of contamination of components bought from Pakistan, probably through the A.Q. Khan network. The origin of the uranium traces has been a highly contested issue until now. The IAEA report is likely to influence the next meeting of the Board, giving Iran the benefit of the doubt once again.

The Board's August 11 decision followed a 20 month-long voluntary suspension of Iran's civilian uranium enrichment activities. The Iranian government, however, notified the IAEA on August 1, 2005 that it intended to resume uranium conversion at Isfahan. The IAEA was requested to make appropriate preparations to accommodate the resumption of conversion activities consistent with Iran's Safeguard Agreements. On August 8, Iran began to feed uranium ore concentrate into the process line at the facility, subsequent to the installation of Agency surveillance measures. Iran subsequently removed the seals on the process lines and the UF4 at the facility following verification of the feed material and installation of Agency surveillance measures.

Iran's decision to resume uranium conversion activities came less than a year after the November 15, 2004 Paris Agreement, which announced Iran's intention to expand and extend its suspension pledge as a confidence building measure to facilitate talks with France, Germany, and the United Kingdom (EU-3) regarding long-term arrangements for Iran's civilian nuclear program that could include eventual supply of light-water reactors and operation of certain enrichment-related facilities on a pilot scale. Prior to the Board's special August 11 session, France, Germany, and the United Kingdom, along with other EU members and the United States, expressed serious concerns over the resumption of Iran's conversion activities at Isfahan, arguing that there is little justification for the resumption of these activities in Iran since it has no current need for a nuclear power program.

Moreover, these States continue to view Iran's claim to the right to peaceful nuclear technology with skepticism considering the country's past discrepancies with the IAEA and furtive nuclear activities. While still in favor of continuing negotiations, France, Germany, and the United Kingdom say they will only resume negotiations under the framework of the Paris Agreement, while Iran maintains that it will return to negotiations "free of pre-conditions and with manifest good will." Iran's strongly worded statement immediately following the Board's decision called the resolution "a vote of no confidence to the credibility of the Agency and its Safeguards system" given that it is based on inconclusive evidence about Iran's nuclear program without applying the same treatment to "so many unsafeguarded facilities spread around in other parts of the world, in particular in (the Middle-Eastern) region.

While some may consider the Board's request for the IAEA Director-General to submit a "comprehensive report" on the implementation of the resolution by September 3, 2005, it is important to note that the Board is not the implementer of the Paris Agreement. The implied threat by the Board is to cite Iran for its previous failures and for not maintaining suspension, which the Board has deemed essential for resolving outstanding issues. Iran's continued claim that it does not seek to create nuclear weapons and that it is willing to respect and comply with the IAEA and the Safeguards system, stands in sharp contrast to the belief by many that Iran has over time deliberately deceived the IAEA and that it continues not to exhibit full compliance with its NPT Safeguard obligations. Although Iran agreed to sign the Additional Protocol to its Comprehensive Safeguards agreement, thereby allowing more extensive inspections by the IAEA, it has not yet ratified this important instrument.

Questions remain whether Iran's signature of this agreement in 2003 was simply a diplomatic ploy to avoid potential referral to the Security Council at that time. As the European Union pointed out at the most recent Board meeting, Iran's recent decision to restart its conversion activities at Isfahan comes at a time when the outstanding questions relating to Iran's nuclear program have yet to be resolved, and when new questions about plutonium related activities have arisen. While the August 11 Board of Governors resolution—as others had done before it—noted that all declared materials have been accounted for and have not been diverted to prohibited activities, it also states that the Agency cannot yet conclude that there is an absence of undeclared nuclear materials or activities in Iran.

Although true that Iran has so far not been found to be in non-compliance, its actions—including the violation of the Paris Agreement—do not instill confidence about the peaceful nature of Iran's nuclear program. The resumption of currently suspended activities, including the uranium conversion, will only further heighten international concern about the real objective of Iran's nuclear program. The Board's recent decision followed several rounds of tough negotiations, mainly between the European Union and the United States on the one side and the Non-Aligned Movement (NAM) on the other. The NAM statement on August 10 supported Iran's quest to develop a civilian nuclear program and opposed any possible referral of Iran to the Security Council.

Playing the peaceful use card, the NAM emphasized that the development of peaceful nuclear energy is an absolute right of all countries, that Iran's two year suspension of nuclear activities was voluntary, and that Iran's willingness to suspend the program should not deprive it of the right to resume nuclear development. The NAM statement is indicative of the strong views held by the Movement that the pressure on Iran to limit or suspend its civilian nuclear activity is indicative of the desire by many developed states to curtail the right to develop peaceful nuclear energy guaranteed to non-nuclear weapons states (NNWS) parties of the NPT.

While the NAM Board members were united in their opposition to stronger action against Iran, it is noteworthy that Western block countries are not as united in their approach. Divergent views, especially among the EU member states, may have impeded the negotiation process and prevented the EU-3 from providing any concrete proposals to diffuse the situation thus far. Also significant is what appears to be another feud between the United States and the United Kingdom on one side and Germany on the other. For example, in sharp contrast to several statements by President Bush that he considers military force against Iran a viable option, already supported by the United Kingdom, Germany's Chancellor Gerhard Schröder made it clear that military force is not being considered.

Although the use of military force is one of several options for the Council to consider, it is unlikely at this stage that Western countries would be unified in supporting any United Nations Chapter VII action. From a legal perspective, Iran's recent decision to resume uranium conversion is not contrary to the requirements of the NPT or its IAEA safeguards obligations, even with the Additional Protocol in place. Bearing in mind that the purpose of safeguards agreements is for the IAEA to verify non-diversion of nuclear material to nuclear weapons, and since the IAEA has reported (as reflected in several Board resolutions including the most recent one) that all declared nuclear material is accounted for and thus has not been diverted to prohibited uses, it raises a serious challenge for the Board, and indeed the Security Council: Does the Board have a legal footing to report Iran to the Security Council, and on what basis could the Council consider Iran in non-compliance with its safeguard undertakings? In this regard, it should be borne in mind that the NPT State Parties have delegated to the IAEA the authority to verify compliance with the Treaty's safeguards obligations. In the event that the Board of Governors finds a Party in non-compliance, the IAEA statute clearly mandates the Board to report such non-compliance to all members of the Security Council and the General Assembly of the United Nations."

The Board is also mandated to take other corrective actions such as suspending assistance to the non-compliant State. Moreover, Iran maintains that the pressure from the European Union and the United States to halt its civilian nuclear program curtails the "inalienable right" of every State Party to the NPT. In a statement issued to the IAEA, Iran noted that protest against peaceful nuclear activity in full conformity with the NPT and the Safeguard Agreements "constitutes a limited manifestation of the exercise of an inalienable right." Iran has stated that it feels a particular responsibility not to bend under the pressure of the West to end its civilian nuclear fuel program because Iran's acquiescence may contribute to the ability of the nuclear weapon states (NWS) to curtail the rights of other NNWS.

Also in this statement, Iran is quick to note that the pressure to halt its uranium enrichment activities comes from states that possess and rely upon nuclear weapons. Iran's position, shared by many states, is that these NWS, some of which hold many tons of separated plutonium available for direct conversion into nuclear weapons, have little justification in demanding that Iran cease its peaceful civilian program—a right enumerated by the NPT—when they do not faithfully pursue their obligation—nuclear disarmament. Moreover, Iran noted that that these states justify their nuclear activities due to their good standing within the NPT, but that they, and the IAEA, ignore the fact that many non-nuclear weapon States who desire civilian programs have not yet had the opportunity to establish good standing. Given a "fraction of that access" afforded to NWS and certain NNWS with developed civilian nuclear programs, Iran claims, the country will also become an example of transparency and "exemplary standing" in Safeguard Agreements. Iran's statement also emphasized that it can only prove its dedication to IAEA compliance once it is able to develop a peaceful nuclear program.

In addition, when Iran decided to resume its uranium conversion activities, it offered open and advance notification to the Agency about its intention to break the Isfahan facility seals while allowing time for the installation of monitoring equipment. It is unclear whether another meeting of the Board of Governors in September would result in Iran's referral to the Security Council, or in light of the most recent IAEA report, lead to further investigations. However, Iran may already be preparing for such a possibility and may decide not only to refuse to suspend its activities at Isfahan, but also resume the uranium enrichment process at Natanz. While Iran's nuclear program remains a divisive one within Iran, the recent replacement of Hassan Rohani, the former moderate leader of Iran's nuclear negotiating team, with ultra-conservative Ali Larijani—a close advisor to Iranian Supreme Leader Ali Khamanei—in the negotiation process may be an intentional strategy by the more radical elements in Teheran paving the way towards a more aggressive pursuit of a nuclear program.

While the best option for Iran would be to seek negotiations with the IAEA over a timeline for resumption at Isfahan and to continue its suspension at Natanz, the close association between nuclear power and national pride in Iran may have already led the government to view referral to the Security Council as a *fait accompli*. Should Iran be referred to the Security Council, it will be important to consider the international implications of such a move. Any decision (by voting) to refer Iran over the protest of the Non-Aligned Movement and other developing countries—

assuming that developing countries influenced by the United States would support such referral— could send a negative message to States inside and outside of the NPT. In this regard, it is important to note that while voting is allowed under the Board's rules of procedure, the "spirit of Vienna" calls for decisions without a vote. However, the latest IAEA report could bolster the NAM's position and result in further deadlock.

To maintain that Iran poses a threat to international peace and security, absent proof of more than the ability to eventually develop a nuclear weapon, ignores countries like India and Iran's Middle Eastern neighbor, Israel. The double standard evident in the treatment of Israel's undeclared weapons program has long been a source of concern not only to its Middle Eastern neighbors, but to most countries. It is ironic that while the United States is leading the charge against Iran for not being in full compliance with the NPT, it again chose to completely ignore another nuclear weapon powered nation outside the treaty. Instead, President Bush promised to award India lucrative nuclear and military related trade deals.

The countries outside the NPT treaty not only possess more than the ability to make nuclear weapons, but they are holding actual nuclear weapons in their arsenals. Moreover, they are not bound by NPT Safeguards and other obligations such as those required by the Nuclear Suppliers Group (NSG). That these countries would not be considered a threat (and in fact receive various forms of aid from the United States) would seem to indicate that a state would be better off outside the confines of the NPT than trying to operate within its boundaries. This might have been a point North Korea understood when it announced its withdrawal from the NPT in 2003, opting to join those nations outside the confines of the NPT. It is ironic that so far no attempts have been made to bring the issue of North Korea to the Security Council despite clear evidence (as stated in several

IAEA Board resolutions) that it has been in non-compliance with the NPT since entering the Treaty in 1985.

In the event that the IAEA Board—at its next meeting or thereafter—decides to report Iran to the Security Council, the Council will be faced with two equally bleak options: The Council could choose to criticize Iran's refusal to terminate its conversion and enrichment activities, calling on it to do so with immediate effect, and request that the IAEA report to the Council on further progress towards this end. This would likely result in the issue being yet again deferred, with negative implications for the Council. An equally bleak option would be to consider Iran as a Chapter VII issue. This leaves the Council two more options: either impose economic sanctions on Iran—the world's fourth largest oil producer—with potential economic implications not only for Iran's trading partners, but the world economy as a whole; or to take military action—as recently intimated by President Bush. Either option could provide further justification by the new conservative government in Teheran to aggressively pursue a nuclear program, if not a military one.

While highly unlikely that the Council would support any form of military action, a resolution by the Security Council threatening Iran with "serious consequences" if it continues to violate its Safeguards and other related agreements, might leave a back door open for unilateral action or action by a coalition of willing forces. Not only would another military campaign led by the United States further exacerbate an already volatile political debate in the United States and elsewhere about the wars in Iraq and Afghanistan, but it would most certainly further destabilize the Middle East peace process. An even more serious potential consequence would be that such a resolution could prompt Israel to launch an attack on Iranian nuclear facilities, claiming that these facilities pose a direct threat to Israel's security.

With China and Russia, and other key peaceful use proponents on the Security Council such as Argentina, Brazil and Algeria, unlikely to support a "punishing" resolution against Iran, the Council may find itself yet again deadlocked and ineffective. This is hardly the time to set the Council up for yet another "failure." At a time when proposals are being considered to revitalize the United Nation in the face of criticism that it is outdated and incapable of taking concrete action, a deadlocked Security Council would lead to further criticism. More daunting, unilateral action by a militarily dominant country using the Security Council's mere consideration of Iran's non-compliance as justification, will lend credence to critics' complaints that the Security Council is illegitimate in its current structure and would further undermine the overall effectiveness of international agreements under its auspices.

Perhaps it would be overly optimistic to hope that Iran and the EU-3 reach an agreement on Iran's nuclear activities prior to the September 3 deadline. It seems that the Iranian government is convinced it is holding all the cards in this game of nuclear poker. The newly elected conservative government Iran is likely to find increasing domestic and international support in its quest to maintain a civilian nuclear program as a right and a matter of national pride. Also, with its divergent views on viable options, the EU-3 do not seem likely to develop a plan for a middle ground, especially with the United States pushing a doctrine of force over diplomacy in the background.

The situation needs to be defused urgently. Instead of continuing with its bluffing game, Iran should fold its hand, and fully cooperate with the Agency in setting a timeline that will ensure Iran's right to a civilian nuclear program while still allowing the IAEA to develop a conclusive report on its nuclear weapons program. Iran should under all circumstances avoid a situation in which the Security Council be requested to consider its case. While conclusive action by the Security Council, in particular under Chapter VII, may not be possible at first, the pressures resulting from a deadlocked Council may eventually force less powerful members to acquiesce to the desires of states such as the United States, the United Kingdom, and even France. Moreover, the positions of the Russians and Chinese are unpredictable at best. These two veto-wielding members may out of self interest decide not to oppose a Security Council resolution on Iran.

Finally, leading members of the NAM, such as South Africa and India, as well as other influential developing countries such as Brazil, in cooperation with longstanding Iranian allies Russia and China, should increase their mediation efforts and use their influence in Tehran to resolve the matter before the IAEA Board is forced to play its hand and report Iran to the Security Council.

While true that Iran has repeatedly maintained that it embraces the tenants of the NPT and does not plan to withdraw from the Treaty, a failure by all concerned to find an area of convergence prior to the September 3 deadline that prompts the Board to report Iran to the Security Council may force Iran's hand, with potential disastrous consequences for the nuclear nonproliferation regime and international security in general. Given the hard-line approach by the new Iranian leadership, they may conclude—as others have—that staying inside the NPT without nuclear weapons is no longer in Iran's supreme national interest. Such a development would seriously undermine the nuclear treaty regime, with potentially fatal consequences.

4

New Chemical Terrorism Weapon

Osmium Tetroxide

Appearance in Recent Terrorist Plot

A highly toxic chemical has emerged as a key component of an alleged terrorist plot in London. Serving legitimate functions in biological research and in specialized chemical industry, osmium tetroxide's suitability as a terrorist agent - a dual use compound - is limited, despite the characterizations of it generating "chemical fallout."

On 30 March 2004, hundreds of British anti-terrorism police conducted raids throughout the London area after tracking a group of terrorist suspects over the course of several months. Authorities subsequently arrested eight British citizens of Pakistani origin, who were allegedly involved in the planning stages of a terrorist attack. In the following week, reports emerged that these suspects, including a Canadian and a British-Algerian, were researching the potential of detonating a chemical bomb in a crowded, civilian location within London.

Authorities conducted the raids at 24 locations within London after learning from GCHQ, the British electronic eavesdropping intelligence agency, that these terrorist suspects were discussing the use of osmium tetroxide during phone calls among themselves within Britain and to Pakistan. Some sources claim that the U.S. National Security Agency collaborated with its British counterpart to help intercept the phone calls implicating the suspects in planning a chemical attack. The British Home Office would not, however, comment on the alleged scenario, as the case is still under investigation by authorities. The suspects reportedly were not able to acquire the osmium tetroxide before authorities were able to intercept members of the group.

Those involved are allegedly sympathetic to al-Qa'ida and were preparing to target Gatwick airport, the London subway, or other enclosed high-traffic areas. Al-Qa'ida has previously produced training manuals containing plans for use of choking agents as a method of attack, yet this is the first instance of osmium tetroxide being included among the list of possible chemical agents.

This is the first incident in the open literature in which the chemical has been connected with terrorism. Although this plot did not progress beyond the planning stages, the potential use of osmium tetroxide has raised new fears about al-Qa'ida's pursuit of dual-use chemicals as terrorist weapons and has encouraged discussion about the potential lethality of such a substance when combined with a conventional explosive.

Characteristics of Osmium Tetroxide (OsO_4)

Scientists are already familiar with the use and effects of osmium tetroxide (OsO_4) even as these recent reports have introduced the general public to the compound for the first time. OsO_4 is a colorless to pale yellow solid at room temperature, occasionally called osmic acid. The solid readily evaporates at room temperature (has a high vapour pressure). An open canister left in an enclosed area would be readily noticeable based on the characteristic pungent, ozone- or chlorine-like smell.

For the numerically inclined: the vapour pressure of OsO_4 is 7 mm Hg at 20°C/68°F, compared to a vapour pressure of 17 mm Hg for water, 2.10 mm Hg for sarin nerve agent (GB), and 0.0007 mm Hg for VX nerve agent (the latter three are liquids). The vapour pressure of a chemical is important in determining the inhalation hazard. Solids and liquids with no vapour pressure don't evapourate and therefore don't pose an inhalation hazard unless they are mechanically aerosolized. Liquids with very low vapour pressures, like VX nerve agent, don't evaporate readily and therefore are considered a much more significant threat for exposure via direct skin contact.

Physiological Effects of OsO_4 Exposure

Osmium tetroxide is highly toxic and a rapid oxidizer. Severe reactions may result through all routes of exposure: inhalation, ingestion, contact with the eyes and other mucous membranes, and contact with skin. Because of its volatility, the vapour hazard is usually emphasized. Exposure to the vapour can cause severe chemical burns to the eyes, skin and respiratory tract. Very short-term contact with the vapour may generate a lachrymation (tear-causing) response, accompanied by coughing, headaches, and dizziness.

Among the most insidious effects of osmium tetroxide is its capacity to cause irreversible blindness - literally turning the corneas black. Symptoms may not be noticed until several hours following exposure, which may be an attractive feature for terrorists. People may not realize the extent of the toxic effects of a compound to which they have been exposed immediately; rather the damage will be occurring while they continue on their day. Another delayed effect of substantial inhalation exposure is a build up of fluid in the lungs (edema) leading to "dryland-drowning." Exposure to osmium tetroxide dissolved in water will turn the skin black. Painful burns or dermatitis may result depending on the concentration. It is not known, however, to be cancer-causing.

OsO_4 can be compared to traditional chemical warfare agents. The first appearance of a physiological response, also known as a threshold effect, is observed at a lower concentration for osmium tetroxide vapour exposure than phosgene (CG), sulfur mustard (HD), or sarin nerve agent (GB). At first glance, the inhalation hazard associated with OsO_4 is comparable to that of the traditional asphyxiant phosgene and blister agent sulfur mustard based on lethal inhalation concentrations (LCt_{50}). Phosgene is a gas at ambient conditions, so all of the material will be available as an inhalation hazard. On the other hand, sulfur mustard is a liquid with a fairly low vapour pressure (0.072 mm Hg), which will result in a decreased volatility relative to OsO_4 (626 mg/m3 for sulfur mustard versus 97,300 mg/m3 for OsO_4 at 20°C/68°F). So there will be over 150 times more OsO_4 vapour available in an enclosed area relative to sulfur mustard vapour.

While the lethal inhalation concentration of OsO_4 is substantially larger than that for sarin, again the decreased volatility of the traditional warfare agent (16,090 mg/m3) should be considered in evaluating the relative threat. Under similar conditions, there will be six times more OsO_4 vapour in an enclosed area compared to sarin vapour. The overall inhalation risk for osmium tetroxide is estimated to be closer to sarin nerve agent than sulfur mustard or phosgene gas.

Table 4.0: Toxicity Comparison of Osmium Tetroxide with Three Traditional Chemical Warfare Agents

	Threshold effects *(mg/m3)*	LCt_{50} *(mg-min/m3)*	LD_{50} *(mg/kg)*
OsO_4	0.1 - 0.6	1316	162
Phosgene	2	3200	n/a
Sulfur mustard	12-500	1500	100
Sarin (GB)	2	70	24.3

Legitimate Uses of OsO_4

This substance is used primarily in the preparation of biological samples, a technique called "fixation" or "fixing," to help maintain cellular and sub cellular structures that would otherwise be damaged during further processing. Fixing is an important step in most biological applications of electron microscopy - looking at very small structures with electrons rather than light. OsO_4 reacts with the olefins in fatty acids and other tissues.

Fixing has some similarities to staining used in traditional microbiology - the osmium atomic nucleus helps make the biological structures more easily "seen" under an electron microscope. Osmium tetroxide is also used in specialty organic chemistry reactions, such as the synthesis of the synthetic human-hormone norestradiol and industrially significant glycol compounds. These reactions using solid osmium tetroxide are most commonly done on the laboratory scale.

Commercial Availability

Osmium tetroxide is commercially available as either a solid or as an aqueous solution (less than 6% OsO_4 by weight, due to limited solubility in water). Commercial quantities are typically very small and prices are high. Cost for the largest, commercially available units from a leading U.S. chemical supplier range from $118 for 1 gram of the solid compound to $195 for a 25 mL ampoules containing 2.5% OsO_4 by weight, dissolved in water (0.625 grams OsO_4 per vial). A terrorist attempting to use OsO_4 in the creation of a chemical terrorist weapon would most likely be hindered by the high cost of the substance. There would also be a danger to the terrorist in attempting to prepare an improvised explosive device containing large quantities of the chemical compound. In packages of five grams or more, larger quantities of material are commercially available in which osmium tetroxide is bound to a polymer backbone.

The polymer backbone, or support, eliminates the vapour hazards associated with solid OsO_4. If a potential terrorist were to seek to acquire large quantities of this type of immobilized OsO_4, the utility as a weapon would be extremely low. Such materials were designed specifically to protect industrial workers. A leading U.S. chemical supplier of OsO_4 does not take any special precautions regarding sale of the chemical. Because of the potential dual-use nature of many chemicals with legitimate industrial and research purposes, all orders are screened prior to shipment.

Decontamination

If an OsO_4-containing solution were to be used as a chemical terrorist weapon, it could be decontaminated with copious amounts of any "unsaturated" cooking oil or dry milk. Once a solution is black, the risk of rampant oxidation (burning) is abated.

As a Chemical Terrorism Weapon

The feasibility of using a bomb to disburse OsO_4 is highly suspect. When heated OsO_4 rapidly decomposes to OsO_2, which is effectively a rock. OsO_2 is used as a ceramic resistor in specialty electronic applications. The inhalation hazard would be destroyed with the bomb explosion rather than generating "chemical fallout" as in a dirty bomb scenario. In addition to the difficulties and hazards faced by anyone seeking to use osmium tetroxide as a dirty bomb, the effect of the compound would be minimal in an open space, and it would not leave lasting contamination in an area in the same manner as a radioactive bomb. Because it is such a rapid oxidizer, it would most likely first enhance the combustion of the materials used for the bomb. As an oxidizer for an improvised explosive device, OsO_4 would be a very expensive choice and very risky for the bomb assembler. Thus, its utility in the creation of a dirty bomb, when combined with conventional explosives, is questionable. Chemical terrorism incidents are not limited to those events involving explosives or incendiary materials. The likelihood of OsO_4 to cause harm as a chemical agent alone is substantially greater than as part of a dirty bomb. The major danger from the solid is via inhalation. An enclosed space with poor ventilation would present the greatest hazard. OsO_4 would not be an effective chemical terrorism weapon for a large, open air venue. The major danger in solution form is via the skin (percutaneous) or ingestion.

As a terrorist weapon, however, the biggest problem with osmium tetroxide is its nature as a rapid, indiscriminate oxidizer. OsO_4 doesn't distinguish between membranes in the human eye and lungs, plants, rubber, or cooking oil. While it has the potential to inflict horrifying damage to the body in the form of chemical burns and blindness, the chemical does not specifically target a critical physiological function as nerve agents do. A second limitation as a terrorist weapon is its volatility. The persistency of both sarin and VX substantially exceed that of OsO_4.

OsO_4, although unquestionably a lethal compound, is not estimated to be a viable dirty bomb hazard as it will readily decompose if utilized with explosives. In comparison to traditional chemical warfare agents, OsO_4 has similarities to the choking agents in its high volatility and targeting of the respiratory system. It resembles the blister agents, like sulfur mustard in that it attacks the eyes, burns the skin (by a different molecular mechanism than sulfur mustard), and some effects may be delayed. The blindness from OsO_4 vapour exposure, however, may be permanent unlike sulfur mustard.

Because of its high volatility combined with high toxicity, the inhalation risk of OsO_4 vapour verges on that of sarin nerve agent, but it does not target critical nerve connections that control the cardiovascular and respiratory systems as the nerve agents do. Additionally, the persistency of osmium tetroxide vapour is low in comparison with the nerve agents and sulfur mustard. The incorporation of osmium tetroxide, a fairly obscure inorganic compound, suggests some familiarization with advanced undergraduate level chemistry.

The British terrorist suspects recognized the deleterious health effects, but their plan to incorporate OsO_4 into a conventional explosives bomb shows a lack of sophisticated and detailed understanding of inorganic chemistry. Such knowledge might be indicative of a graduate-level individual or technician in a research or industrial biochemistry, molecular biology, or biomedical engineering laboratory with access to OsO_4. Such a plot does not point to a person with graduate-level experience in synthetic chemistry or significant experience in an industrial setting. This incident may also hint at an escalating terrorist interest in pursuing non-traditional chemicals as improvised weapons. Recent events have forced British authorities to investigate such a threat, and such a possibility has caused scientists to speculate on the utility of OsO_4 for use by a terrorist group.

The Suicide Bombings in Iraq

Suicide bombing attacks are becoming a weekly if not daily fixture in post-war Iraq. To date, there have been more than 40 suicide bombing attacks. In the last few weeks, numerous suicide bombings were carried out in Baghdad, Basra, Karbala', and other Iraqi cities and towns. Suicide bombers in Iraq have targeted numerous military, police, and civilian targets, and many hundreds of Iraqi civilians have been victims. The most egregious of these attacks was the Ashura bombings on March 2, 2004, that targeted *Shi'a* worshipers in the Shrine of Imam Husayn in Karabala' and in a *Shi'i* mosque in Baghdad and on that day, alone more than 181 Iraqi civilians were killed.

A number of coalition and Iraqi officials have blamed various actors for the wave of recent suicide bombings attacks that have plagued Iraq. Some have pointed the finger at the alleged al-Qa'ida affiliate Abu Musab al Zarqawi and his network of foreign Jihadis that have allegedly infiltrated Iraq with aspirations of starting a civil war to hinder the U.S. occupation of Iraq. Others have argued that this is the work of former regime remnants who are attempting to hinder Iraq's transition following the fall of the Saddam regime. This report explores the possible suspects and motivations behind the current wave of suicide bombings attacks in Iraq.

Various Coalition officials have declared that Abu Musab al Zarqawi is the main culprit behind the wave of suicide attacks; they claim that much of the intelligence points to him. U.S. Brigadier General Mark Kimmitt named Zarqawi as "one of the chief suspects." Members of the Iraqi Governing Council (IGC) have also supported this assertion — in the immediate aftermath of the Ashura attacks in Karbala` and Baghdad, Mowaffaq al-Rubaie a member of the Iraqi Governing Council stated: "the civil war and sectarian strife that Zarqawi wants to inflict on the people of Iraq will not succeed."

According to the Coalition and IGC, the evidence against Zarqawi is mounting. They claim that Hasan Ghul, a known Pakistani al-Qa'ida courier, was captured by the Kurdish forces in Northern Iraq carrying a 17-page letter from Abu Musab al Zarqawi to al-Qa'ida that details Zarqawi's current operations in Iraq, in which he details a plan to spark a civil war by targeting *Shi'a* religious targets in the hope that such attacks will drag the *Shi'a* into the fighting. According to the Coalition Provisional Authority (CPA), which published the text of the alleged Zarqawi letter on its website, the current wave of suicide bombing attacks in Iraq follows the scenario outlined in the alleged Zarqawi letter and thus proves Zarqawi's and, by extension, al-Qa'ida's complicity in the attacks in Iraq. As a result, Coalition authorities have offered a $10 million dollar reward for information leading to the capture of Zarqawi.

The 38-year old Jordanian militant Abu Musab al Zarqawi was also mentioned in Secretary of State Colin Powell's presentation in front of the United Nations Security Council (UNSC) in February 2003, in which he highlighted the Iraqi threat and the need for military action against Iraq. At that time, Colin Powell told the UNSC that Abu Musab al Zarqawi was an active and known al-Qa'ida associate who sought medical treatment in Baghdad in May 2002. In the letter that was seized with the alleged Pakistani al-Qa'ida courier Hasan Ghul, Abu Musab al Zarqawi describes to the recipient of the letter the makeup of his network in Iraq. He says that his network consists mainly of Iraqi *Sunnis* who have little experience in insurgency operations, a problem he will remedy through training. As he states, they "are the quintessence of the *Sunnis* and the good sap of this country. In general, they belong to the *Sunni* doctrine and naturally to the Salafi creed.... Most of them have little expertise or experience, especially in organized collective work.... Most of the groups are working in isolation, with no political horizon, farsightedness.... But matters are still in their initial stages."

Equally important, Zarqawi claims in his letter that the number of foreign fighters who infiltrated Iraq and are helping his network to carry out suicide bombings in Iraq is rather small. Referring to these "Immigrant Mujahidin," Zarqawi indicates that "their numbers continue to be negligible as compared to the enormity of the expected battle." If the text of the Zarqawi letter is indeed authentic, it is abundantly clear about its goals and methods. Zarqawi claims that his objective is to hinder the U.S. occupation of Iraq and to motivate the majority of the Iraqi *Sunna* to join the ranks of Islamist organizations. He believes the way to accomplish both these goals is to collectively target the *Shi'a* institutions and leadership in an effort to drag the Iraqi *Shi'a* majority into a civil war. A civil war would make Iraq ungovernable to the Americans and would scare the Iraqi *Sunnis* into the arms of his radical fundamentalist *Mujahidin* network.

According to the text of the Zarqawi letter:

The only solution is for us to strike the religious, military, and other cadres among the *Shi'a* is with blow after blow until they bend to the *Sunnis*. Someone may say that, in this matter, we are being hasty and rash and leading the [Islamic] nation into a battle for which it is not ready, [a battle] that will be revolting and in which blood will be spilled. This is exactly what we want, since right and wrong no longer has any place in our current situation....

If we are able to strike them with one painful blow after another until they enter the battle, we will be able to [re]shuffle the cards. Then, no value or influence will remain to the Governing Council or even to the Americans, who will enter a second battle with the *Shi'a*. This is what we want and, whether they like it or not, many *Sunni* areas will stand with the *Mujahidin*.

Then, the *Mujahidin* will have assured themselves land from which to set forth in striking the *Shi'a* in their heartland, along with a clear media orientation and the creation of strategic depth and reach among the brothers outside [Iraq] and the *Mujahidin* within.... As for the *Shi'a*, we will hurt them, God willing, through martyrdom operations and car bombs...along with the anticipated incitement of the wrath of the people against the Americans, who brought destruction and were the reason for this miasma. Abu Musab al Zarqawi has claimed credit for carrying out more than 25 attacks against Coalition and *Shi'a* targets including the killing of the *Shi'a* Ayatollah Mohammed Baqr al-Hakim in the Najaf bombing of August 2003.

As it pertains to attacks against the *Shi'a*, the situation on the ground most definitely affirms the scenario portrayed in the Zarqawi letter. Since the fall of the Saddam regime, *Shi'a* holy sites, neighborhoods, and political leaders have been targeted extensively by the current insurgency forces in Iraq. However, that does not exclude that attacks on the *Shi'a* may also be the work of the secular Ba'ath remnants. In the past three decades, Saddam's regime killed tens of thousands of Iraqi *Shi'a* and executed and tortured many of the *Shi'a* political leaders. There is no reason to believe that regime remnants will not attack *Shi'a* targets in post-war Iraq.

Table 4.1: Major Attacks on Shi'a Targets in Post-war Iraq

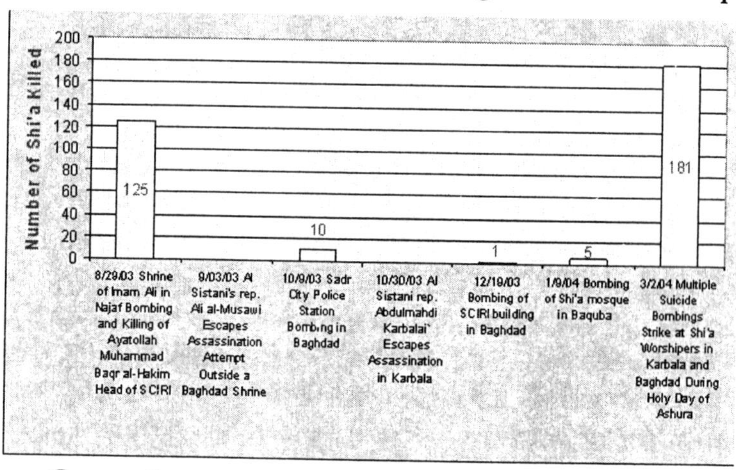

Currently post-war Iraq is unstable; in the last few weeks, a report was given to the Pentagon indicating that there is a strong possibility of a civil war breaking out. Up to this point and despite numerous attacks on *Shi'a* holy sites, the Iraqi *Shi'a* leadership has shown immense restraint; however, as more of these attacks are perpetrated against *Shi'a* targets, the *Shi'a* leadership, especially Grand Ayatollah Ali al-Sistani, will be under increased pressure from his *Shi'a* constituents to form *Shi'a* armed militias and to retaliate for these murders. Such vociferous calls from members of the Iraqi *Shi'a* community have already started. If the United States and the Iraqi Governing Council are unable to find a way to convince Grand Ayatollah Ali al-Sistani and his many *Shi'a* followers to continue to show restraint and work on building a stronger unified Iraq there is a possibility that some *Shi'a* elements will seek revenge against whomever they perceive to be directly responsible.

There is also the possibility that some *Shi'a* elements will begin to target Coalition personnel whom they may view as indirectly responsible for the harm visited on their holy shrines. As long as these terror attacks continue, Paul Bremer and the Coalition Provisional Authority must go the extra mile to placate Sistani by addressing his concerns and providing the *Shi'a* with the necessary tools to better defend their holy sites. The CPA has released $100,000 to aid the victims of the Ashura bombings. This is a good first step in placating the Iraqi *Shi'a*, and it encourages their restraint. In this delicate period, enhancing the restraint of the long victimized Iraqi *Shi'a* majority is paramount.

Fortunately the United States is not alone in this task. Following the Ashura bombing, there have been unanimous regional condemnations of these criminal attacks on holy sites in Karbala. More so, all the important regional actors, including the governments of Egypt, Jordan, Lebanon, Iran, Syria, Saudi Arabia, and even regional militant organizations such as Hizbullah have all called on Grand Ayatollah Sistani and the Iraqi *Shi'a* to show restraint, maintain Iraq's national unity, and to avoid being dragged into a civil war that would exact a terrible toll on Iraqi society.

Hizbullah's Secretary General Hassan Nasrallah, during Ashura ceremonies in South Lebanon, called on both *Sunni* and *Shi'i* Muslims to reject actions that target all Muslims as a whole, and warned against delving into the turmoil and civil war that the perpetrators are attempting to foment. He added that such a civil war would give the United States a pretense to stay in Iraq. He called the perpetrators of these attacks "a group of dark, stonehearted, living in the middle ages, mindless, heartless, religion-less, radicals without manners, who claim to belong to Islam."

There is a lot of contradictory information on whether Abu Musab al Zarqawi is a subordinate of al-Qaida. Some in the Iraqi Governing Council and the Coalition claim that Abu Musab al Zarqawi is an al-Qa'ida associate who works at the behest of Osama Bin Laden. Various U.S. officials, including Paul Bremer, have stated that Zarqawi is connected to the Kurdish Islamist organization, Ansar al-Islam, or its subset Jaish Ansar al-*Sunna* that is connected to al-Qa'ida. This view is supported by the characteristics of the attacks in Iraq. The attacks in Iraq have unmistakably been carried out by a group of professionals who have been able to undertake multiple attacks simultaneously — the trademark of a sophisticated terror organization such as al-Qa'ida. In addition, the March 2 Ashura bombings in Iraq were paralleled by attacks on a *Shi'a* shrine in Quita, Pakistan which resulted in the death of 44 Pakistani *Shi'a*.

If these attacks are indeed related, this coordination of attacks in more than one country is the hallmark of al-Qa'ida, which previously attacked U.S. embassies simultaneously in Kenya and Tanzania. This view, however, is not unanimous. Some European intelligence analysts claim that al Zarqawi is actually a competitor to Osama Bin Laden. While they were both prominent members of the Afghani Arabs Mujahidin in the 1980s, some contend that Abu Musab al Zarqawi attempted to head his own independent terrorist outfit called *al Tawhid*. In the aftermath of the Soviet withdrawal from Afghanistan, Zarqawi returned to his homeland of Jordan, but was imprisoned for seven years for conspiring to overthrow the Hashimite monarchy. It is believed that upon his release, Zarqawi fled to Europe, where he headed a militant cell of Jordanians who did not want to join al-Qa'ida.

The letter seized by Hassan Ghul portrays a complex relationship between Abu Musab al Zarqawi and al-Qa'ida. The text of the Zarqawi letter gives the impression that Zarqawi is not a subordinate of al-Qa'ida. It appears that he operates an independent terror outfit as he writes in his letter to al-Qa'ida: "You, gracious brothers, are the leaders, guides, and symbolic figures of jihad and battle. We do not see ourselves as fit to challenge you, and we have never striven to achieve glory for ourselves."

Furthermore, it appears that Zarqawi is attempting to solicit al-Qa'ida's help and support, and is offering the services of his organization in the global battle against the United States and the Iraqi *Shi'a* who are cooperating with the Coalition. He adds:

All that we hope is that we will be the spearhead, the enabling vanguard, and the bridge on which the [Islamic] nation crosses over to the victory that is promised and the tomorrow to which we aspire. This is our vision, and we have explained it. This is our path, and we have made it clear. If you agree with us on it, if you adopt it as a program and road, and if you are convinced of the idea of fighting the sects of apostasy, we will be your readied soldiers, working under your banner, complying with your orders, and indeed swearing fealty to you publicly and in the news media, vexing the infidels and gladdening those who preach the oneness of God.

The text of the letter also makes it evident that Zarqawi is uncertain whether his appeal for support from al-Qa'ida will yield support for his operations in Iraq. He states, "If things appear otherwise to you, we are brothers, and the disagreement will not spoil [our] friendship." In the last few months, there has been a great deal of contradictory information regarding the role of Abu Musab al Zarqawi and his whereabouts. Some have alleged that Zarqawi was being harbored in Iran with other al-Qa'ida personnel including Osama Bin Laden's son Saad.

In a conflicting report, a statement circulated in Fallujah in early March by Iraqi militants claiming to belong to the "Leadership of the Allahu Akbar Mujahedeen" group stated that Abu Musab al Zarqawi was killed some time ago during the U.S. bombings of Ansar al Islam's strongholds in the Sulaimaniyah Mountains in Iraqi Kurdistan.

The group stated that Zarqawi's injury and artificial leg prevented him from escaping the bombings. The "Leadership of the Allahu Akbar Mujahedeen" also alleged that al-Qa'ida is not present in Iraq, and that the text of the 17-page "Zarqawi letter" to al-Qa'ida is a forgery fabricated by the Coalition and the Iraqi Governing Council "to back up their theory of civil war." Time will tell if any of these conflicting reports are accurate.

Current suicide attacks on civilian targets in Iraq may also be the work of domestic Iraqi *Fida'iyin* and remnants of the Ba'ath regime. This theory contradicts conventional wisdom that leads many to believe that such suicide bombings are consistent with the *modus operandi* of fundamentalist Jihadis and not the work of secular nationalist, but immediately following the onset of the war various Iraqi men and women carried out suicide bombings against U.S. forces on behalf of the regime. On various occasions in the first few weeks of the war, numerous Iraqis got close enough to Coalition Forces to detonate explosive-laden vehicles and kill U.S. soldiers.

Also, on their way to Baghdad, many coalition vehicles were ambushed by members of *Fida'iyin* Saddam, who attacked them with reckless abandon using RPG's, mortars, and rifles. As a result, many hundreds of these *Fida'iyin* Saddam were killed by Coalition Forces on the road to Baghdad. It is quite possible that after the fall of Baghdad many of these elements expanded their tactics to include the suicide vests and car bombs that have been the culprits in the recent attacks on Iraqi *Shi'a* and Kurdish targets.

It appears that in spite of the secular nature of the Ba'ath regime — a staunch opponent and oppressor of organized religion in Iraq — since the invasion of Kuwait, the Iraqi military and intelligence apparatus may have planned to instill a secular patriotic Iraqi version of the martyrdom concept among its forces. Months after the occupation of Kuwait, when a looming military coalition campaign aimed at liberating Kuwait became evident, the Iraqi security and intelligence apparatus was in the process of creating a new force called the *Fida'iyin* (a secular Arabic term meaning "those who are willing to sacrifice their lives for the cause"). Internal Iraqi correspondence from December 1990 reveals that the regime of Saddam Hussein embarked on a search for volunteers from the ranks of the Iraqi military and civilians to create a volunteer force of *Fida'iyin*. The Iraqis planned to deploy this force behind enemy lines to carry out special suicide operations by sabotaging Coalition equipment and killing Coalition personnel.

In addition, other recovered Iraqi correspondence from the 1991 Gulf War suggested that concepts of martyrdom and sacrificing one's life in defense of the Iraqi motherland in the face of U.S. "aggression and colonialism" were instilled by the Iraqi regime and designated as the ultimate demonstration of a soldier's patriotism and duty. As an example, the following classified Iraqi internal correspondence in February 1991 from an *AMN* (General Security) Captain at the 18th Field Engineering Battalions to a subordinate Lieutenant ended with the following words:

Victory is ours because up until now we have done what God has promised, up until now the new colonialism and aggression on Iraq aims at our present and our future as Iraqis. Their goals will not be achieved, the land of the motherland will remain pure, the flag of Iraq will continue to fly, and the people of Iraq will remain full of joy and happiness. Due to its ultra secular orientation, the Iraqi

Socialist Ba'ath regime has consistently seen organized religious fundamentalist organizations as the prime threat to its rule in Baghdad. In its internal correspondence prior to the 1991 Gulf War, the Iraqi regime classified its various enemies on a list of its most significant security threats.

For Iraqis to carry out suicide martyrdom operations is somewhat peculiar because of their secular orientation. As stated by former U.S. Central Intelligence Agency analyst Judith Yaphe, "the real question is the suicide bombers that are not strictly an Iraqi thing." Moreover, some members of the Iraqi National Congress have claimed that Iraqis do not undertake suicide bombings due to their culture, insinuating that the suicide bombings must be the work of foreign Jihadis that have infiltrated Iraq. However, when looking at all other areas in the Middle East in which suicide bombing tactics have been utilized extensively, it appears they all have one thing in common: the perpetrators of the suicide bombing are intimately familiar with the areas which they target.

During the onset of the tactic of suicide bombing in Lebanon in the early 1980s, members of the *Shi'a* militias AMAL, Lebanese Islamic Jihad, and later Hizbullah who carried out more than 30 suicide bombings against Israeli and American targets in Lebanon were all native Lebanese who could easily mingle through their indigenous population. They knew the Lebanese cities, towns, roads, and location of facilities utilized by the Israeli Army. In the case of Palestinian suicide bombings in Israel, hundreds of thousands of Palestinians from the West Bank and Gaza have worked inside Israeli cities since the onset of Israeli occupation in 1967. Most of these Palestinians are employed as cheap labor in Israeli restaurants, gas stations, hotels, farms, construction companies, factories, and hospitals. They have utilized Israeli public buses and taxis as their major source of transportation. Thus, thousands of Palestinians are intimately familiar with the locations of various would-be targets within Israeli cities and are proficient in getting around within Israel. Integral parts of the Palestinian population are also intimately familiar with the language and mannerisms within Israel.

The vast majority of Palestinian bombers are residents of the occupied territories, with the possible exception of very few foreigners such as Asif Hanif, the English suicide bomber who carried out the Tel Aviv bombing in April 2003 on behalf of Hamas, killing three Israelis and wounding 55 more. Many of the Palestinian suicide bombers who operated in Israel were disguised as Israeli soldiers or Hasidic Jews. When taking all these trends into account, it becomes clear that acquiring a target for a suicide bombing is not an easy task, even when chosen randomly.

A bomber must have intimate familiarity with the society which it seeks to target. The bomber must speak the native language and dialect and be familiar with the location of targets in order to successfully navigate within a city and acquire a suitable, if not specific, target. Even in Israel, where the targets are often random restaurants or buses in Tel Aviv or Haifa, the bombers needed to make their way through various Israeli population centers without raising suspicion until they acquired the target. Security services in Middle Eastern nations routinely employ racial and ethnic profiling, and perpetrators who are not able to efficiently assimilate within the target societies are more easily identified and engaged.

In light of this information, the theory that suicide bombings in Iraq are exclusively the work of foreign Jihadi infiltrators does not hold water. It goes against common sense to believe that a large group of non-Iraqis who are not proficient in Iraq's colloquial Arabic dialect, customs, traditions and mannerisms and, most importantly, not familiar with Iraqi cities and towns, are somehow able to move around through major Iraqi cities and identify specific targets within these cities, and carry out dozens of suicide bombings. It would be a challenge for a non-Iraqi who is not fluent in Iraqi dialect to move freely under the watchful eye of the Coalition Forces, the Iraqi Police, and the naturally suspicious and territorial sectarian militias such as the Kurdish Pesh Merga and the *Shi'a* Badr Brigades who have been patrolling and guarding Iraqi *Shi'a* and Kurdish targets in anticipation of such acts.

Such a scenario of foreign fighters targeting sectarian Iraqi facilities would have been more likely during the early suicide attacks in Najaf in August 2003, but since then the local population and security services have been much more vigilant in looking for outsiders. A more likely scenario is that many of the actual martyrs are young Iraqi men who are intimately familiar with the location of these targets within Iraqi cities and who can enter a *Shi'a* Mosque or Kurdish building without raising alarm. It would take a non-Iraqi much more than few weeks or months to learn to master the Iraqi dialect, mannerism, look, customs and, most importantly, the location of specific *Shi'a* or Kurdish targets within a relatively big city such as Baghdad, Basra, or Karbala'.

In short, it may have been relatively easy for foreign infiltrators to carry out some early suicide bombings, but it is extremely difficult for a non-native group to sustain a seven-month effort of more than 40 suicide bombings on random and select specific targets without extensive aid and involvement by local Iraqi elements. Simply put, whether the suicide bombings are being organized by the Zarqawi's Islamist network, remnants of the Iraqi intelligence services or a combination of both, it is quite clear that some Iraqi elements are playing an integral role in the planning, dispatching and the execution of suicide bombings in Iraq. To a large extent Iraqi suicide bombings are the work of domestic forces.

The current suicide bombings in Iraq could be the work of various actors. They might be carried out by the Zarqawi terror outfit, which claims to have conducted more than 25 attacks. The attacks might also be the work of Saddam loyalists or former members of the Iraqi security and intelligence apparatus. While it is unclear who is ultimately behind them, it is very likely that local Iraqis play a major role in the organization and execution of these suicide bombings on various *Shi'a*, Kurdish, and Coalition targets, be it for the sake of Zarqawi and his holy Jihad, the old regime, or for Iraqi nationalism and the removal of foreign troops. All of these actors have one thing in common; they all want to turn Iraq into an ungovernable turmoil with the ultimate goal of driving the United States and the Coalition out of Iraq.

5

Suitcase Nukes

On February 8, a London-based Arab newspaper, *Al-Hayat,* reported that in 1998, in Kandahar, Afghanistan, al-Qaeda had bought nuclear weapons from Ukraine using the services of a Ukrainian scientist, whose first name was Viktor. Multiple news sources immediately linked this story to the 1997 statement by the late General Alexander Lebed, who claimed that a special commission established by the Russian government in 1996 could not account for about 100 portable nuclear devices (commonly known as "nuclear suitcases"). These allegations are not new. In 1998 another London-based Arab daily, *Al-Watan Al-Arabi,* reported that 20 "suitcase nukes" had been acquired by Chechen separatists, who then sold them to al-Qaeda for cash, arms, and drugs. Another similar story, also from Arab sources, surfaced in 2000, but this time it pointed at Kazakhstan.

As in earlier cases, the *Al-Hayat* story was immediately and firmly denied by both Ukrainian and Russian officials, all of whom declared that all nuclear weapons had been removed from Ukraine by 1996, and consequently there simply were no weapons to sell.

The Foreign Ministry of Ukraine further stated that "the so-called 'suitcase weapons' had never been kept in the territory of Ukraine and had never fallen under its control."

Official denials closely coincide with the findings of a study conducted by CNS in 2002: "'Suitcase Nukes:' A Reassessment." That study concluded that the loss of any nuclear weapons, including portable devices, during the withdrawal of nuclear weapons from Ukraine and other former Soviet republics was highly unlikely (that report was quoted on February 10 by ITAR-TASS along with the statement of Deputy Chief of the General Staff Yuri Baluevski to the same effect).

The relevant findings of the CNS report include the following:

First, portable nuclear devices did, indeed, exist in the Soviet Union, notwithstanding the many denials made by Russian officials in the mid-1990s.

Second, these weapons most likely remained in the custody of the Ministry of Defense's 12th GUMO - the department charged with handling nuclear devices, which also oversaw the withdrawal of these weapons from the newly independent states in 1992-96. Consequently, that department was in a position to ascertain that no weapons remained outside Russia (following Lebed's allegations, a well-known Russian ecologist, Academician Alexei Yablokov, claimed that "suitcase nukes" had been under the control of the KGB, and consequently the records of the Ministry of Defense were incomplete).

Third, these devices, if any had been located outside Russia, were most likely removed to the territory of Russia in 1992. Although the withdrawal of all nuclear weapons was completed only in 1996, tactical weapons were withdrawn by May 1992. Fourth, the withdrawal from Ukraine was conducted according to a special procedure, which made the loss of any weapons even less likely than in the case of other former republics. Namely, after a temporary freeze on the withdrawal, Ukraine and Russia concluded a special agreement in April 1992, which established strict accounting rules.

One is left to speculate about the reason for publishing yet another story about "al-Qaeda suitcase nukes." Judging by *Al Hayat*'s claim that its source was in Pakistan, the goal of that source might have been to shift attention from the ongoing scandal over secret sales of nuclear equipment and technologies by that country's nuclear scientists. An unexpected benefit of that story is the availability of additional information about Soviet portable nuclear devices, which allows us to verify and augment the data contained in the CNS 2002 report.

Two years ago, based on scanty information, CNS concluded that such weapons (a) existed and (b) were intended for Special Forces of the Ministry of Defense (Spetsnaz). We also tentatively sketched the likely characteristics of these weapons. Newly available information confirms and expands these conclusions. It has been disclosed that these weapons were indeed intended for Spetsnaz. Two versions of these devices were created - RA-155 for the army and RA-115-01 for the navy (to be used under water). The weight of one device was 30 kilograms and it could be armed by a single operator in just 10 minutes. These weapons, which were called "nuclear backpacks" ("*yadernyi ranets*"), had a yield of 0.5 to 2 kilotons and could contaminate areas of up to 10 square kilometers. They were kept at only two secret storage facilities and had never been released to troops.

Information vital for the assessment of the threat presented by these weapons if fallen into the wrong hands been confirmed, namely that "nuclear suitcases" have a very short shelf-life and have protection against unauthorized use. The former director of Research Institute No. 4 (the research arm of the Strategic Rocket Forces) General (ret.) Vladimir Dvorkin confirmed that portable nuclear devices were designed in such a way that they could not remain in the ready-to-use status for a long time because certain components had to be periodically replaced by experts (sources quoted in the CNS report mentioned regular maintenance at six-month intervals). In addition to some type of permissive action link (PAL) device, they were also protected against attempts to forcibly remove electronic locks. In the event of such an attempt, the weapon automatically switched into a "non-use" mode and would not explode.

Finally, the CNS report concluded that the sensational statement by General Lebed was based on an incomplete study. That study was launched in 1996 in response to reports that several portable nuclear devices had been stolen and landed in the hands of Chechen separatists, but it was not completed by the time Lebed was forced to resign from the position of the Secretary of the Security Council. It remained unknown whether the study was completed and which methods were used, specifically, whether the commission only checked records or also matched records to actual weapons. The chairman of the commission established by Lebed, Vladimir Denisov, has now come forward to say that the commission was able to complete its job. Furthermore, he disclosed that its members were able to match records to actual weapons or, as he put it, "counted them on fingers." The latter statement also implies that at least in the mid-1990s, a number of portable nuclear devices still existed, contrary to the common belief that they had been eliminated years before.

Thus, even though the *Al-Hayat* allegations are apparently groundless, it still seems advisable to continue closely monitoring the situation surrounding portable nuclear devices. The most intriguing question remains open: whether such weapons still exist or have been eliminated? Russia was supposed to have eliminated all "nuclear mines" - the category, into which "nuclear suitcases" should fall - according to the 1991 unilateral statements by Presidents George Bush and Mikhail Gorbachev, but implementation of these initiatives has not yet been completed. In 2002, Russia announced that the deadline for completion was extended from 2000 to 2004 due to insufficient funds. To date, there has been no official update on the status of this work.

A Reassessment

Attention to portable nuclear devices (often referred to as "suitcase nukes") peaked in 1997-early 1998 following well-publicized allegations by the late governor of Krasnoyarsk Krai and former Russian Security Council Secretary, General (Ret.) Alexander Lebed, that an unknown number of these weapons (possibly as many as several dozen) could not be accounted for. These devices represent probably the greatest threat if they end up in the hands of terrorists due to the combination of small size and full-scale nuclear explosion effects. Interception of "suitcase bombs" is difficult along land borders and practically impossible along maritime borders. At the same time, the political, psychological, and economic effects of a blast from a portable nuclear weapon would be far greater than, for example, those of a "dirty bomb."

The first and only reliable line of defense against the acquisition or use of "suitcase nuclear weapons" by terrorists lies in the countries that possess such devices or have the capability to produce them. Lebed's 1997 statements are particularly unnerving because the early 1990s (when, according to him, a number of portable nuclear devices were lost) represented the time of greatest risk with regard to nuclear weapons security in Russia. Governmental institutions were radically weakened; and a dramatic drop in the standard of living made individuals with access to these weapons extremely vulnerable to the temptation of easy illegal profit. Official denials, including the denials that such weapons even existed, are not a sufficient reason for complacency.

This paper revisits open-source information about suitcase nukes to assess the level of threat stemming from the possibility that a number of them could have ended in the hands of terrorists or states that support them. It seeks to achieve that task by concentrating on the following objectives:

- Reassess information from publicly available sources about portable nuclear devices and try to determine, in particular, whether these weapons actually existed;
- Analyze the scenarios of their loss that were offered by the special commission charged with the accounting for portable nuclear devices in the mid-1990s; and
- Based on these scenarios, assess the probability that portable nuclear devices could have fallen into the hands of international terrorist organizations or states that support them, as well as the probability that such devices could be used for terrorist purposes.

The paper reaches two main conclusions:

First, the probability that any portable nuclear devices were lost prior to or after the breakup of the Soviet Union appears low; the scenarios of loss offered by the special commission in 1996 are actually the least plausible among other possible scenarios. This does not mean that the threat does not exist, but rather that at this moment; it is probably not the most immediate threat to the home security of the United States or to U.S. armed forces abroad.

Second, even if any devices were lost, their effectiveness should be very low or maybe even non-existent, especially if the loss occurred during the period of the greatest risk, in the early 1990s. Without scheduled maintenance, these devices apparently can produce only minimal yield and eventually possibly no yield at all, and can only serve as a source of small amounts of weapons-grade fissile materials. That being said, open-source information has limited usefulness and can only yield probabilistic analysis instead of definitive answers. Consequently, it is necessary to continue efforts aimed at acquiring better and more reliable information about the status of Soviet/Russian portable nuclear devices, as well as about the parameters of threat they might pose in the hands of terrorists.

Portable Nuclear Devices

In a recent interview, the deputy chairman of the Duma Defense Committee, Alexei Arbatov, noted that complete silence had surrounded the subject of portable nuclear devices since the debate of the mid-1990s. Indeed, suitcase nukes often seem a matter of fiction rather than that of fact. The "mythological" qualities of suitcase nukes derive not only from limited information—this is a common feature in almost everything concerning Russian nuclear weapons—but primarily from the fact that almost all available information dates to a very brief period (the second half of 1997 and early 1998) and is not very reliable. Comments about suitcase nukes are conspicuously absent in open sources prior to 1997. For example, one of the most authoritative Russian treatises on nonstrategic nuclear weapons published by the Institute of World Economy and International Relations does not mention them.

There are only two stories in which references to them could be suspected, and then only in hindsight. The first is a statement in 1995 by the director of the Ministry of Defense Ecological Center, Col. Boris Alexeev, about nuclear devices that weighed 90 kilograms (kg). The other was made by Anton Surikov, an outspoken nationalist expert on defense issues and son of a leading figure in the Soviet military-industrial establishment, who said in an interview with the Estonian newspaper *Postimees* in 1996 that in a scenario of NATO landing on the Russian Baltic Sea shores, Russia would resort to "miniature" nuclear weapons. Both statements are not conclusive proof; however, as it is not entirely clear whether the authors meant portable nuclear weapons or some other types of weapons. Silence continued in the post-1998 period. It is hardly surprising that official sources remained mute, but non-governmental organizations did as well.

For example, in the manuscript of a major study of Russian tactical nuclear weapons, an expert from the Moscow-based PIR Center, Ivan Safranchuk, referred to them as "so-called" and ultimately dropped the reference in the final version of the study published in 2000. A subsequent study of these weapons written by the deputy director of the PIR Center, Yuri Fedorov, did not mention them either. Alexei Arbatov, who earlier was cited complaining about the absence of information about portable nuclear devices, did not mention them in his 1999 study, which treated the subject of Russian nonstrategic nuclear weapons in considerable detail.

Scarcity of information notwithstanding, hindsight has its advantages, and a reassessment of available data can yield tangible results, especially utilizing new information about the state of the Russian nuclear weapons complex that has become available in the last five years. The "suitcase nukes saga" began in the fall of 1997, when General (Ret.) Alexander Lebed made several statements to the effect that during his short tenure as the Secretary of the Security Council in 1996, he received information that the separatist government in Chechnya possessed small nuclear devices. In an attempt to clarify the situation, he created a special commission under the chairmanship of his assistant, Vladimir Denisov. According to Lebed, the commission was only able to locate 48 such munitions of a total of 132, an indication that 84 were lost (subsequently Lebed changed the total number of suitcase nukes several times, stating in the end that the number was between 100 and 500, but probably closer to 100).

It should be noted that almost nothing is known about the methods of the commission's work: for example, whether it checked only records or was able to compare the actual inventory to records as well (if only records were checked, it cannot be said with certainty whether more warheads were missing or whether any warheads were missing at all).

Since the commission was disbanded before it was able to complete its work, it has remained unclear whether it was able to confirm the alleged loss of warheads (i.e., it looked everywhere and failed) or simply did not have time to clarify the situation (Denisov's statement seems to imply the latter). It is not even known who the members of the commission were.

A well-known leader of the Russian ecological movement, academician Alexei Yablokov, immediately confirmed and expanded on Lebed's statements. He announced that 700 such devices, which he called "nuclear mines," had existed in the Soviet Union. Responding to statements from Ministry of Defense (MOD) officials that there were no portable nuclear devices in the records, Yablokov announced that these devices had been in the hands of the KGB, and thus, by definition, MOD records could not include them.

Official and semi-official Russian sources immediately denied Lebed's and Yablokov's stories, but their testimonies gradually revealed bits and pieces of information, raising suspicion that small nuclear devices did exist and even providing a glimpse of their properties. For example, the press secretary of Minatom, Georgi Kaurov, stated that, like the United States, the Soviet Union produced "very small nuclear weapons," and that "the ability to manufacture miniature nuclear weapons demonstrates a state's high level of technology and its ability to create multipurpose and even aesthetically attractive nuclear weapons." Another official said that these devices did not exist, but that if they had existed, their production and maintenance would have been very expensive.

The chief of the 12th GUMO, Igor Valynkin, recently disclosed that the serial number of one of the "suitcases" that Lebed made public, RA-115, represented a "production index" (i.e., the type of munitions) and that the whole type had already been eliminated. The difficulty of assessing the situation stems, first and foremost, from the fact that many, if not all, participants to the 1997-98 scandal could have had ulterior motives. At that time, Lebed was running for the governor of Krasnoyarsk Krai, with an option of running for President again in 2000. Yablokov, a perennial fighter against Minatom, was (still is) prepared to support anything that would help his cause; from a technical point of view, his testimony is particularly questionable. Russian MOD and Minatom officials could be expected to deny anything, regardless of whether allegations were completely or even partially correct. Several remarks about suitcase nukes from Arab sources in the late 1990s-early 2000s could have been prompted by a desire to promote or expose Usama bin Laden's terrorist organization. In the end, not a single source can be considered entirely reliable.

The Mini-Nuke

In hindsight, it is clear that statements made by both sides in the 1997-98 debate could have referred to different classes of nuclear devices. One class mentioned was nuclear mines, while another was the portable nuclear devices for Special Forces, which were the subject of Lebed's statement. Even if portable devices did not exist, one can suspect that some types of nuclear mines were sufficiently small to generate "suspicious" statements by officials. Indeed, statements by MOD and Minatom representatives were worded very carefully and denied the existence of "nuclear suitcases," but not necessarily the existence of other small nuclear devices. They could thus claim that they were telling the truth even if they knew all along that other small nuclear devices could be portable. The uncertainty about classification could also explain the silence of non-governmental experts.

Nuclear mines are a well-known class of nuclear weapons. They were used by the Engineering troops and deployed along Soviet borders, primarily along the border with China. Nuclear mines were intended to create obstacles in the path of advancing enemy troops by altering the landscape and creating areas with high levels of radioactive contamination. The total stockpile was 700—incidentally, the number Yablokov claimed represented the stockpile of suitcase nukes (and, potentially, evidence that Yablokov did not have adequate knowledge of the subject). Russian official sources reported that, in accordance with the 1991 Presidential Nuclear Initiatives (PNIs), all nuclear mines had been withdrawn to central storage facilities, and their elimination was "almost complete."

Judging from the available information, including from official and semi-official Russian sources, some of these devices were relatively small and could be portable. The often-cited weight was 90 kilograms (kg), and they could have low yield (0.02 to 1 kt). On the other hand, the existence of smaller devices custom-designed for Special Forces, probably analogous to American small atomic demolition munitions (SADMs), should not be ruled out either. Lebed apparently referred to such munitions in his statements (some sources, including himself, mentioned the weight of 30 kg). Several broad considerations suggest that the story about portable nuclear devices should be taken seriously, with a caveat that their existence cannot be viewed as an established fact.

First and foremost, the very fact that the United States possessed such munitions makes it feasible that the Soviet Union produced them as well, if only to replicate the American experience (the habit of Soviet designers to duplicate American weapons systems or use them to justify their own research is well known from other major projects, such as development of solid-fueled missiles or MIRVed ICBMs). Furthermore, Soviet scientists are known for their propensity to explore every possible avenue, including the most powerful nuclear device; it is only logical to assume that they tried miniaturization as well.

An artillery shell for 152-mm howitzers (which, in the Chelyabinsk-70 museum, is advertised as the smallest nuclear munition in the world) testifies to the ability to create a reasonably small and light nuclear explosive device. According to one Russian expert, the size of these shells (15 cm in diameter and 50 cm in length) apparently represents the smallest size of the nuclear device Russian designers were able to achieve (the 130-mm naval guns did not have nuclear shells). Sifting through available evidence, one can conclude that if such devices existed, they likely had the following characteristics:

- Small size (60x40x20 cm) and relatively light weight (probably upward of 30 kg). These parameters are generally consistent with available information about Soviet 152-mm artillery shells, as well as with the U.S. SADM.
- Low yield (less than 1 kt, maybe as low as 0.1 kt).
- Remained under control of the 12th GUMO (the Main Department at MOD in charge of handling all nuclear devices), were kept at or near MOD Special Forces (Spetsnaz) bases, as well as at central storage facilities, and were intended for transfer to Spetsnaz at short notice.
- Short life span between scheduled maintenance. According to the chief of the 12th GUMO, Igor Valynkin, small munitions required replacement of components every several months (other sources mentioned six months). Valynkin's statement is the most direct corroboration of the allegations about the existence of portable nuclear devices. Stationary nuclear mines with such a short warranty period simply did not make sense, while portable devices for use behind enemy lines could still be acceptable.

- Were likely equipped with reasonably sophisticated permissive action links (PALs), which should preclude unauthorized use. Also, there is unconfirmed information that some small nuclear devices (munitions for 152-mm howitzers) were kept during peacetime in "half-assembled" state, i.e., parts were kept separately, although quick assembly in the case of war was possible.

Several of these statements require an in-depth discussion. Control of portable nuclear devices is a highly contentious issue, and there has been little data except the claim of the 12th GUMO that it controlled all nuclear weapons and Yablokov's claim that nuclear suitcases were controlled by the KGB. The latter claim appears insufficiently credible for two reasons.

First, the mission of portable nuclear devices should have been explosions in the enemy's rear position during or just prior to the outbreak of war for the purpose of disrupting the infrastructure as well as sabotaging the enemy's command and communications. This directly points to the MOD Spetsnaz as the likely custodian of these weapons since this use of the devices closely matches its type of missions. Spetsnaz representatives flatly denied possession of nuclear weapons, but their statements might refer to the fact that in peacetime, nuclear weapons remained in the custody of the 12th GUMO and were released to troops at a special command.

In contrast, the first KGB Spetsnaz group, *Alpha*, was created in 1974, whereas miniature nuclear devices were probably created in the 1960s, as in the United States or, at the latest, in the early 1970s. Until the end of the 1970s, KGB Spetsnaz was small and consisted of just one group. Furthermore, its mission was, from the very beginning, antiterrorist operations, in particular, rescue of hostages (the group was established immediately following the terrorist acts during the Olympic Games in Munich). The first combat mission of KGB Spetsnaz was in 1979 in Kabul, where they participated in the capture of Amin's palace. Thus, possession of nuclear weapons was simply not in line with its mission.

One should be sensitive to the possibility that GRU Spetsnaz, as well as KGB Spetsnaz, if necessary, could have used the smaller versions of nuclear mines, which were technically within the purview of the Engineering Troops. Valynkin's statement that one type of nuclear device mentioned by Lebed had been completely eliminated is an indirect corroboration of that hypothesis since all or almost all nuclear mines were eliminated during the 1990s. In that case, however, it cannot be doubted that during peacetime, portable nuclear mines remained in the custody of the 12th GUMO.

A short maintenance schedule is an intriguing feature of portable nuclear devices, which is particularly important from the counterterrorism perspective: If that information is correct, such devices would be useless or have limited utility after only a few years, begging the question of whether terrorists would envision the same purpose for such devices as the Soviet Union. The period between routine maintenance—only six months—might seem very short, but short maintenance periods appear to be a typical feature of all Soviet warheads.

Without detailed knowledge of the design of Soviet warheads, it would be impossible to know which components needed replacement at what time intervals. Two potential candidates are tritium and the neutron generator, which may use radioactive materials that decay over time.

It seems possible, for example, that Soviet designers balanced on the threshold, using only just enough plutonium to achieve critical mass and relied on tritium to generate required yield. In that case, even modest degradation of tritium could have resulted in a significant drop of yield. Thus, it would be safe to assume that without proper maintenance, portable nuclear devices might still produce chain reaction, but yield would be minimal, and with time, possibly non-existent.

PALs were apparently introduced no later than in the mid- to late 1970s. Consequently, portable nuclear devices produced before that time probably did not have sophisticated means of preventing unauthorized use. Regardless, there is reason to believe that most of them eventually were equipped with such devices. Due to their short service life, they had to return to production facilities for a major overhaul (reportedly, service life of Soviet strategic warheads was about 15 years). During the disassembly-assembly process, the devices could have been fitted with better protection devices. Warheads produced in the late 1960s or in the 1970s should have undergone major maintenance at least once by the time of the breakup of the Soviet Union.

The Scenarios of Loss

It is, of course, impossible to reliably verify Lebed's claim that nearly a hundred of these miniature nuclear devices could not be accounted for in 1996. According to Vladimir Denisov, the chair of the special commission established by Lebed in 1996 to account for suitcase nukes, the commission was able to account for the portable nuclear devices that had been present in the territory of Russia prior to 1990 or 1991, but could not vouch for the ones that could have remained in the territories of other former Soviet republics. This leaves three possible scenarios of loss of such devices:

- Some of them remained outside Russia when nuclear weapons were consolidated in the early 1990s;
- A handful of such devices were assembled outside Russia using components that could have been produced or stolen; or

- They were lost inside Russia, most likely in the early 1990s. The first two scenarios were implied by Denisov, while the third simply appears logical and requires attention. The following section assesses the probability of loss under each of these three scenarios.

The loss of nuclear explosive devices might have occurred in the early 1990s, just prior to or during the transfer of all nuclear weapons to the Russian territory. Tactical nuclear weapons were stored in the territories of all 15 republics that made up the Soviet Union. According to Lebed, portable devices were kept in republics around the perimeter of Soviet territory, which makes the Baltic states, Belarus, Ukraine, and South Caucasus particularly suspicious from the point of view of control of portable nuclear devices (since the Soviet Union was geared for a war with NATO, it is likely that nuclear weapons intended for use by Spetsnaz forces would be kept close to borders with NATO). The period of 1990-91 was marked with increasing chaos, the emergence of nationalist and/or pro-independence movements in some republics, in particular in Ukraine, the Baltics, and South Caucasus. Many servicemen joined these organizations, whether openly or secretly, and thus opportunities for unauthorized access to nuclear warheads could not be ruled out.

Several stories published in Russian newspapers in the mid-1990s concentrated on this scenario. One such story, which fit Lebed's allegation about Chechnya, described the purchase of two 30 kg "rucksack" nuclear devices by Chechen representatives in Lithuania in November 1991-January 1992. Another report about a "Chechen bomb" appeared in the fall of 1999, when Russian troops were starting a new war in Chechnya. The devices were reportedly stolen prior to the transfer of nuclear weapons to Russia and hidden there until sold to Chechnya. It should be noted, however, that Russian newspapers, which published stories about the sale of nuclear weapons to the Chechens, are among the least reliable sources of information in Russia, so their evidence should be taken with a grain of salt. Lebed himself stated that the story about the diversion of portable nuclear devices to Chechnya, which prompted his investigation in the first place, was eventually found to be false. Incidentally, according to former Deputy Secretary of State, Strobe Talbott, Chechen President Jokhar Dudaev approached the U.S. government in 1993 claiming he possessed Soviet nuclear weapons, but could not support his claim.

The assessment of the validity of that scenario should take into account two considerations. First, accounting and control of nuclear weapons in the Soviet Union was reasonably reliable, if primitive by today's standards. The troops of the 12th GUMO, which controlled all nuclear devices, were privileged and passed through, by Soviet standards, a very rigorous selection process. In the general chaos of the late 1980s-early 1990s, troops charged with the control of nuclear weapons (the 12th GUMO, the SRF, parts of the Navy and the Air Force) were the last to see the weakening of morale and loyalty. In addition to other selection criteria, these troops were comprised, with few exceptions, of officers, sergeants, and privates of Slavic and, on rare occasions, Baltic origin. Representatives from the Caucasus (especially North Caucasus) or Central Asia, as well as non-Slavic people of Russia, were usually avoided.

In this regard, the Baltic republics were, indeed, a likely candidate for the location of possible diversion of nuclear weapons, especially given the intensity of anti-Soviet and anti-Russian sentiment in the late 1980s-early 1990s. Still, the probability of an "insider job" should be judged as remote. Chances are, in 1990-91, the loss of one or several nuclear devices would have been noticed. Second, all nuclear weapons were withdrawn from the Soviet republics, with the exception of Belarus, Kazakhstan, and Ukraine, to Russia as early as 1990 and definitely no later than the beginning of 1991. The early removal was usually conducted in secret and, in many cases apparently avoided the attention of U.S. intelligence services (Presidential Nuclear Statements in September-October 1991 were reportedly motivated in part by the desire to facilitate the removal of tactical nuclear weapons to Russia from other Soviet republics).

This action was motivated by the increasing risk that nuclear weapons might fall into the hands of various political movements that were rapidly developing at that time. In at least one case, in Azerbaijan, the local pro-independence Popular Front attempted to prevent the removal; the Soviet military had to fire warning shots to disperse the crowd that was blocking the runway at the Air Force base from which bombers with nuclear weapons were taking off.

Troops were authorized to use deadly force if necessary, but luckily warning shots were sufficient. This case demonstrated the length to which the Soviet MOD was prepared to go to prevent the seizure of nuclear weapons. Consequently, the possibility that nuclear weapons could have been intercepted and captured by a local group seems low: Information about such an event could not have been concealed within the MOD and, furthermore, we would have known about the use of force to defend or recapture nuclear weapons.

This leaves Belarus, Kazakhstan, and Ukraine as possible candidates for diversion. Tactical nuclear weapons were withdrawn from their territories in 1992, already after the dissolution of the Soviet Union. According to Arab sources, Usama bin Laden attempted to acquire (bought, some newspapers claimed) nuclear weapons in Ukraine (the Ukrainian government denied this) and Kazakhstan, among other countries (including Russia). One uncorroborated report in December 2000 claimed that the intelligence agency of an unnamed European country intercepted a shipment of approximately 20 nuclear warheads—originating from Kazakhstan, Russia, Turkmenistan, and Ukraine—intended for bin Laden and the Taliban regime of Afghanistan. An attempt to acquire "suitcase" weapons was specifically mentioned in relation to Kazakhstan. An Israeli military intelligence report, which was supposedly leaked, claimed that bin Laden paid over £ 2 million to a middleman in Kazakhstan for a "suitcase" bomb. This claim, however, was also uncorroborated by other sources or physical evidence.

Among these three scenarios, the presence of portable devices in Kazakhstan is the least likely, since it was not a border republic. The removal of tactical nuclear weapons from Belarus and Kazakhstan proceeded smoothly, following the same procedure as the removal from other republics in 1990-1991 (i.e., the 12th GUMO remained part of an integrated command and was formally under the authority of the CIS Strategic Deterrence Forces, but in practice answered to the Russian MOD and the President of Russia). In other words, chances of diversion in these two republics should be assessed as about the same as with regard to other republics, except that the situation in 1992 was more chaotic and difficult to control.

Ukraine represented a different case. In 1991, the government announced a decision to become non-nuclear, but in early 1992 began to explore the possibility of keeping nuclear weapons. Of particular concern was the fact that in May 1992, the personnel of "Facilities S"—nuclear storage facilities controlled by the 12th GUMO—began to take the oath of allegiance to Ukraine, effectively meaning that the chain of custody and accounting began to break down.

It is impossible to say with any certainty when erosion began—probably not earlier than February, when the transfer of tactical nuclear weapons to Russia was stopped for the first time. Air Force bases, including those with aircraft equipped for nuclear weapons (and with nuclear weapons stored inside the bases) began to take the Ukrainian oath in March 1992.

On the other hand, the removal of tactical nuclear weapons from Ukraine was conducted under a special procedure codified in a Russian-Ukrainian agreement signed in March 1992.

This procedure included thorough authentication of each warhead delivered from Ukraine by representatives of both sides, including the checking of serial numbers against the logs kept at the 12th GUMO in Moscow. In effect, the tense Russian-Ukrainian relationship generated a more reliable accounting and verification procedure than was the case with other republics. Consequently, the chance that any weapon entered in central logs remained in Ukraine is very low.

Based on this information, it seems unlikely that any nuclear devices, including portable ones, were lost or stolen outside Russia prior to their removal to the Russian territory. It is practically certain that, contrary to recent (1999-2001) reports, no nuclear warheads could have been bought in Ukraine or Kazakhstan simply because there have been no reports about the presence of non-strategic nuclear weapons in their territories after 1992.

This conclusion, however, rests on two assumptions: first, that original records were complete and accurate and, second, that all withdrawn warheads were checked against these records. These assumptions need further exploration in light of the above-quoted statement by Denisov—which his commission was unable to verify whether any portable nuclear devices remained outside Russia—since that statement implicitly questions the status of the records.

The following hypotheses are possible:

- Records are full and complete, as Igor Valynkin announced. No warheads are smissing, and Denisov's commission was simply unable to complete its job (Denisov admitted that the commission was, indeed, disbanded prematurely).

- As Yablokov speculated, portable nuclear devices were not entered into logs of the 12th GUMO, since they were under control of the KGB. This explanation does not seem very plausible, the special status of the KGB notwithstanding. Yablokov's assertion contradicts all available information about the chain of custody of nuclear weapons, which were supposedly the sole responsibility of the 12th GUMO. In addition, it should be possible to check MOD records against logs of production facilities, and then any "unaccounted" devices would be revealed. This means that, in theory, the 12th GUMO or the Denisov commission had the opportunity to ascertain the existence or the absence of unaccounted warheads.
- A small number of nuclear weapons could have been moved to republics other than Russia in 1990-91, when Soviet institutions were weakened. This theory does not seem plausible either, simply because it would be illogical to send nuclear weapons to republics from which other weapons were being hastily withdrawn (again, possible exceptions are Belarus, Kazakhstan, and Ukraine, where substrategic nuclear weapons remained until mid-1992).
- There is (or was) no single, complete, readily accessible repository of records, and comprehensive checks conducted before the creation of the Denisov commission in 1996. For example, records could be divided between the 12th GUMO and four production (dismantlement) facilities in Russia. In that case, the whereabouts of warheads withdrawn from outside Russia and subsequently eliminated or stored would be particularly vague. This appears a plausible explanation for Denisov's statement about the inability

to locate warheads that had been kept outside Russia prior to the collapse of the Soviet Union. One hopes such a check has been conducted since 1996.

Thus, the hypothesis that a number of portable nuclear devices remained outside Russia or were stolen during the transfer to Russia does not appear convincing. Both the circumstances of that transfer and the likelihood that reasonably complete records exist (even though they might be divided among several holders) lead to a conclusion that former republics of the Soviet Union are an unlikely source of unaccounted for suitcase nukes.

The possibility that a handful of warheads could be produced outside Russia using components left, purchased, or stolen after the transfer of warheads to Russia were raised during the debate in 1997-98. However, this does not seem plausible: Design and production of nuclear weapons were concentrated solely in Russia, and, in all probability, nuclear research centers in other republics simply lacked specialized knowledge. However, it is possible that such information exists outside Russia, perhaps procured by officials contemplating the possibility of retention of Soviet nuclear weapons. Official and unofficial sources in 1997-98 asserted that the design of miniature nuclear devices was more complex than that of common warheads and could not be performed "at home" (thereby indirectly confirming that small devices did exist in the Soviet Union). In any event, the probability of assembly of a portable nuclear device is much smaller than the probability that a crude nuclear weapon could be assembled in a non-nuclear state or by terrorists.

Like all nuclear weapons that are not permanently deployed on delivery vehicles, portable nuclear devices should be kept at storage facilities, controlled by the personnel of the 12th GUMO. Consequently, they should be subject to the same risks as other weapons, exacerbated by their small size. Another potential weak link in the chain of custody is dismantlement facilities, where these devices are kept for some time prior to elimination. According to reports in late 1998, including a detailed one in the London-based, Arab daily, *Al-Watan Al-Arabi,* Chechens acquired approximately 20 "tactical" nuclear weapons from Russian facilities, to be subsequently transferred to bin Laden for a sum of $30 million in cash plus two tons of opium. These claims, too, were not corroborated by other sources or physical evidence. In the end, the feasibility of this scenario depends on the level of security provided by facilities, some of which in the last decade have benefited from American assistance.

Security risks at storage facilities have been well researched. It is sufficient here to briefly list the most relevant factors for the case of portable nuclear devices:

- There is an uncomfortably high probability of "insider threats" from personnel that work or previously worked at storage facilities. Although their salaries and living conditions are usually somewhat better than that of ordinary officers and sergeants, the standard of living is still low by today's standards. Many officers are forced to take additional jobs "on the side" and could be easily co-opted by criminal organizations or foreign intelligence.
- All, or at least the majority, of key personnel live inside the outer security perimeter of storage facilities and often do not leave upon retirement unless provided housing by the government, as required by law. In the mid-1990s, for example, nearly 3,500 retired officers continued to live within the closed compounds of the 12th GUMO facilities. Close personal relations among active-duty officers, and between them and retired officers, can facilitate access to inner security perimeters. In at least one case, a retired officer who was still living at a nuclear weapons storage facility was able to arrange access for local criminals to the inner (most secure) zone to steal small arms intended for guards.

- Security systems at many storage facilities are old and often inadequate; only 47 percent of these facilities so far have been equipped with new fences and other equipment purchased through U.S. funding under the Cooperative Threat Reduction (CTR) program. The power supply is often unreliable. The accounting systems at many of the facilities are antiquated. All these problems continue to haunt nuclear weapons storage sites even today, but conditions were considerably worse in the early 1990s. It is difficult to be confident that any thefts that might have occurred a decade ago would have been noticed.

The situation is similar at production and dismantlement facilities, where components of warheads could be stolen by employees. Workers and engineers were and are plagued by the same woes, and the challenges are further exacerbated by the absence of military discipline (or what remains of it in post-Soviet conditions), as well as greater numbers of facilities and their location in large cities (the "closed" status of these cities offers only limited enhancement of security).

The early 1990s was a period of particularly high risk both due to socioeconomic conditions and also because the massive removal of nuclear weapons to Russia from outside the Soviet Union and from other former Soviet republics put an unusual stress on the system. At that time, storage facilities were literally overflowing, and many of them contained more warheads than allowed by safety regulations. The open-source data on suitcase nukes is sketchy and incomplete. Still, even using this data, one can assess the nature of these weapons, the probability of an unknown number of them having been stolen, and the level of associated threat.

In spite of official denials, there are sufficient grounds to believe that the Soviet Union had one or more types of portable nuclear devices. Most likely, these were devices designed for the use by Special Forces (Spetsnaz), analogous to the American SADM, or using the physics package similar to that contained in artillery shells. The widely used word "suitcase" is misleading since these devices were quite heavy (no less than 60 lb, probably considerably more), but they could have been moved by one, but more likely, two people.

Without additional data, it is impossible to say with an acceptable level of certainty whether any number of these weapons was stolen during and following the breakup of the Soviet Union, as Alexander Lebed and a few other Russians claimed. Available evidence suggests that these stories were most probably not true, and that they were generated by incomplete information or ulterior motives. The probability that such weapons could be used by terrorists (assuming some were stolen) appears even lower. The reasons for that conclusion are the following:

- Probably the most convincing evidence is the fact that no terrorist group has used such a device or even credibly threatened its use. There have been many instances, especially during the first and the second, ongoing wars in Chechnya. Yet, the worse case so far was limited to the burying of a container with radioactive isotopes in a Moscow park. Since the majority of feasible scenarios involve Chechens, and since the period of greatest risk was in the early 1990s, the inactivity of Chechens in this matter is significant.
- The scenario offered by Denisov, namely, that a number of portable nuclear devices were left outside Russia when nuclear weapons were withdrawn to its territory, appears unlikely. In most cases, the removal took place more than a year before the breakup of the Soviet Union, when the Soviet military, in particular troops charged with custody of nuclear weapons, were in relative order. In the only case in which an attempt to "conceal" a limited number of nuclear weapons

could be suspected—in Ukraine—the removal was subject to enhanced accounting procedures.

- The risk of loss of nuclear weapons was the greatest in the early 1990s within the territory of Russia itself. At that time, large numbers of nuclear weapons were transported across the country, often by trains ill-suited for that purpose; accounting could be relatively lax, and personnel was undergoing the period of deepest uncertainty, depression, and precipitous drop in the standard of living. With time, the probability of the loss of portable nuclear devices decreased with gradual increase of stability and, even more important in terms of immediate effect, American assistance, which helped to improve accounting, transportation, and security of nuclear weapons.
- Yet another scenario offered by Denisov—assembly of portable nuclear devices from parts "forgotten" outside Russia—is the least believable. There was no nuclear weapons production outside Russia; consequently, the probability that parts of nuclear weapons could be found outside its territory is very unlikely. In addition, there was very little specialized expertise and know-how outside Russia, whereas portable nuclear devices were apparently very complicated in design and required highly skilled professionals to oversee their production and assembly.

  Even assuming that some portable nuclear devices were lost, it would be very difficult to use them, and it is almost certain that the features that make portable nuclear devices so dangerous (small size and full-scale nuclear explosion effects) will not be taken advantage of.
- Information about unusually short maintenance periods for these weapons is probably true, although the extent and the pace of deterioration of nuclear weapons' features cannot be determined from open sources.

Since, as it was noted above, the period of greatest risk was in the early 1990s, the stolen devices, if any, have already missed as many as 20 routine component replacement procedures and are probably nearing the end of their service life. Consequently, it is nearly certain that they will be unable to produce the design yield and maybe will not be able to produce any yield at all.

- Most, if not all, portable nuclear warheads are equipped with some protection devices (e.g., PALs), making their unauthorized use difficult, though not completely impossible.

In effect, portable nuclear devices, if stolen, will hardly be usable, at least not in the fashion that they were originally designed for. They could be, of course, dismantled to extract weapons-grade plutonium, which could then be used in a cruder nuclear device or for a "dirty bomb"; but in this case, the problem of suitcase nukes is virtually indistinguishable from the broader problem of safety and security of all Russian nuclear weapons and weapons-grade fissile materials.

That being said, low probability is not a sufficient reason for comfort or lower vigilance. Until the situation is sufficiently clarified, it will be necessary to guard against the infiltration of a portable nuclear device into U.S. territory and, probably of even greater importance, to keep in mind the possibility that nuclear mines might be used against U.S. troops abroad in more or less the same way the Soviet Union planned to use them against advancing NATO or Chinese troops.

Above all, it is necessary to strengthen the effort to obtain additional information about suitcase nukes, including the types of small (portable) weapons and their status (eliminated or stored; whether any were lost; and the safety and security procedures applied to the ones that are still kept), as well as the possible performance of the ones that could have been stolen and remained hidden for long periods of time.

Placating the *Shi'a*

The United Nations Secretary-General has just announced his intent to dispatch a team of experts to Iraq to explore whether it is possible to hold open elections. This new UN mission to Iraq comes on the heels of week-long mass demonstrations held in most of Iraq by the tens of thousands of Iraqi *Shi'a* who answered the call of their Grand Ayatollah Ali al-Sistani to oppose the Coalition plan to appoint a new provisional government. This presents a serious obstacle to the U.S.-led Coalition in post-Saddam Iraq.

Many leading figures among the Iraqi *Shi'a* majority reject the current Coalition plan to transfer Iraqi governance to a provisional government, and are demanding direct and open elections to determine the legitimate leadership of Iraq prior to the July 1st deadline. The Coalition has claimed that flaws in the current Iraqi infrastructure seriously hamper the possibility of direct elections, and instead proposed that power be transferred to a selected provisional government by the end of June. This argument has fallen on deaf ears. Iraq's foremost *Shi'a* cleric Grand Ayatollah Ali al-Sistani has issued a *fatwa* (religious decree) opposing this plan and demanded full and open elections in the absence of an UN-certified finding that supports the Coalition's claims. The following essay will discuss the major Iraqi *Shi'a* organizations in Iraq and their sources of discontent with the transfer of power plan presented by the U.S.-led Coalition.

Due to its long history of oppression and bitter experience with perceived betrayal the Iraqi *Shi'a* have a mistrust of Coalition intentions. The support of the *Shi'a* has the potential to "make or break" any new Iraqi government, and thus it is essential for the occupying forces to understand how this aspect of *Shi'i* history affects the current political climate.

Although they constitute a majority of the population, the *Shi'a* of Iraq have long been subjugated by the ruling power, be it the Ottomans, the British, or most recently, the *Ba'ath* Party. Following the U.S.-led invasion of Iraq, the *Shi'a* majority will play an integral part in the establishment of a new Iraqi government. At present, there are four predominant *Shi'i* factions in Iraq: the "Quietists," the al-Sadr faction, the Supreme Council for the Islamic Revolution in Iraq, and the *D'awa* Party. The "Quietist" movement evolved under the leadership of Sayyid Abu al-Qasim al-Khoei in the first few decades of Ba'athist rule and following al-Khoei's death in 1992, the Grand Ayatollah 'Ali al-Sistani assumed control of the movement. Quietism, a long-standing *Shi'i* tradition, discourages religious clerics from becoming directly involved in politics.

According to the Quietists, the clergy may monitor and debate politics, but it should refrain from becoming directly involved in the development of policy. Thus, the Quietist view is a challenge to the ruling elite in Iran, where the Grand Ayatollah Ruhollah Khomeini launched *velyat al-faqih,* or the rule of the jurisprudent. In fact, Khomeini's establishment of clerical rule is considered anathema to a majority of leading clerics in both Iraq and Iran. Under the rule of Saddam Hussein, Quietism served as a survival mechanism for a number of Iraqi *Shi'a*. Their opposition to *velyat al-faqih* portrayed the Quietists as posing a limited threat to Hussein's regime. Quietists, however, do not necessarily renounce politics completely. With the threat of Ba'athist rule no longer looming over their heads, the Iraqi *Shi'a* may turn to Sistani, one of the *maraji' al-taqlid* (sources of emulation), for political guidance. Having been subject to minority rule for so long, Sistani and the Quietists may have found that they must take a more active role in politics, or lose their popular support.

Following the onset of Operation Iraqi Freedom in March 2003, Grand Ayatollah Ali al-Sistani was helpful to the Coalition's war effort. He adhered to the Quietist tradition and rarely issued political statements. On some occasions al-Sistani has also advocated the separation of religion from the state in post-war Iraq. Moreover, he issued religious decrees asking his *Shi'a* followers not to resist Coalition troops and not to hinder the Coalition's effort to overthrow the Ba'ath regime. For that, on various occasions al-Sistani was repeatedly praised by American forces. But he is the most vociferous proponent of open elections now.

The *al-Sadr Faction*

The *al-Sadr faction* is led by Muqtada al-Sadr, whose father, the popular Sayyid Muhammed Sadiq al-Sadr, was assassinated by the Iraqi government in 1999. Another member of the al-Sadr family, the extremely influential Ayatollah Muhammed Baqir al-Sadr, was also killed by the government in 1980. Muqtada al-Sadr, young and inexperienced, has relied on his family name to attract followers. The core of the Sadr faction is the *Jama'at al-Sadr al-Thani* (Association of the Second al-Sadr). Muqtada al-Sadr has used this association as a vehicle to propel himself to fame among the *Shi'a* of Iraq, primarily in and around Baghdad. The *Shi'a* dominated area of Baghdad once known as "Saddam City" has been renamed "Sadr City" in honor of the Sadr faction.

Muqtada al-Sadr is known for fostering discord within the *Shi'a* community, often targeting the Quietists. Following the U.S.-led invasion, al-Sadr declared that al-Sistani and two other prominent clerics, Baqir al-Hakim and Muhammed Ishaq al-Fayyad, should leave Iraq. Following the death of 'Abd-al-Majid al-Khoei in April 2003, rumors circulated that al-Sadr was involved in the murder, though no evidence of this has been brought to light. Muqtada al-Sadr has targeted a number of leading clerics based on their ethnicity. He is leading a "nativist" campaign to drive clerics of foreign descent out of Iraqi politics. Several prominent Iraqi clerics were actually born elsewhere, such as al-Sistani, who is of Iranian origin. The nativist line touted by al-Sadr eschews Iranian interference in Iraqi *Shi'i* politics. Should al-Sadr's faction emerge as the dominate *Shi'i* force in the state, Iraq will pose a serious challenge to Iran's influence over *Shi'i* Muslims in the region.

The Supreme Council for the Islamic Revolution in Iraq (SCIRI) was founded in Tehran in 1982, by then-exiled Ayatollah Muhammed Baqir al-Hakim. SCIRI has received considerable support from the Iranian government, and lingering ties to the Islamic regime could endanger SCIRI's popularity among Iraqis. While al-Hakim created a vast power base for SCIRI, including the 10,000-strong Badr Brigade that followed him from Iran to Iraq in the spring of 2003, he also developed a number of enemies. Much of the animosity directed toward al-Hakim stemmed from his ties to Iran, and his support for Iran during the 1980-88 Iran-Iraq war.

Though some believed that al-Hakim would be to Iraq what Khomeini had been to Iran, al-Hakim adopted a rather moderate stance upon returning to Iraq after 20 years of exile in Iran. Al-Hakim denounced the possibility of a puppet government installed by the United States, but encouraged Iraqi *Shi'i* to work with the United States in order to develop a new Iraqi government. Also, he began to promote a separation of church and state in the future Iraqi government. Al-Hakim then turned his focus toward more spiritual issues. His brother, Abdel Aziz al-Hakim, assumed leadership of SCIRI's political objectives, joining the interim Governing Council.

Under the leadership of Ayatollah Muhammed Baqir al-Hakim, SCIRI developed ties with the United States, despite U.S. reservations about SCIRI's relationship with Iran. SCIRI is also an important part of the Iraqi National Congress (INC), which has received substantial backing from the United States for several years. SCIRI suffered a serious blow when al-Hakim was killed by a car-bomb on August 29, 2003, outside the sacred Imam Ali Mosque in Najaf. More than 120 Iraqi *Shi'a* civilians were killed in the blast, for which no one has claimed responsibility.

Following the assassination of al-Hakim, more than 400,000 *Shi'a* attended these funeral ceremonies in Najaf in a display of great support and solidarity that highlighted the immense popularity of Baqir al-Hakim and his SCIRI organization. Moreover, the assassination of this popular *Shi'i* Ayatollah and bombings of the shrine of Ali have driven many *Shi'a* groups in Iraq to form their own armed militias to defend themselves from threats. SCIRI was among the major organizers of the mass *Shi'a* demonstrations against the U.S. transfer of power plan, in the cities of Karbala', Dajil and in the province of Nissan.

The *D'awa* Party

Founded in 1957 by Sayyid Baqir al-Sadr and his associates, the *D'awa (call to Islam) Party* predates the other major *Shi'i* movements in Iraq. The party attacked Saddam Hussein's regime in an effort to establish an Islamic state in Iraq. A vast number of *D'awa* members suffered at the hands of the regime and consequently the Iraqi *Shi'i* populace developed a great reverence for the party. Although it played an active role in the founding of SCIRI in 1982, the *D'awa* leadership's support for *velyat al-faqih* led to a rift within the organization. Members opposed to the rule of the clergy and Iranian influence in the *D'awa* movement broke with the party. Today, there are two main factions behind the *D'awa* movement.

One faction, Islamic *D'awa*, remains affiliated with SCIRI and maintains a base of power in Iran. The other faction is based in London and promotes a more "Iraqi" character for the movement. The true extent of *D'awa's* influence in post-Saddam Iraq is still unknown. Thus far, the *D'awa* leadership has cooperated with the occupation forces, but it may well align itself more closely with the al-Sadr faction should popular opinion continue to turn against the U.S.-led forces.

Self-Restraint in Post-War Iraq

In the aftermath of the fall of the Ba'ath regime, the long subjugated Iraqi *Shi'a* majority have shown restraint. Up to this point and contrary to the predictions of many, there have been very few cases of revenge killing by the majority *Shi'a* against the *Sunni* minority who brutally ruled Iraq for many decades. Moreover, Iraq's *Shi'a* majority has shown immense restraint in the face of continuous provocations by Ba'ath regime remnants. The most egregious provocation was the attack on the Shrine of Ali on August 29, 2003, which damaged a part of the holy mosques and killed more than 120 *Shi'a,* including the head of SCIRI Ayatollah Baqr al-Hakim.

Many in and outside Iraq feared the beginning of a campaign of *Shi'a* revenge killings and possibly a civil war. Yet, for the most part the Iraqi *Shi'a* has shown high levels of restraint and has not been dragged into a cycle of revenge. A reflection on events at this time shows that heads of SCIRI and other major Iraqi *Shi'a* groups abstained from full-blown violence so that Coalition rebuilding efforts and the upcoming transfer of power could take place. Many in the *Shi'a* leadership may have reasoned that revenge killings and civil war would only hamper the *Shi'a* long-term strategy of supporting free elections in which they would surely win due to numerical majority.

However, in the event of a Coalition-appointed provisional government made up of Iraqi expatriates vs. a freely elected government headed by a domestic *Shi'a* figure, it may be that the *Shi'a* leadership's motivations for cooperation and restraint could be replaced with animosity and hostility toward the Coalition and the appointed provisional government. In that event, it would not be surprising if Grand Ayatollah Ali al-Sistani and other influential local *Shi'a* leaders begin to encourage the Iraqi *Shi'a* population to reject the Coalition's efforts and plans for post-war Iraq.

The Coalition's plan is somewhat complicated. Local caucuses are to convene in each of Iraq's 18 regional governorates. Each governorate will then elect delegates from their caucus to become part of the Iraqi Transitional National Assembly. By June 30, 2004, this National Assembly is to elect Iraq's leaders from its ranks, who will then assume full sovereignty of the country. If all goes according to plan, Iraq's interim governing council and the Coalition Provisional Authority will be dissolved on that date, thereby ending the UN-specified responsibilities of the Coalition as an occupying power. The plan has some snags, however. First, the Iraqi population has no accurate electoral roll and it is unlikely that the more than 20 million people in the country could be registered in time for the June 30 deadline.

Second, direct elections at this stage might give undue representation to Ba'athists, fundamentalist groups, or the *Shi'a*. Moreover, the United States believes the security situation is currently too volatile to hold free and fair elections - a position UN Secretary-General Kofi Annan has agreed with. The June 30, 2004, date is significant. Washington wants to bring the occupation of Iraq to a close as soon as it is safe and feasible to do so, and in the atmosphere of upcoming U.S. presidential elections, George Bush stands to regain the political ground that he has lost as a result of American troop losses and failure to locate WMD in Iraq.

While most of the Iraqi *Shi'a* and their leaders had been largely supportive of the U.S.-led effort to overthrow the oppressive Ba'ath regime in Iraq, it appears that in the last few months *Shi'i* support and hope have given way to suspicion and opposition. The root of the current disagreement between the Coalition and the most influential leaders of the Iraqi *Shi'a,* including al-Sistani, SCIRI, and Sadr, seems to stem from various *Shi'a* concerns. First and foremost, the majority of the Iraqi *Shi'a* community wants the Coalition to transfer power to a freely elected government and not a government that is selected by the U.S.-led Coalition by the July 1, 2004 deadline. Many *Shi'a* leaders justify open elections by pointing out that their community has long been subjugated by a ruling minority (Ottomans, British and the *Sunni* Ba'athists).

Moreover, due to the *Shi'a* numerical majority, they will surely win the elections and elect a leadership that will grant them the long-awaited control over Iraq. It is important to note that two leading *Shi'a* figures in Iraq the Grand Ayatollah Ali al-Sistani and the late Ayatollah Mohammed Baqr al-Hakim have adhered to the *Shi'i* Quietist tradition and have advocated an Iraqi democratic secular state and not an Islamic Republic a la Iran. As al-Hakim told Reuters in May: "We should not make a copy of the Iranian revolution and establish it in Iraq."

Second, in recent weeks al-Sistani and many of his assistants have rejected the possibility of a U.S.-selected government made up primarily of Iraqi expatriates who returned to Iraq following the overthrow of the Ba'ath regime. On January 14, al-Sistani told a meeting of local tribes and clans in the holy city of Najaf: "The authority should be given to you and not to those who came from abroad.... The next council should be made up from the elected sons of the people." Sistani and other *Shi'a* leaders have stated that any imposed, un-elected transitional government devoid of local representation will not be considered legitimate by the local Iraqi Ayatollahs, who will not adhere to its authority. Hashem al-Awad, a representative of al-Sistani warned: "The sons of the Iraqi people demand a political system based on direct elections and a constitution that realizes justice and equality for everyone... Anything other than that will prompt people to have their own say."

Third, in spite of their tacit support for the overthrow of Saddam's regime, many in the Iraqi *Shi'a* mistrust U.S. intentions in Iraq. Some of this mistrust is fueled by the *Shi'a* sense of betrayal by the United States in the aftermath of the liberation of Kuwait in February 1991. Following the liberation of Kuwait, President George Bush Sr. called on the Iraqi people to revolt against the Saddam regime stating: "There's another way for the bloodshed to stop, and that is for the Iraqi military and their people to take matters into their own hands and force Saddam Hussein, the dictator, to step aside." However, when the *Shi'a* and Kurds succeeded in taking control of over 14 of Iraq's 18 provinces and overpowering many of Saddam's forces, the United States allowed Saddam Hussein to deploy helicopter gun ships and crush the rebellion, killing thousands of *Shi'a*. Finally, much of Iraqi *Shi'a* mistrust is fueled by the current administration of various *Shi'a* areas, including the holy city of Karbala'. According to Dr. Hussein Shahristani Iraq's former leading Nuclear Chemist and founder of a *Shi'i* relief organization in Karbala', the Coalition has failed to live up to its promise of dealing with former members of the Ba'ath party.

Shahristani told "60 Minutes" in December: "The expectations were that the Ba'athists would be immediately arrested and put on trial for their crimes against humanity, for their crimes against the Iraqi people. Now this hasn't happened. And people were alarmed when the Ba'athists was actually reinstated back into the government." Dr. Shahristani indicated that the local *Shi'a* population is very concerned with this turn of events and the fact that various local *Shi'a* figures who spoke against this governing arrangement were arrested by the Coalition forces. He added, "People feel vulnerable."

In the last few weeks various moderate Iraqi *Shi'a* leaders have expressed distrust of the Coalition's intentions.

On January 7, Al-Sistani stated: "the (occupation) authorities are not entitled to name the members of the assembly charged with drafting the constitution.... There is no guarantee that such a convention will draft a constitution upholding the Iraqi people's interest and expressing their national identity." By mid-January, Sheikh Abdul Mahdi, Ayatollah al-Sistani's local representative in the *Shi'a* holy city of Karbala` warned during Friday prayers: "In next few days, we will see protests, strikes and many clashes with the occupation troops if they insist on their colonialist scheme and on designing Iraq's policy according to their own interests."

Shi'a disenchantment and agitation with Coalition plans culminated in a letter from Iraq's second most senior *Shi'a* cleric, Hojat al-Islam Ali Abd al-Hakim al-Safi, to President Bush and Prime Minister Blair. The letter calls into question their sincerity in transferring power to an Iraqi provisional government and warns the Coalition leaders that, if they deny Iraqis the ability to choose their leaders, the United States and England will face an unwinnable war. Mr. al-Safi expressed distrust of the Coalition's claims of logistical difficulties, stating that it was simply a pretext to deny the Iraqi people their legitimate aspirations. The current powder keg situation may ignite into outright opposition between the *Shi'a* and Coalition forces if the Coalition selects a provisional government and denies the *Shi'a* free elections. As summed up by Dr. Hussein Shahristani, "If that process doesn't happen, god only knows what will be the consequences of such a move."

A possible way to defuse the currently brewing crisis between the Coalition and the leadership of the Iraqi *Shi'a* is to proactively enlist the help of the United Nations. On more than one occasion, Grand Ayatollah Ali al-Sistani and other Iraqi *Shi'a* leaders have agreed to give the Coalition more time to set up the necessary institutions and infrastructure to conduct free elections at a later date, possibly by 2005, if an official, unbiased UN survey shows that Iraq currently lacks the potential to hold open, free elections. In the last few days, Paul Bremer and members of the Coalition-appointed Iraqi Governing Council were in the midst of negotiating such an effort with UN Secretary-General Kofi Annan.

As a result, Kofi Annan has just announced that he will send an international team of experts to asses the feasibility of holding Iraqi free elections prior to the July 1, 2004 deadline. If the UN team concurs with the Coalition's assessment, it is likely that such international, legitimized finding will encourage Grand Ayatollah Ali al-Sistani and his followers to moderate their demands. During the Friday prayers on January 23, 2004, al-Sistani urged his *Shi'a* followers to halt mass protests against the current plan until the UN Secretary-General rules on the possibility of direct elections, after which the Grand Ayatollah will address his followers. This is a positive development that gives the Coalition much needed breathing room.

In the immediate aftermath of Israel's invasion of Lebanon on June 6, 1982, initial Lebanese *Shi'a* reactions were mostly encouraging to the Israelis. The majority of the Lebanese *Shi'a* wanted the Palestine Liberation Organization (PLO) and their forces removed from their areas; they were mostly indifferent to the Israeli presence in Southern Lebanon. However, all that changed within a year. Misguided Israeli policies resulted in the death of many Lebanese *Shi'a*. On October 16, 1983, an Israeli Army convoy tactlessly interrupted the *Ashura* ceremonies in Nabatiya that were attended by 50,000 Lebanese *Shi'a* to commemorate and mourn the Martyrdom of Imam Husayn Bin Ali.

The following day, Sheikh Mehdi Shamseddin, the head of Beirut's Higher *Shi'a* Council, issued a *fatwa* (religious decree) calling for "civil resistance" against Israeli forces. Similar calls were soon issued by other Lebanese *Shi'a* leaders. These events marked the beginning of the end of the Israeli occupation of Lebanon. Shortly thereafter, an umbrella organization called the Lebanese National Resistance (LNR) was formed and became dominated by AMAL. In the following years, AMAL and other militant *Shi'i* militias (the Lebanese Islamic Jihad and Hizbullah) entered and dominated the Lebanese civil war, which up to that point was mainly fought among the Christian Phalanges, *Sunni*, and Palestinian militias.

While reflecting on this troubling new situation in Lebanon, former Israeli Prime Minister Yitzhak Rabin's remarked, "We have let the *Shi'a* genie out of the bottle." In the next three years, militant *Shi'i* militias became the most formidable force in the Lebanese civil war. These groups re-invented and perfected the notion of martyrdom and the tactic of suicide bombings. AMAL, and Lebanese Islamic Jihad militias killed more than 600 Israeli soldiers and 241 U.S. marines. Following the U.S. withdrawal from Lebanon, *Shi'a* militants overwhelmed the Christian Phalanges and on June 10, 1985, forced the Israeli Army to withdraw from most of Lebanon. Continued guerilla resistance by Hizbullah against the Israeli Defense Forces in the next 15 years resulted in Israel's complete withdrawal from Lebanon in 2000, after which Hizbullah decimated the Israeli-sponsored South Lebanon Army.

The U.S.-led Coalition in Iraq would do well to learn from Israel's mistakes in South Lebanon. Failure to placate the 14 million Iraqi *Shi'a* by attempting to impose an un-elected outsider government in Iraq may very well result in an open conflict between the Coalition and the *Shi'a* population. Such a conflict has the potential to deteriorate into a Beirut-style cycle of violence that result in the death of many thousands. One cannot overstate the apparent danger in a policy that would alienate the Iraqi *Shi'a*, who constitutes more than 60% of the Iraqi population. Most insurgent attacks against Coalition targets that claimed the lives of hundreds of Coalition forces have come from the

Sunni triangle, which accounts for only 15% of the Iraqi population. An armed *Shi'a* uprising as in South Lebanon has the potential of turning Iraq into a truly ungovernable quagmire.

The Coalition will do well to heed Prime Minister Rabin's advice and not let the "*Shi'a* genie out of the bottle" again. With the ongoing U.S.-led occupation and nation-building effort in Iraq, the Coalition may be running into a potential conflict with the Iraqi *Shi'a* population over plans to hand over control to a provisional government. Last week's mass demonstrations in Baghdad and Southern Iraq have brought to light the concerns of Iraq's *Shi'a* majority. These demonstrations have also revealed the formidable power that Grand Ayatollah Ali al-Sistani and his followers possess among the Iraqi *Shi'a* community. Shortly after al-Sistani issued his *fatwa* opposing the Coalition plan, the streets of Baghdad, Basra, and Karbala` and many other Iraqi cities and towns were filled with tens of thousands of peaceful Iraqi *Shi'a* demonstrators who condemned the Coalition plan and demanded free elections.

Currently post-war Iraq is still unstable; in the last few weeks a report was given to the Pentagon indicating that there is a strong possibility of a civil war breaking out. In such a tense situation, understanding the concerns of the Iraqi *Shi'a* leadership and opting to address them by reaching out to the long victimized *Shi'a* population of Iraq might be the difference between success and failure in rebuilding Iraq. If the United States and the Iraqi Governing Council are unable to find a way to placate Grand Ayatollah Ali al-Sistani and his many *Shi'a* followers there is a possibility that a cycle of violence may break out among Coalition troops and some of the *Shi'a* militias. If and when that happens, the occupation and rebuilding of Iraq will become a much more difficult undertaking and may deteriorate to Lebanon-style violence. In post-war Iraq, enhancing the American - Iraqi *Shi'a* peace is paramount.

6

The Current Terrorist Tactics and Methods

The bloody scenes from Istanbul the target of four devastating bombings in a single week have become all too familiar in recent years. Indiscriminate suicide bombings against civilian and military targets have become a constant fixture in Middle Eastern politics. This tactic has been used in the Palestinian fight against Israeli occupation, Ba'athist insurgency against the American presence in Iraq, and in al-Qa'ida global terrorism targeting civilians in Africa, Asia, the Middle East and the West. Organized systemic suicide bombings have become a very popular method of warfare in the Middle East, used by various political and religious groups to further their goals and objectives. This trend that started in the 1980s in war torn Lebanon has become a popular tactic that is widely used by various regional militant groups, and multinational terror organizations with global reach. The historical roots of Middle Eastern suicide warfare methods and tactics can be traced to early Islamic history.

Fourteen centuries ago an important schism occurred within the Islamic *umma* (community of believers). From this rift, two main factions emerged: the *Sunna* and the *Shi'a*. In addition to generating the concepts of *Sunna* and *Shi'a*, this schism sparked yet another idea that would have a tremendous impact on the course of Middle East history. The origins and justification for the concept of *shahada*, or martyrdom, stem from this schism. Gaining notoriety in the 1980s, *shahada* has become a popular military paradigm used by various *Shi'i* and *Sunni* militant groups to justify their use of suicide bombings as a legitimate method of warfare. To best understand the motives behind self martyrdom, one needs to return to the roots of the *Shi'i-Sunni* conflict and explore how early Islamic history continues to affect the attitudes and religious interpretations of militant Islamist groups that rely upon suicide operations as integral parts of their military operations. This story will trace the historical root of modern Middle Eastern suicide warfare tactics and methods.

The Origins of *Shi'i* Islam

Shi'i Islam grew out of a schism that developed within the Islamic community after the death of the Prophet Muhammad in 632 A.D. The majority of Muhammad's followers believed that his successor should be selected from his tribe, the Quraysh, by elders close to the Prophet. The elders chose Abu Bakr, the father-in-law of the Prophet and the first adult male convert to Islam, to succeed him as leader of the Islamic community. The successor, or caliph, would rule the community according to Islamic law, or *Shari'a*, which had been established under Muhammad. Those who believed in this method of succession became known as *Sunni*; from the Arabic word *Sunna*, meaning custom or tradition. Thus, the term *Sunni* has the connotation of being a follower of the example of the Prophet. Today, *Sunnis* comprise approximately 90 percent of the Muslim population.

Unlike their *Sunni* counterparts, a minority of Muslims believed that Muhammad's eldest male relative, Ali ibn Abi Talib, should succeed him. The cousin and son-in-law of the Prophet, Ali was viewed by this faction (or *shi'a*) to be the true leader of the community (known as the *Imam*). In addition to being a blood relative of the Prophet, Ali had repeatedly proven himself to be devoted to the nascent religion. In fact, a number of Ali's supporters regarded him as the Prophet's intended heir. Thus, *Shi'i* Islam grew out of the belief that only descendents of Ali (and thus of the Prophet) could be leaders of the Islamic community. Initially members of this faction were called *Shi'at Ali* (partisans of Ali); later their name was shortened to *Shi'a.*

The Early Caliphate

The *Sunni* majority would select four caliphs in close succession in the three decades following Muhammad's death. The first caliph, Abu Bakr, was followed first by 'Umar ibn al-Khattab and then by 'Uthman ibn 'Affan. Finally, in 656 A.D., the *Sunni* elders selected Ali as the fourth caliph. Ali would rule only four-and-a-half years, until 661 A.D. These first four caliphs are known as the rightly guided caliphs, or *al-khulafa' al-rashidun.* This era, during which Islam took root across the Arabian Peninsula, is viewed by many *Sunnis* as a continuation of the "golden age" of the Prophet Muhammad. For most *Shi'a,* however, the true height of the Islam occurred only during Muhammad's rule in Medina (622-632 A.D.) and Ali's brief reign as caliph (656-661 A.D.)

The Advent of Islamic Fundamentalism

Ali's term as caliphate was marred by controversy. His legitimacy as successor to the Prophet was challenged by Mu'awiyah ibn Abi Sufyan, a member of the powerful Ummayad tribe. Mu'awiyah, the governor of modern Syria, accused Ali of supporting the assassination of his cousin, the late caliph 'Uthman. In 657 A.D., the two men's armies met at the battle of Siffin. Neither side could claim victory, although according to *Shi'i* tradition, Mu'awiyah's troops faced certain defeat. The battle ended before Ali was able to secure his victory, however, when Mu'awiyah's troops carried *Qu'rans* onto the field of battle, calling for arbitration that would "Let God decide." Ali consented but the arbitration, like the battle itself, was inconclusive. Consequently, Ali and Mu'awiyah remained locked in a struggle for leadership.

In the wake of the arbitration, there emerged a *Shi'i* faction known as the Kharijites (or *Khawarij* from the Arabic *"kharaja,"* meaning to exit or secede). The Kharijites had initially regarded Ali as the rightful successor to Muhammad. They also considered Mu'awiyah to be an infidel for his opposition to Ali's reign. After Ali consented to arbitration, the Kharijites became convinced that he, too, was guilty of *takfir*, or unbelief. By submitting to arbitration, Ali had flouted God's right to decide the victor of the battle at Siffin. The Kharijites withdrew their support from Ali and formed their own religious community that preached strict adherence to the *Qu'ran* and the *Sunna* (example of the Prophet).

Central to the fundamentalist beliefs of the Kharijites was the concept of *jihad*. This concept existed long before the advent of the Kharijites. The *Qu'ran* places great emphasis on *jihad*, the Arabic term for "struggle." According to the Qu'ran, followers of Islam must struggle to remain on the path of God and the Prophet. Over time, there have been various interpretations of what form this struggle should take. Often, *jihad* is believed to be a peaceful struggle; an effort to foster virtue and charity in the face of evil and adversity. Most interpretations of *jihad* often focus on improvement within an individual or the Islamic community. Fundamentalist and militant interpretations take a more aggressive view, believing that *jihad* justifies force and violence in order to spread God's word to nonbelievers and to combat perceived injustices.

The Kharijites placed a great emphasis on violent *jihad*, believing that force was often necessary to "command the good and forbid evil," as they construe the *Qur'an* to mandate. The Kharijites viewed the world in dualist terms as "us against them"; "them" being both non-Muslims and those Muslims who deviate from the Kharijite vision of Islam. The Kharijites' fundamentalist interpretation of the *Qu'ran* led them to equate the majority of other Muslims with infidels. In order to protect and purify Islam, the Kharijites believed that it was their duty to kill any unbelievers who did not repent. One of their more notable victims was Ali himself, whom the Kharijites assassinated in 661 A.D., as punishment for his consent to arbitration with Mu'awiyah.

Ali's assassination took place in the southern Iraqi town of Najaf, and his shrine there remains among the most sacred sites in *Shi'i* Islam. The assassination itself was carried out by sleeper cells that infiltrated Ali's ranks, waiting patiently for the opportunity to strike. Although the Kharijites comprised a small minority of Muslims that remained on the fringes of the Islamic community, the impact of fundamentalism and violent *jihad* has echoed throughout Islamic history. In particular, it has taken center stage in the twentieth century with the resurgence of extremist *Sunni* Islamic fundamentalist groups.

Present-day terrorist groups, such as al-Qa'ida and Egyptian Islamic Gihad, have adopted strict interpretations of the *Qur'an* and embraced the practice of *takfir*, casting all Muslims who disagree with them as apostates. Like the Kharijites, these groups organize sleeper cell formations that assimilate within various communities and target opposing political leaders and civilian institutions that they regard as infidels or non-believers.

Following Ali's assassination, his eldest son, Hasan, became the second *Imam*. Hasan quickly ceded the caliphate to Mu'awiyah, who launched the Ummayad dynasty that would rule the *Sunni* Muslim community from 661 until 750 A.D. Although Hasan did not act as caliph, *Shi'a* Muslims continued to regard him as their *Imam* until his death, sometime around 670 A.D. *Shi'i* tradition states that Hasan abdicated to Mu'awiyah in order to prevent another conflict, but with the understanding that Hasan would one day be Mu'awiyah's heir to the caliphate. Mu'awiyah then allegedly went back on his word and had Hasan assassinated.

Shortly before his own death, Mu'awiyah named his son, Yazid, as his successor. Yazid came to power in 680 A.D. Hasan's younger brother, the third Imam, Husayn, refused to declare his loyalty to the new caliph and took haven in the Sacred Mosque of Mecca. Supporters of his late father, Ali, encouraged Husayn to organize a revolt against new caliph's regime in Kufa. Located in southern Iraq, Kufa had been the seat of Ali's rule. *Shi'i* tradition holds that Husayn accepted the call to rebellion in order to combat the growing hedonism of the Umayyads and to guide the Muslim people back to the path of Muhammad.

According to *Shi'i* accounts, Husayn left for Kufa knowing that he would not return. It is reported that before departing Mecca, he proclaimed that he would become a martyr in the struggle against the Umayyad "government of injustice and tyranny." In fact, Husayn met his end before reaching Kufa. The caliph's forces lashed out at the *Shi'i* leaders in Kufa before Husayn reached them to lead the revolt. On October 10, 680 A.D. Husayn and his small band of close supporters were routed and killed at Karbala in southern Iraq. Although his head was taken to Damascus as a sign of Yazid's victory, Husayn's body was entombed in Karbala and, like his father's tomb in Najaf, remains one of the most important holy sites in the *Shi'i* faith.

The Arabic term for martyr is *shahid*, meaning "witness" (just as the Greek word *martyr* literally means "witness"). As a result of his death at Karbala, Husayn is revered in the *Shi'i* faith as *Sayyid al-Shuhada'*, Lord of the Martyrs. The death of Husayn illustrates the strong bond between the concepts of martyrdom and *jihad*. To sacrifice one's self in the struggle for Islam guarantees one entry into Paradise. Thus, the example set by Husayn has served as a source of faith and inspiration to the *Shi'i* community for several centuries. In the twentieth century in particular, his example has been heralded as a battle cry in numerous conflicts, from the Palestinian struggle against Israel to the Iran-Iraq War.

Martyrdom and Origins of Suicide Bombings

On November 11, 1982, a new method of warfare debuted: the first human bomb. Seventeen-year-old Ahmad Qassir, a *Shi'i* from southern Lebanon, drove a white Mercedes filled with explosives into the Israeli military headquarters in the Lebanese city of Tyre, killing 141 people. This was the beginning of new era, the inception of a deadly trend of suicide bombings. Over the course of the next three years, there would be more than 30 similar attacks against Israeli targets. The *Shi'a* suicide bombers drove cars, carried suitcases, and in one instance, even detonated a bomb while riding a donkey. The legitimacy for these instances of "self martyrdom" stems directly from the death of Husayn Bin Ali. The image of Husayn and his small band of devotees, marching bravely toward certain death at the hands of Yazid and his vast army, has had a particularly profound impact on *Shi'a* resistance movements in the twentieth century.

Shi'i theology glorifies the act of "self martyrdom" against overwhelming odds, claiming to provide the "martyr" with a direct path to heaven. What is more, the *shuhada'* (martyrs) see themselves as continuing Husayn's tradition of "self martyrdom." The following Hizb`allah fighter echoes these sentiments:

I, Salah Mohammed Ghandour, known by my alias *Malak* [angel], ask God to grant me success. I will be meeting the master of martyrdom Imam Hussein, this great Imam who taught all the free people how to avenge themselves on their oppressions. I shall, *inshaallah* [God willing], shortly after saying these words, be meeting my God with pride, dignity and having avenged my religion and all the martyrs who preceded me on this route. In a short while I shall avenge all the martyrs and oppressed of Jabal Amel, South Lebanon, as well as the children and sons of the Intifada in ravished Palestine. While religious fervor may have inspired the first suicide bombings, strategic acumen has perpetuated their use. Suicide bombs are notoriously cost effective and enable groups to inflict extensive destruction upon the enemy while incurring minimal damage themselves. Consequently, groups such as Hizb'allah consider suicide bombing to be the ultimate method of attack, religious ideology aside.

In the early 1980s, the growing trend of *Shi'a* suicide bombings in Lebanon took a heavy toll on the Israeli military, killing more than 650 soldiers in three years. These bombings marked the beginning of the end for the Israeli occupation of Lebanon. On June 10, 1985, the Israeli forces withdrew from most of Lebanon, limiting their presence to a "Security Zone" in the South, from which they withdrew in the year 2000. On December 16, 1992, Israeli Prime Minister Yitzhak Rabin sought to disrupt Hamas and Palestinian Islamic Jihad's activities by deporting 415 Islamic militants to a deserted area in southern Lebanon. The deportations came in response to Hamas' abduction and murder of Israeli border policeman Nissim Toledano. The decision to deport the Hamas and Islamic Jihad militants to southern Lebanon would soon return to haunt Israel.

The deportation immediately drew sharp international criticism and romanticized the Islamic militants in the eyes of their constituents in the West Bank and Gaza Strip. Popular support for Hamas and Islamic Jihad rose dramatically within the Palestinian community. Additionally, the militants' desire for revenge against Israel only grew more potent during their time in exile. Stranded in "no man's land" just north of Israeli Occupied Southern

Lebanon, the Palestinian deportees initially had little or no support system in Lebanon. The Lebanese government resented their presence, contesting Israel's use of its territory as a prison. The Palestinian exiles, however, soon received support from another powerful force within Lebanon. Hizb`allah, the perpetual thorn in Israel's side, provided the Palestinians with food and medicine. The advent of the relationship between Hizb`allah and the Palestinian militants represents an important juncture in the Palestinian-Israeli conflict. It was during their exile in Southern Lebanon that the Palestinian Islamists learned the value of *shahada,* or "martyrdom," from the Hizb`allah religious leaders.

Until 1992, the Palestinians had relied upon secular nationalism as the justification for their resistance to Israeli occupation. From the birth of the Palestine Liberation Organization (PLO) in 1964 until the Islamist exile in 1992, all Palestinian fighters were regarded as *fida'iyin,* or freedom fighters. Although the *fida'iyin* were willing to sacrifice their lives for the cause, their intent was not suicide, which Islam considers *haram* (forbidden).

Graph 1: Suicide Bombings in Israel

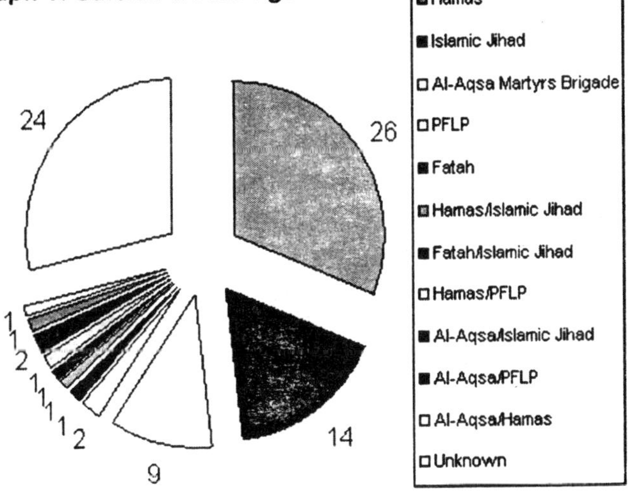

Lebanon continued to voice its opposition to harboring the militants. Consequently, Israel was forced to readmit the Islamic militants nine months after the initial deportation. In southern Lebanon, the Palestinian *Sunni* Islamists had adopted Hizb'allah's *Shi'i* paradigm of *shahada*. Upon returning to the West Bank and Gaza, they imported this deadly paradigm, giving rise to Palestinian suicide bombings. Sacrificing one's life for the liberation of Palestine ceased to be a nationalistic obligation of the *fida'iyin*. For the Islamist fighters, it also became a religious duty, rewarded with a direct path to heaven. In the years that followed, many young Palestinian men and women follow this path.

Although the Palestinian Islamists are *Sunni*, the sheer efficacy of suicide bombings drew them toward the *Shi'i* concept of *shahada*. The use of suicide bombers against Israeli targets had enabled Hizb'allah to significantly impair Israel's 1982 invasion and occupation of Lebanon. While the Israeli military easily overcame both Syrian troops and PLO guerrillas, the *Shi'a* of south Lebanon killed hundreds of Israeli soldiers, forcing the Israeli Defense Forces (IDF) to withdraw from most of Lebanon. The Hamas leadership found inspiration in these successes, and reasoned that by emulating Hizb'allah's tactics they could force the Israelis to end their occupation of the West Bank and Gaza.

The first wave of Palestinian suicide bombings began in April 1994. The attacks came in response to the massacre of 29 Muslims in the Tomb of the Patriarchs in Hebron, carried out by Jewish settler Baruch Goldstein on 25 February 1994. Palestinian Islamic Jihad and Hamas unleashed an unprecedented onslaught of attacks on Israeli military personnel and civilians, killing more that 40 Israelis in five separate operations. Since that time, the suicide bomber has become the weapon of choice for Palestinian radicals. Over the course of the current *intifada*, there have been more than 70 confirmed suicide bombings and 50 other attacks, which have killed more than 800 Israeli civilians and soldiers and wounded thousands more.

The hundreds of casualties inflicted by *Sunni* Palestinian suicide bombers in Israel have inspired Islamist radical groups such as Al-Qa'ida, Egyptian Islamic Gihad, Ansar al-Islam and others to adopt the *Shi'i* paradigm of martyrdom. Thus, suicide bombers have come to represent a legitimate method of warfare across the spectrum of Islamic militancy. In August 7, 1998, two suicide car bombs struck the American embassies in Tanzania and in Kenya, killing hundreds of civilians and injuring thousands more. These attacks marked the first stages in a pattern of Al-Qa'ida suicide terror attacks, culminating in the deaths of almost 3,000 Americans on September 11, 2001. Similar attacks by al-Qa'ida and associates were carried out more recently in Riyadh, Casablanca, Bali, and Istanbul.

Graph 2: Major Suicide Bombings in Post War Iraq 2003

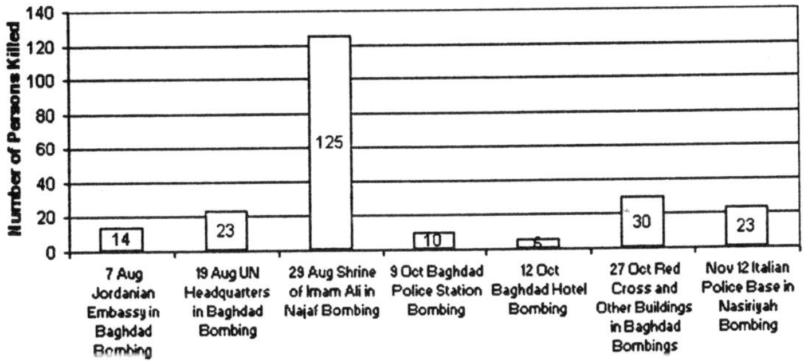

Currently in Iraq suicide car bombings have become a weekly fixture. Since early August 2003, suicide car bombings have blown up the Jordanian embassy, the UN headquarters, the Turkish Embassy, Iraqi hotels, the Shrine of *Imam* Ali in Najaf, the Red Cross building in Baghdad, and the Italian Police Base in Nasiriyah. In Iraq it is still uncertain who is behind the suicide attacks, it may be Ba'ath loyalists, foreign fighters that infiltrated Iraq from Saudi Arabia or other borders, and/or Iraqi *Sunni* and *Shi'a* Islamists who are targeting American personnel and their allies in the hope of hindering the American occupation and reconstruction efforts in Iraq. Recent statements by American officials in Iraq indicate that they consider Saddam loyalists as the main culprit behind these attacks.

Considering the increasing violent attacks on American personnel in Iraq, which presently average 35 attacks per day, it is possible that in the near future, Beirut-style suicide bombings will be unleashed on American forces and their allies in Iraq. It appears that since 680 A.D., *Shahada* has come full circle and returned to the vicinity of Karbala. The historical roots of current terrorist tactics stem from militant interpretations of early Islamic history. Gaining fame in the 1980s, *shahada* has become a popular military paradigm used by various *Shi'i* and *Sunni* extremist militant groups to justify their use of suicide bombings as a legitimate method of warfare.

In addition, many current Islamist extremist groups like al-Qa'ida and Egyptian Islamic Gihad also utilize the tactics of *takfir*, sleeper cells, and infiltration strategies that were initially used by the Kharijites in 661 A.D. to target the army of the fourth caliph Ali ibn Abi Talib. To best understand these tactics, one needs to return to the roots of the *Shi'i-Sunni* conflict and explore how early Islamic history continues to impact the attitudes and religious interpretations of militant extremist Islamist groups that rely upon these tactics as integral parts of their military operations.

The Contribution of the Scientific Literature to the BW Threat

Since World War II, security analysts and policymakers have worried that information published in open scientific literature could benefit military adversaries. Recently, research in the biosciences has caused particular concern because of dramatic advances in this field and their potential application to biological warfare and terrorism. Some open scientific publications in microbiology and related fields contain information potentially relevant to the development, production, formulation, and/or delivery of biological weapons. A workshop in August 2002 organized by the Center for Nonproliferation Studies and supported by the U.S. Defense Threat Reduction Agency, discussed possible approaches to minimize the risk that "sensitive" research findings could be misused for biological warfare (BW) or terrorism.

The workshop brought together two groups of professionals who usually do not communicate, the first consisting of scientists, journal editors, and grant administrators and the second of intelligence and security experts. Conference participants sought to develop guidelines that the Department of Defense might use when reviewing proposed bioscience research projects and sensitive findings stemming from those projects. They acknowledged that to be effective, any guidelines would have to be applied more broadly, potentially by all sponsors of bioscience research, and would have to offer a reasonable balance between enhanced security and scientific freedom.

The participants generally agreed that the most serious threat arises not from lone terrorists or organizations with limited scientific expertise, but from scientists working in sophisticated, well-funded national BW programs or affluent terrorist organizations such as Aum Shinrikyo. Such experts read the scientific literature and are capable of using basic research findings to pursue weapons-related developments. A major challenge facing those who seek to stem the spread of biological weapons is the dual-use nature of applied microbiology and biotechnology. The same scientific knowledge, technical know-how, and equipment involved in the peaceful development and production of commercial products could be misused by those seeking to acquire biological weapons. This dual-use dilemma carries over into the scientific literature.

When research papers are published that elucidate the infectious process, describe the molecular basis of pathogenesis, or examine the action of toxins on physiological systems, they add to the general body of scientific knowledge and facilitate the development of new medical treatments. Yet, the same information could be used by bioweaponeers to devise more deadly biological agents or means of delivery. To give just one example: an article on aerosol spray drug-delivery systems benefits those trying to replace insulin injections for diabetes and to develop intranasal delivery of a vaccine against influenza. But it could also be used by those seeking to disseminate biological warfare agents through aerosolization, the most effective means of attack.

Prior to the terrorist attacks of September 11, few scientific journal editors worried about whether a research finding such as this could be misused. After the terrorist attacks and the subsequent incidents of anthrax-tainted letters, several new regulations on sensitive information and foreign scientists were proposed. In one of the most recent examples, the White House Office of Management and Budget announced its intention to develop rules for "the discussion and publication of information that could prove sensitive to national security."

Regulating Scientific Regulation

The conference participants reviewed the historical precedents for government-imposed restraints on the communication of scientific information. They noted that the U.S. government has long classified information that bears directly on national security, including technical data generated by universities performing government contract work. Some universities have set up subsidiary institutions that perform classified research for the federal government. Also, the U.S Patent and Trademark Office can prevent the release of information contained in a patent on security grounds. However, the guidelines for patent examiners reviewing applications for national security implication were developed in 1972, when modern biotechnology was in its infancy, and thus they are probably outdated.

The Current Debate

Biological scientists and their professional associations generally assert that the government should not restrict the dissemination of unclassified fundamental research, even when the findings are potentially hazardous. They argue that such restrictions would: 1) hinder valuable advances in the biosciences that might offer therapeutic benefits, 2) hamper research needed to develop effective countermeasures against bioterrorism, 3) delay only temporarily the spread of sensitive information, and 4) prevent scientists from replicating the claimed results to prove or disprove their validity. Other authorities counter that restrictions on sensitive research for national security reasons are warranted in cases where such information could be directly relevant to the production of biological and toxin weapons.

This contingent argues that 1) some types of scientific knowledge are inherently dangerous, 2) publishing scientific advances in open literature could abet the development of new types of biological weapons that might not be countered effectively by defensive applications of the same research, 3) scientific research is already subject to numerous ethical guidelines and regulations, such as those on recombinant DNA research, and 4) some scientists are already voluntarily requesting that journal editors withhold key pieces of information from their papers to avoid providing details that might aid terrorists.

Restricting Scientific Communications

Whether or not restrictions on scientific information are advisable, the question of their feasibility remains. The original aim of the workshop was to suggest guidelines that the Department of Defense could consider when reviewing research contracts in the area of microbiology. But after preliminary discussions it became clear that the issue affects other government funding agencies as well.

Since a wide range of scientific research funded by both military and civilian agencies might be misused, workshop participants decided to broaden the focus to include all government-funded research in microbiology and related fields. Given this scope, workshop participants agreed that if research is to be assessed for its potential national security implications, the review should take place when the project proposal is being considered for funding by a government agency. Also, the agency could require as a condition of funding that any papers resulting from the research project undergo security review prior to publication.

Currently, such conditions can legally be imposed on research contracts but not on grants, the primary form of support for university research. The workshop discussed guidelines for the security review of research proposals, and procedures for restricting the distribution of sensitive research results so that only *bona fide* scientists are granted access to it. The effectiveness of the proposed guidelines and procedures would be judged by whether they are voluntarily accepted by the scientific community, and whether they strike a reasonable balance between scientific freedom and national security.

The Security Review of Research Proposals

In brief, most participants agreed that to limit damage to the scientific enterprise, restrictions on the dissemination of unclassified research results, if any, should be confined to the small proportion of findings directly relevant to the military or terrorist use of pathogens and toxins. One proposal put before workshop participants would consider placing restrictions on research that involves a Select Agent and aims to achieve one or more of six weaponization-related goals:

- Enhance pathogen infectivity, pathogenicity, antibiotic resistance, or resistance to host immunological defenses;
- Improve the ability of a microbial pathogen to remain viable and virulent during prolonged storage and/or after release into the environment;
- Facilitate the dissemination of biological agents as a fine-particle aerosol;
- Facilitate the dissemination of a biological agent by contamination of food or water sources;
- Create a novel pathogen or one whose characteristics have been altered to evade current detection methods or host immune defenses; and
- Assemble oligonucleotides to synthesize the genome of a pathogenic microorganism.

Under this proposed security review process, reviewer(s) would place a research proposal in one of two categories. Studies involving a Select Agent that did not contain any of the six weaponization criteria listed above would be designated "Unrestricted," with no limits on public release. Studies that involve a Select Agent and one or more of the six weaponization criteria would be considered for placement in the "Restricted" category, which would entail certain controls on public release of the research results.

"Restricted" designations—expected to be applied to only a small fraction of academic research projects—could also be applied in the later stages of the research project. Investigators would be obligated to notify the funding agency if an experiment was modified in such a way as to invoke listed criteria, or if unexpectedly sensitive results were obtained.

Compliance of research institutions could be encouraged by withholding federal funding from those that refused to participate; non-governmental funders could apply the same security review criteria voluntarily.

The Dissemination of Sensitive Results

Under the proposed guidelines, when a paper containing results of a "Restricted" research project was submitted to a scientific publisher, it would be accompanied by a letter from the funding agency denoting which portions of the paper were sensitive and warranted restrictions on distribution. Dissemination of the restricted material to legitimate scientists would then be controlled by the journal editor, in cooperation with the funding agency, perhaps through passwork-controlled web sites and other secure means.

Given the wide range of print and electronic outlets for communication of research findings, sensitive information could not be restricted effectively unless the author was persuaded not to distribute it publicly in any form. Moreover, because scientific publishing is an international enterprise, a system focused exclusively on U.S. scientists or publishers would be ineffective. Many implementation questions remain to be answered, such as who should be given access to the sensitive information and how long the restrictions on public access should apply.

Workshop participants identified significant problems with the proposed regulatory system, including several issues that would have to be addressed by any scheme for controlling research or the information it produced. Some of the drawbacks mentioned include:

- The proposal appears to establish a system of national censorship, with scientific journals as the guardians of sensitive materials;
- Research universities and scientific journals would not agree to the proposed mechanism;
- The proposal ignores the fact that the intellectual

knowledge generated under grants (as opposed to contracts) is the property of the investigators, many of whom are foreign nationals;

- Scientists may be unwilling to take on the responsibility of reviewing a potentially "sensitive" paper;
- Scientific journals are not set up to deal with the segregation of sensitive data or to provide for secure means of review and publication;
- Once a document has been designated "Restricted," it must be tracked and its security monitored; and
- The proposed system would impose high legal and professional risks on journals, with minimal benefits.

It was the sense of the workshop that if a system for restricting the publication of "sensitive" information is to be workable, it requires the broad support of the international scientific community, which must perceive that the security benefits of restricting open publication outweigh the possible costs to science. The two groups of professionals attending the workshop—scientists and security experts— could not reach a consensus on how sensitive information from scientific research should be handled. Most participants did agree that under rare circumstances, the open communication of unclassified research could pose such a high risk of substantial harm as to warrant controlling the distribution of that information. It is essential that bioscientists and their professional organizations take the lead in informing security experts about how best to meet the threats of biological warfare and terrorism in a way that will not cause undue harm to the scientific enterprise.

7

Chemical Terrorist Plot

On February 20, 2002, Italian police arrested four Moroccan nationals for allegedly plotting a chemical terrorist attack on the U.S. Embassy in Rome. The suspects were apprehended with approximately nine pounds of a cyanide compound (potassium ferrocyanide), as well as maps in their possession detailing the location of the water pipes that serve the U.S. Embassy. In the days following the initial arrest, five additional Moroccan nationals were taken into custody, and all nine suspects are being held on charges of subversive association. According to media reports, police have thus far been unable to make much headway in the investigation. None of the suspects has a credible explanation for the maps and chemicals in his possession, and, as of this writing, no link have yet been determined between the suspects and the al-Qa'ida terrorist network.

On February 25, this case garnered even more attention with the discovery of a hole dug into an underground passageway next to the U.S. Embassy. Fears emerged that the terrorists were planning a chemical attack on the embassy from underneath the compound. The concrete tunnel, located under the street Via Boncompagni, is normally closed at each end by a wall three feet thick. However, Italian authorities claimed that someone had hacked through one of the walls, leaving an opening two feet high—enough space to enable someone to crawl through and reach the pipes of the water system of the embassy. It is by no means certain that the hole was intended for nefarious purposes, as it may have been created earlier by local employees in order to pass tools back and forth.

Although it first appeared that Italian police had thwarted a major chemical terrorist attack against the U.S. Embassy, details that emerged regarding the specific chemical compound possessed by the Moroccans raised more questions about the nature of the incident and the intent of the alleged perpetrators. The substance reportedly in the possession of the would be attackers was potassium ferrocyanide (also known as yellow prussiate of potash), a chemical commonly used as an anti-caking agent and food additive. Because of its low toxicity in mammals and humans, potassium ferrocyanide is an unlikely choice to cause poisoning, especially in a water system.

When combined with acid or heated to a very high temperature, potassium ferrocyanide can be induced to release hydrogen cyanide gas, a potent poison. But if the alleged attackers intended to generate the highly toxic gas—perhaps with the intent to deliver it through the ventilation system of the embassy—it is not clear how this goal could have been achieved from the underground tunnel. With these facts in mind, it is possible that the perpetrators intended to poison the water supply of the U.S. Embassy, but that their lack of technical expertise led them to choose a widely available but ineffective chemical agent (potassium ferrocyanide) for the attack.

In a potentially related case, on March 3, 2002, Italian police arrested six men in Rome who are believed to have ties to Usama bin Laden. These men were overheard discussing plans to assassinate President George W. Bush and to supply terrorist training camps in Afghanistan. In addition, they were reportedly heard making references to the use of a cyanide compound. Italian police believe that this reference suggests a link between al-Qa'ida and the alleged plot to attack the U.S. Embassy in Rome.

Cyanide

Also referred to as prussic acid, hydrogen cyanide (NATO code AC) has been known as a classic poison for centuries. In modern times, cyanide compounds have been used for mass murder and terrorism. Nazi Germany employed hydrogen cyanide—used at the time as a commercial rodenticide—to murder millions of Jews and others at Auschwitz and other death camps. In 1978, potassium cyanide (dissolved in water) was used by the Reverend Jim Jones and his cult followers in Guyana to commit mass-suicide, resulting in the deaths of over 900 people. Hydrogen cyanide (HCN) gas has also been used in political assassination. Using a contraption that combined ampoules in a metal tube, in 1959 the Soviet KGB murdered Ukrainian nationalist and exile Stefan Bandera by spraying him directly in the face with HCN.

HCN is a member of the "blood agent" category of chemical weapons, so-named because it interferes with the energy metabolism of all living tissues. The French military made many attempts to use hydrogen cyanide as a weapon during World War I, with mixed results. Although HCN is a liquid at room temperature, its high volatility makes it difficult to achieve high enough concentrations for effective use on the battlefield. During World War II, some Japanese soldiers were equipped with glass bottles of a stabilized hydrogen cyanide compound. It is not known to what extent these chemical weapons were used, or what effects they had against Allied forces in the Pacific theater.

Because the chemical ingredients for making hydrogen cyanide are relatively accessible, terrorists might utilize this agent to attack localized targets. For example, in May 1995, members of the Japanese Aum Shinrikyo cult left a "binary" chemical bomb in a Tokyo subway restroom that was designed to generate hydrogen cyanide gas. Fortunately, the device was deactivated before it inflicted any casualties. Other evidence obtained from the October 2001 arrest of Ahmed Ressam, convicted in April 2001 for plotting to detonate a bomb at the Los Angeles International Airport, revealed that al-Qai'da operatives had received training in employing cyanide against buildings, apparently by combining powdered cyanide with acid. According to Ressam, other plans included using a form of liquid cyanide that would be applied to doorknobs. He stated at the trial, "The poison would go through the skin and kill you." It is not clear how this material was prepared.

Whether delivered as a gas (HCN) or a salt (-CN), cyanide forms an inhibitory complex with the cellular enzyme cytochrome oxidase and blocks the normal utilization of oxygen by tissues, causing death. The lethal inhaled dose of HCN is 50 milligrams (mg), and the ingested dose of either potassium or sodium cyanide is 200-300 mg. About 100 mg of HCN liquid on the skin is reportedly fatal for most adults. The median lethal concentration (LCt_{50}) of hydrogen cyanide (inhaled) is estimated to be approximately 5 grams-min/m3 (versus about 11 grams for another blood agent, cyanogen chloride).

In industry, hydrogen cyanide has been produced by a number of methods, including synthesis from ammonia and carbon monoxide. It can also be generated by mixing cyanide salts with acid and is the basis for the gas chamber method used to execute prisoners in some U.S. states. HCN is listed in Schedule 3 of the Chemical Weapons Convention annex of controlled chemicals. In addition, cyanide salts (e.g., sodium cyanide) are included in the voluntary export control list developed by the Australia Group.

$$C{\equiv}N{-}H$$

Hydrogen Cyanide (AC)

Relaxes HEU Export Controls

Experts have long recognized that highly enriched uranium (HEU) is the nuclear material of choice for terrorists, since HEU is the easiest material to use in manufacturing an improvised nuclear explosive device. HEU at civilian facilities is particularly vulnerable, since such facilities are often inadequately secured. To mitigate this risk, the United States has led efforts since the 1970s to reduce the civilian use of HEU. Beginning in 1992, the United States restricted its exports of HEU in order to encourage other countries to convert civilian facilities to low-enriched uranium (LEU), which cannot be used directly to make nuclear weapons. The latest step in this campaign was the unveiling of the Global Threat Reduction Initiative (GRTI) in May 2004, which among other goals, seeks to "minimize and eventually eliminate any reliance on HEU in the civilian fuel cycle, including conversion of research and test reactors worldwide from the use of HEU to the use of low-enriched uranium fuels and targets."

In the current environment of increased terrorist threats and proliferation concerns, further restrictions on civilian commerce in HEU should be a top priority. Instead, on July 29, 2005 Congress passed the Energy Policy Act of 2005, which includes provisions relaxing restrictions on HEU exports for medical isotope production. The primary beneficiaries of the new law are producers of medical radioisotopes, who claim that conversion to LEU is too costly and could disrupt production of needed medical isotopes. The new law will permit the export of U.S. HEU to medical isotope producers even if they refuse to convert to LEU. Passed after heavy lobbying efforts by Canadian medial isotope producer MDS Nordion, the new legislation establishes an unfortunate precedent legitimizing continued international commerce in HEU.

It essentially places the economic interests of medical isotope producers above the nonproliferation interests of the United States and the international community. It is virtually certain to complicate ongoing efforts to reduce the risk of nuclear terrorism.

For example, the new law stands in contradiction with established U.S. efforts—like GTRI—to eliminate the civilian use of HEU. It will also complicate a promising initiative, led by Norway at the 2005 Review Conference of Parties to the Treaty on the Non-Proliferation of Nuclear Weapons (NPT Review Conference), to seek an international consensus on eliminating the civilian use of HEU. The new law thus represents a step backward for nonproliferation.

There are currently three principal uses of HEU in the civilian nuclear sector: in research reactors, for medical isotope production, and as fuel in icebreaker propulsion reactors. Historically, the proliferation risks posed by civilian uses of HEU have been underestimated. HEU at civilian facilities, for example, is less well-protected than that at military or weapons production facilities, and more vulnerable to theft by terrorists. While reducing all stocks of HEU is a worthy nonproliferation goal, eliminating the civilian use of HEU would address the most vulnerable and thus highest priority material.

The two most widespread civilian uses of HEU are as research reactor fuel and as targets for the production of medical isotopes. While the United States and the Soviet Union exported large quantities of HEU for these purposes in the 1950s-1970s, by the late 1970s both countries, citing proliferation concerns, began to limit these exports. Initiatives were also launched at the time to begin converting research reactors and radioactive isotope production from HEU to LEU, although Russia has yet to convert any of its domestic research reactors. In 1978, the United States launched the Reduced Enrichment for Research and Test Reactors (RERTR) program, which aims to develop new LEU fuels and targets to replace HEU.

In 1992, in order to provide foreign users of U.S.-origin HEU with an increased incentive to convert their reactors and production processes, Congress adopted the Schumer Amendment. This legislation restricted U.S. exports of HEU to facilities that meet the following conditions: 1) there is no existing alternative LEU fuel for the reactor or production process; 2) the facility has agreed to switch to LEU fuel as soon as it is available; and 3) the United States is actively developing an alternative LEU fuel suitable for the facility. While U.S. exports of HEU had already declined prior to the Schumer Amendment, they subsequently fell to very low levels.

According to data from the U.S. Nuclear Regulatory Commission (NRC), in recent years there have been only a handful of HEU exports for medical isotope production. As nuclear material at greatest risk of theft during transit, reducing international commerce in HEU is an effective way to reduce proliferation risks and bolster international security. Considering current terrorist threats, civilian uses of HEU should be eliminated, unless their benefits are so great and so difficult and/or expensive to obtain by other means that they justify the increased risk of nuclear terrorism.

Radioisotope Production

HEU continues to play a major role in the production of radioactive isotopes for medical applications. HEU targets are irradiated in a reactor, producing the fission product molybdenum-99, which has a 2.7-day half-life and decays to 6-hour half-life technicium-99m, a gamma ray emitter used in medical imaging. There are currently four major international producers of radioisotopes who use HEU: MDS Nordion (Canada), Mallinckrodt (Netherlands), Institute National des Radioelements (Belgium), and the Nuclear Energy Corporation of South Africa. All four have resisted efforts to convince them to convert to LEU, citing concerns about cost and disruption of production. According to a

2004 U.S. Government Accountability Office report, these four producers use about 85 kg of HEU each year.

That is enough material to make a few improvised nuclear devices, considering that the IAEA regards 25 kg of HEU as a significant quantity, and independent experts believe that terrorists could fabricate a simple gun-type nuclear weapon with 40-55 kg of HEU. Three of these producers—those in the Netherlands, Belgium, and South Africa—either use domestically produced HEU or import it from sources outside the United States. One, Nordion, located in Canada, has continued to receive some HEU exports from the United States in recent years, based on its pledge to convert to LEU. Critics, however, contend the company is not serious about converting its operations to LEU. According to its press materials, Nordion is "the world's largest supplier of short-lived radioisotopes for medical diagnostic nuclear imaging and therapeutic applications," and generated $343 million in revenues in 2002, most of it from exports to 95 countries.

The company claims to provide medical isotopes for most of the 15 to 20 million nuclear medicine procedures performed around the world every year. Nordion produces molybdenum-99 in Canada's more than 50-year old NRU reactor at Chalk River, using HEU targets supplied by the United States. Nordion has planned for a number of years to switch to a new pair of reactors, the MAPLE reactors, also located at Chalk River, and to construct a new processing facility for the isotopes. The NRU reactor was to have shut down years ago, but technical problems have repeatedly delayed the start-up of MAPLE. NRU is now slated to run until the end of 2005, and perhaps longer.

Nordion also now argues that it will take additional time to develop LEU targets, stating that the increased waste produced by the LEU targets during the production process presents a serious technical and financial challenge to conversion. This posture reflects a change from earlier plans and pledges made by Nordion and Atomic Energy of Canada, LTD, which operates the reactors. As early as 1990, the companies promised to switch to the use of a new LEU target by 1998, and to "phase out HEU use by 2000."

Later, when it was granted a U.S. export license for HEU in 1999, Nordion pledged to submit annual progress reports on its conversion efforts, but its conversion efforts appear to have been minimal, and the company now contends that it could not convert to HEU without interrupting the supply of critically needed medical isotopes, and has said it cannot proceed with conversion unless provided with $90 million in financing to construct a new LEU-based processing facility. Officials from Argonne National Lab, who are in charge of the RERTR Program efforts to develop LEU targets, do admit that it will take a few more years to implement conversion to LEU. But they also insist that it is technically feasible, and have even suggested that it could ultimately result in a more economic process, compensating for the costs of conversion.

Repeal the Schumer Amendment

While dragging its feet on conversion, Nordion also began lobbying efforts to modify the Schumer Amendment so it would no longer be required to convert. Working with Mallinckrodt, Nordion lobbied the U.S. Congress to remove the restrictions on HEU exports for medical isotope production. The company drafted an amendment to the 2003 energy bill under consideration in the U.S. House of Representatives, and persuaded Congressman Richard Burr (D-NC), who has since been elected Senator from North Carolina, to sponsor it. The amendment would lift restrictions on HEU exports for medical isotope production pending the completion of a study on the restrictions' effectiveness and economic impact.

Senator Christopher Bond (R-MO) sponsored a similar amendment in the Senate. Nordion's lobbying activities were also supplemented with well-targeted campaign contributions. According to the *Washington Post*, the principal energy lobbyists of the Alpine Group, a firm hired to promote the change in HEU export restrictions, donated $25,000 to members of the House and Senate energy committees. Nuclear medicine groups also made large campaign contributions to these members of Congress. The Alpine Group lobbyists, James D. Massie, Richard C. White and Rhod Shaw, for example, contributed $6,400 to Burr's campaign war chest in 2003 and 2004, according to Federal Election Commission data collected by the Center for Responsive Politics.

Nevertheless, the amendments, which drew substantial opposition from several nonproliferation organizations, did not pass, since the entire bill died in the U.S. Senate. Nordion did not give up its efforts, however, and the 2005 version of the energy bill passed in the House on April 21, 2005 again included the language from the Burr Amendment, allowing exports of HEU for medical isotope production, even if the recipient did not agree to convert to LEU. This change in the law would take away any incentive for Nordion to convert to LEU, and will also ripple through the entire radioisotope industry, as other producers will similarly have no incentive to convert. Supporters of relaxing the restrictions have argued that the limits imposed by the Schumer Amendment are creating a crisis in medical isotope production, and they also claim that conversion is simply too costly.

Opponents, including a number of scientists and nonproliferation specialists, as well as the editorial board of the *New York Times*, contend that smaller producers have already successfully converted to LEU, that there is no shortage of medical isotopes, and that continued HEU exports are too risky under current circumstances. In the Senate, the provisions gutting the Schumer Amendment and relaxing HEU export restrictions were removed following the approval of an amendment sponsored by Senators Charles Schumer (D-NY) and Jon Kyl (R-AZ), by a 52-46 vote on June 23, 2005. However, in the House-Senate Conference committee, efforts to retain the Schumer Amendment or to at least draft compromise language retaining some of its key provisions failed.

The conference report retained the Burr Amendment language passed by the House in April 2005, and the House and Senate passed the conference report on July 27 and 29, respectively. President Bush signed the bill into law on August 8, 2005. Under the provisions of the newly-passed legislation, restrictions on HEU exports for medical isotope production will be relaxed, and the National Academy of Sciences will conduct a study of the effectiveness of efforts to convert isotope production to LEU. In an era of increased terrorist threats, when the main obstacle standing between terrorists and nuclear explosives is the difficulty of obtaining fissile material, it makes no sense to relax export controls on HEU.

It is particularly short-sighted to place the economic interests of a few companies ahead of the international interest in reducing the risk of terrorist access to HEU. While it may be reasonable to study the costs of conversion more thoroughly and consider whether additional incentives to foster conversion are needed, such a study should be done before making any changes in existing law, which is encouraging many facilities to convert to LEU, rather than after relaxing it and potentially giving terrorists easier access to HEU.

The strongest reason to regret the change to U.S. law, however, is that is that the Schumer Amendment had not only been working directly to reduce proliferation risks, but was also catalyzing additional steps in that direction. The changed U.S. law on HEU exports will almost certainly make it harder for these efforts to succeed, exacerbating the risk of nuclear terrorism. Many research reactors around the world have already converted to LEU with help from RERTR and ongoing efforts under GTRI are securing and eliminating civilian HEU stocks in countries around the world. But these efforts to convince other countries to give up their stocks of civilian HEU will be less effective now that the U.S. has set a contrary example by relaxing its own controls on HEU exports. Countries that are already reluctant to part with their civilian HEU, like Ukraine, will now be less likely to respond to U.S. appeals.

In addition, the change in U.S. law will complicate ongoing efforts to build an international coalition to support delegitimizing civilian use of HEU. Many countries are coming to agree that the benefits of civilian use of HEU do not justify the risks involved. A recent step reflecting the emergence of a broader international consensus on this issue was a working paper presented to the 2005 NPT Review Conference by Norway on behalf of itself and Iceland, Lithuania, and Sweden. This paper also enjoyed the support of many other countries, including Austria, Canada, Germany, Kyrgyzstan, Japan, and the United States. The paper endorsed as a goal "the elimination of HEU in the civilian nuclear sector as soon as technically feasible."

It is likely that additional steps to follow up on this proposal will be made this fall at either the UN General Assembly or the General Conference of the IAEA. The recently adopted changes in U.S. law stand in contradiction to this initiative, and may hamper its progress. In its consideration of revoking the Schumer Amendment, Congress should have placed more emphasis on broader nonproliferation efforts than on the interests of medical isotope producers. Those efforts will now have to be redoubled in the face of this unfortunate decision.

North Korean Nuclear Weapons Statement

On February 10, 2005, the North Korean Foreign Ministry issued a statement declaring that North Korea possessed nuclear weapons and that the country would "increase its nuclear arsenal to defend the ideas, system, freedom and democracy that were chosen by the North Korean people." The declaration was made in response to "the hostile policy of the U.S. towards the DPRK," which "requires North Korea to possess a nuclear deterrent." The Foreign Ministry also declared that North Korea wants to participate in the Six-Party Talks, but that they have indefinitely suspended participation until the atmosphere surrounding the talks changes and until they can expect positive results.

The statement concluded that there is no change in North Korea's position of resolving the nuclear issue through negotiations and that North Korea's ultimate goal is a nuclear-free Korean Peninsula. The statement made several references to Pyongyang's future actions being contingent upon U.S. policies and behaviour towards the DPRK. For years, Pyongyang has expressed its desire to improve relations with the United States, while paradoxically issuing belligerent statements towards Washington. For example, on February 2, 2005, the North Korean media broadcast a statement by a North Korean Air Force officer declaring that the North Korean military would turn U.S. military bases into a "sea of fire" if the United States attacked the DPRK.

The Foreign Ministry statement on February 10th also followed two seminars held during the previous week in Pyongyang for scholars, military personnel, government officials, and Korean Workers Party members to extol the *son'gun* (military first) politics of Kim Jong Il. The seminars received extensive coverage in the North Korean media to display the close unity between the party and the military prior to the Lunar New Year holiday and nuclear declaration. In a telephone interview with a South Korean newspaper following the statement on February 10th, Han Song Ryol, North Korea's Deputy Ambassador to the UN, said that North Korea is prepared to return to the Six-Party Talks under the right conditions. He said that direct talks between the United States and North Korea would be a sign that Washington is dropping its "hostile policy" towards Pyongyang.

According to Han, the format of the talks (bilateral vs. multilateral) is not important, but he stressed the importance of a change in the U.S. position. He added that North Korea is not "begging for talks with the U.S., but Washington's failure to talk directly with Pyongyang can only be interpreted as a desire to obliterate our system."

North Korean Nuclear Capabilities

The U.S. intelligence community estimates that North Korea has possessed enough weapons-grade plutonium for one and possibly two nuclear weapons since the early 1990s. During 2003, North Korea likley reprocessed the plutonium from 8,000 spent fuel rods that had been in a temporary storage facility in the Yongbyon Nuclear Complex. This reprocessed spent fuel would provide about 25-30 kg of weapons-grade plutonium, or enough for about five to six nuclear weapons. North Korea has also been operating a 5 MW (e) reactor in Yongbyon since late February 2003. This reactor can produce enough plutonium for about one bomb per year. However, there is no evidence that North Korea has shut down the reactor to discharge the spent fuel and reprocess it into plutonium. North Korea has two larger nuclear reactors (50 MW (e) and 200 MW (e)) that were under construction but frozen under the 1994 Agreed Framework. These reactors, if completed, could provide enough plutonium for about 37-50 nuclear bombs per year.

North Korea also has a uranium enrichment program, but there is no evidence that North Korea has a large-scale uranium enrichment facility in operation. In the 1980s, North Korea began to acquire dual-use items that could be applied to a uranium enrichment program, but North

Korea is probably still years away from operating a full-scale uranium enrichment facility, even though it can apparently produce uranium hexafluoride. North Korea appears to have pursued its uranium enrichment program more aggressively in the late 1990s after becoming dissatisfied with the implementation of the Agreed Framework.

The intelligence community is divided over whether North Korea has assembled its fissile material into nuclear bombs, and it is uncertain whether North Korea has miniaturized any weapons that could be loaded onto a North Korean delivery vehicle. If miniaturized into nuclear warheads, North Korea could deliver its bombs with Hwasong-5, Hwasong-6, Nodong, and Paektusan-1 (Taepodong-1) ballistic missiles.

The North Korean Air Force has a number of fighter-bombers and bomber aircraft that could potentially deliver nuclear bombs, but their ranges are very limited and North Korea has no in-flight refueling capability. Moreover, it is unlikely that North Korea has miniaturized its weapons sufficiently for delivery by aircraft, and North Korean aircraft would be highly vulnerable to air defense systems in South Korea, Japan and surrounding international waters.

Transfer of Nuclear Weapons or Fissile Material

The possibility that North Korea might transfer nuclear weapons or fissile material to states or terrorist groups is a major concern of the United States and its allies. This fear has increased with recent reports that North Korea could have exported uranium hexafluoride (UF6), the feedstock for gas centrifuges; to Libya prior to Tripoli's decision to abandon its nuclear weapons program in December 2003. However, exporting UF6 and exporting nuclear weapons or fissile material are two different things, and our assessment is that North Korea is unlikely to export nuclear weapons or fissile material at this time. If North Korea expands its production capability and increases its fissile material stockpile, the marginal domestic value of the fissile material will decline and the likelihood of export will increase.

First, North Korea's current stockpile of fissile material is relatively small and extremely valuable if the North Korea leadership is convinced it needs a nuclear deterrent. Second, the risk and cost of exposure after transferring nuclear weapons or materials would be high, and North Korean leaders are unlikely to accept these risks or potential costs. Third, North Korea has renounced terrorism and has not engaged in terrorist activities for almost two decades. Critics argue that terrorist groups have acquired North Korean conventional arms, but Pyongyang is more likely to hold onto its small number of nuclear weapons for its own defense. Therefore, the probability of transfer is low, but cannot be completely discounted, and contingency plans should be available for such a development.

The U.S. Response

U.S. Secretary of State Condoleezza Rice called the decision by North Korea "an unfortunate move...because it only deepens the North Korean isolation from the rest of the international community." White House Press Secretary McClellan downplayed the announcement, saying that "we've heard this kind of rhetoric from North Korea before." In response to North Korea's allegation that the United States is seeking to topple the regime, Secretary Rice said, "The North Koreans have been told by the president of the United States himself that the United States has no intention to attack or invade North Korea.

The North Koreans have been told that they can have security assurances on a multilateral basis. Those security assurances will of course include the United States, if they are prepared to take a definitive decision to dismantle their nuclear weapons programs and to do so in a way that is verifiable."

The White House has so far rejected North Korea's demand for bilateral talks, instead emphasizing the Six-Party Talks as the only way to resolve the crisis diplomatically. White House Press Secretary Scott McClellan said, "It's not an issue between North Korea and the United States. It's a regional issue. And it's an issue that impacts all of its neighbors." McClellan added, "There's [sic] plenty of opportunities for North Korea to speak directly with us in the context of the Six-Party Talks."

The Chinese Response

North Korea's announcement that it has produced nuclear weapons and that it is withdrawing from the Six-Party Talks puts China in a difficult position. The timing of the statement at least allows Beijing to save some "face," since it was issued prior to a planned Chinese envoy's visit to North Korea and places the blame on Washington and, to some extent, Tokyo as well. But Pyongyang's abrupt announcement also preempts Beijing's options to mediate.

China's Foreign Ministry spokesman responded to the latest development by reiterating China's long-held position of seeking a denuclearized Korean Peninsula and indicating that Beijing hopes the Six-Party Talks will continue. China seems to have anticipated this dramatic turn of events, as it cautioned the United States not to publicize the reported North Korean transfers of nuclear materials to Libya even as senior U.S. National Security Council officials were hand-delivering a letter from President Bush to Chinese President Hu Jintao earlier in the week. But this still happened, right in the midst of China's one-week holiday marking the Lunar New Year.

Yet Beijing has much to worry about, both with respect to its own reputation and also of the broader ramifications for regional security. China's more proactive diplomacy over the last two years, first as the convener of a trilateral meeting and then as the host of the Six-Party Talks, is not producing the desired results. Beijing knows that the key to any resolution of the Korean nuclear issue will remain North Korea and the United States. In that respect, Beijing at most can provide good offices but nothing more. Pyongyang's announcement that it now has nuclear weapons is also a slap on the face for Beijing. While most U.S. and official western statements and analyses have long held that North Korea possesses the fissile materials for about six to eight nuclear weapons, China has yet to officially acknowledge this and indeed has raised issue with U.S. assertions, in particular after the intelligence debacle on Iraqi WMD capabilities.

Perhaps the most worrisome aspect of the ongoing crisis is its impact on regional security, especially on the potential reactions from Japan, whose recent military activities are of deep concerns to China. However, Beijing's options are limited and any course of action could have potential negative trade-offs. China could express its impatience by subtly applying economic pressure, as it did two years by cutting off the oil supplies for a couple of days to North Korea. It could also indicate its neutrality towards any U.S. proposal to bring the issue before the UN Security Council for possible economic sanctions.

The problem is that these actions probably would not bring about the desired results, and could possibly further escalate tensions. Indeed, should these actions be adopted, China is likely to endure the consequences, including but not limited to massive flows of refuges, disruption of its economic ties with the region's key partners, and a post-conflict environment not entirely to Beijing's liking.

The South Korean Response

The Roh Mu Hyon government has consistently viewed a nuclear North Korea as unacceptable, but Seoul has continued Roh's "peace and prosperity policy" of engagement with Pyongyang. The most visible result of this engagement, which started under former President Kim Dae Jung, is the opening of the Kaesong Industrial Complex in North Korea in December 2004.

Economic exchanges between the two Koreas have increased recently but Seoul could reassess its policy following North Korea's nuclear declaration. The South Korean government fully supports the Six-Party Talks for resolving the North Korean nuclear issue in a peaceful manner. President Roh reaffirmed his support for the talks in a telephone conversation with President Bush on February 5, 2005.

The North Korean announcement came as South Korea's Minister of Foreign Affairs and Trade Ban Ki Moon was arriving in Washington, D.C. Ban said that South Korea will not tolerate North Korean nuclear weapons and that this policy will not change. A spokesperson for the Ministry of Foreign Affairs and Trade later issued a statement asserting the South Korean government "deeply regrets the North declared an indefinite postponement of its participation in the Six-Party Talks." The statement also affirmed that North Korea's nuclear program will not be tolerated.

The Japanese Response

The North Korean Foreign Ministry statement on February 10th accused Japan of "servilely [sic] following the United States and...obstinately clinging to a hostile policy toward our Republic." Pyongyang's declaration that it is indefinitely suspending participation in the Six-Party Talks and that it possessed nuclear weapons will serve to further complicate Japanese-DPRK relations, which recently had become increasingly strained over the abduction issue. In December 2004, DNA tests on remains given to a Japanese delegation in November 2004 by Pyongyang revealed that the remains were not those of a Japanese abductee, Megumi Yokota, as North Korea had claimed.

Pyongyang rebuked the Japanese government's claim and called the DNA tests a scam. In response, Japanese authorities stated that the test gave irrefutable evidence that the remains were not those of Yokota, but of two unknown individuals. In reference to this latest controversy, the North Korean Foreign Ministry statement on February 10th remarked, "How can we sit across from Japan in one place and hold talks with it when it is saying it will nullify the DPRK-Japan Pyongyang Declaration and will not normalize diplomatic relations while going so far as to fabricate the false remains issue over the abductions issue, which has already been settled completely?"

The reaction of the Japanese government to North Korea's statement has been cautious. Prime Minister Koizumi told reporters that Japan would focus on resuming the Six-Party Talks and continue to pressure North Korea to give up its nuclear weapons. However, Koizumi also commented that Japan would continue to apply pressure on North Korea to settle the abduction issue. The issue of Japanese abductees has played heavily on Japanese public opinion with regards to relations with Pyongyang since Kim Jong Il's revelation in 2002 that North Korea had abducted 13 Japanese citizens. In recent weeks, Japanese politicians and commentators have pressured the Japanese government to place sanctions on Pyongyang as a means to pressure North Korea to fully disclose what happened to the abductees. Five abductees were allowed to return to Japan in 2003, and Pyongyang claims the other eight are deceased.

In response to North Korea's declaration that it possesses nuclear weapons, Chief Cabinet Secretary Hiroyuki Hosoda reminded reporters during a press conference that North Korea had previously made outlandish statements and then followed-up by revealing its true intentions. Hosada stated that Pyongyang "has made similar announcements in the past. We need to closely examine North Korea's true intentions." He concluded that Tokyo "will have to watch the development for a little longer."

The Russian Response

Russia's official response to North Korea's February 10th declaration of its possession of nuclear weapons and withdrawal from the Six-Party Talks has been one of "regret." Russian media reports have emphasized the shift from a "nuclear capability" to "nuclear weapons" in the North Korean statement, although they have also cited North Korea's claim to have deployed these weapons for "self-defense" and "deterrence." Russian news articles on the North Korean statement typically note North Korea's expressed desire to return to the talks if the Bush administration drops its threats. In explaining the Korean Peninsula crisis to their readers, Russian journalists have discussed the sharp changes in U.S. policies under President Bush and the U.S. decision (as typically reported) to back out of the Agreed Framework.

None of the recent articles mentioned details of North Korean cheating or the intricacies of the suspected uranium enrichment program. Yet, one reporter noted the extreme restraint shown by Secretary of State Condoleezza Rice (whom he called "the steel magnolia") in responding to the recent North Korean announcement. He commented that this response was "uncharacteristic." But the same article also noted ominously that these developments are taking place on Russia's own border and mean a ratcheting up of a crisis that before could have led to war, and now could lead to nuclear war.

Alexander Zhebin of the Korean Research Center of the Institute of the Far East in Moscow, quoted by the newspaper *Nezavisimaya Gazeta*, said that the DPRK leadership has concluded that further talks with the United

States are "pointless." In his view, Pyongyang now believes that the Bush administration is seeking regime change in North Korea. Zhebin described Pyongyang's past aims in the Six-Party Talks as two-fold: reducing the U.S. threat to the DPRK and obtaining access to international financial credits. The administration's actions, Zhebin argued, have made Kim Jong II decide that these goals are unobtainable. Talks on North Korea's activities, he concluded, will now have to be refocused—from trying to halt a nuclear weapons program to trying to prevent the *export* of nuclear technology and weapons.

Military Options

Three main issues are routinely identified as the key elements involved in successful military strikes against nuclear facilities in North Korea:

- Locating all nuclear weapons and/or facilities and fissile material stocks that could be used in a nuclear weapons program;
- Having the capability to destroy these targets; and
- Preventing full-scale North Korean conventional retaliation, further escalation, or the use of chemical, biological, or nuclear weapons against U.S military bases in the region or against U.S. allies.

Some of North Korea's nuclear facilities have already been located, and together they comprise critical elements in Pyongyang's ability to produce and reprocess plutonium for use in nuclear weapons. However, while it has been deemed unlikely to have secret nuclear reactors, North Korea might possess secret reprocessing facilities, which could be hidden underground or in caves to increase both their secrecy and protection from attack.

Furthermore, no North Korean uranium enrichment facilities have been conclusively located, although some suspected sites have been identified. While very little is known about North Korea's uranium enrichment program, in general such facilities can be housed in relatively small areas, including in underground facilities, which are difficult to locate and destroy.

When assessing the capability of the United States to destroy North Korea's nuclear facilities, North Korea's possible ability to repel such an attack must also be taken into account. With Mig-23 and Mig-29 fighters, SA-2 and SA-5 surface-to-air missiles, and large quantities of anti-aircraft artillery (AAA), North Korea's air defenses are considered reasonably adequate. However, American stealth fighters and bombers armed with precision-guided munitions, as well as cruise missiles would be highly effective against facilities that are located in the open. Therefore, North Korea's reactors, fuel fabrication facilities, and the reprocessing facilities for producing plutonium would be relatively easy to destroy.

But facilities that are unknown or undetected obviously cannot be destroyed. The use of underground and buried facilities presents an additional difficulty to U.S. military planners. The wide-ranging use of tunneling and hardening by North Korea to protect is military infrastructure, and presumably its secret nuclear facilities and storage sites, makes an attack on them with conventional weapons difficult, even if their locations were ascertained by the United States.

The third key element in any military operation aimed at successfully destroying North Korea's nuclear facilities is the one that generates the most concern, both militarily and politically. North Korea's counter to such an attack might not be confined to American bases and warships in the region. North Korean retaliation against Seoul, which lies within range of DPRK artillery, would be devastating. Additionally, North Korea is believed to have between 500-700 Scud missiles capable of delivering both conventional and chemical warheads throughout South Korea. Japan, a key U.S. ally in the region, lies within range of over 175-200 North Korean Nodong missiles. And over 70 percent of North Korea's army ground units are located within 150 km of the demilitarized zone dividing North and South Korea. Finally, the option of nuclear retaliation by the DPRK must be taken seriously.

While the United States would ultimately win such a war, one U.S. military estimate concluded that U.S. and South Korean forces might suffer 300,000-500,000 casualties within the first 90 days of fighting, in addition to hundreds of thousands of civilian casualties. Politically, the outcome of such a military operation would be equally disastrous. Much like the war in Iraq, pre-emptive U.S. military action would engender a great deal of international opposition to U.S.-led efforts in the world. North Korea might possibly use its missiles and threats to skillfully divide the United States politically from its key allies in the region. Additionally, the U.S. launch of a pre-emptive strike on one of China's oldest allies and the prospect of tens of thousands of refugees forging the Yalu (Amnok) River into China might make Beijing side politically, and maybe once again militarily, with North Korea.

Diplomatic and Containment Options

If the Six-Party Talks collapse, the international community will have to decide how best to deal with Pyongyang's status as a *de facto* nuclear power. A number of options are available to the United States and the international community including:

- Increasing diplomatic pressure against Pyongyang;
- A UN Security Council resolution;
- Imposing economic sanctions; and
- Increasing counter-proliferation activities aimed at Pyongyang (such as stopping and boarding North

Korean ships, as set forth in the U.S.-led Proliferation Security Initiative or PSI)

Washington will likely seek an increase in diplomatic pressure, particularly from the other participants in the Six-Party Talks. However, this will probably not be sufficient to resolve the current crisis. There are a number of obstacles to imposing UN sanctions against North Korea, which Pyongyang has declared an "act of war." Since North Korea has withdrawn from the NPT, Pyongyang is not technically violating any international commitments, and it is unclear that China and Russia would support such measures. Furthermore, while Japan might cooperate, economic sanctions will have little or no effect without the full participation of China and South Korea, which is unlikely at this time.

If Tokyo joins Washington in adopting stronger measures against Pyongyang, this could have the negative effect of splitting the United States and Japan from the other parties in the Six-Party Talks. The United States could step up counter-proliferation activities initiated under the PSI with the aim of cutting off North Korea's ability to trade in WMD-related materials. With North Korea having declared it possesses nuclear weapons, the United States and other PSI members will have an increased incentive to halt this trade. As a result, there could be an increase in maritime patrols and search and seizure operations in East Asian waters. However, Beijing and Seoul could object to these actions out of concern that they would antagonize Pyongyang.

Prospects for the Six-Party Talks

North Korea declined to participate in a fourth round of Six-Party Talks that had been scheduled for September 2004. Pyongyang was waiting for the outcome of the U.S. presidential election in November and wanted to assess any possible changes in Washington's policy towards

Pyongyang given the personnel changes in Bush's second term. North Korea has been particularly sensitive to rhetoric by senior administration officials that depicts the DPRK or its leaders negatively. In particular, North Korean officials have cited comments made by Secretary of State Rice during her Senate confirmation hearings whereby she described North Korea as an "outpost of tyranny."

There had been widespread speculation that Pyongyang would accept another round of talks following the Lunar New Year holiday and the celebration of Kim Jong Il's birthday on February 16th. A U.S. House delegation led by Representative Curt Weldon returned in January after a four-day visit to North Korea with the view that Pyongyang was prepared to return to the Six-Party Talks soon. There was more reason for optimism given North Korea's request for 500,000 tons of fertilizer from South Korea on January 13th.

Given the U.S. refusal to engage in bilateral dialogue and the practical alternatives, the United States, North Korea, and other participants will have little choice but to return to the Six-Party Talks. The lack of trust between Washington and Pyongyang continues to be the greatest obstacle to a diplomatic settlement, even though an agreement that leaves all parties better off appears to exist. The United States and North Korea will signal their resolve in the short-term and look for wavering on the other side. This will delay another round of talks, but the other four parties will pressure Washington and Pyongyang to return to the bargaining table. The talks are unlikely to collapse completely unless North Korea conducts a nuclear test, but this is also unlikely unless the United States responds with greater pressure or displays its intention to respond militarily.

8

Bioterrorism

The Threat of Mass Casualty

The September 11, 2001 terrorist attacks that destroyed the World Trade Center in New York, damaged the Pentagon in Washington, D.C., and caused a plane crash in Pennsylvania conclusively demonstrated that mass casualty terrorism has reached the United States. The subsequent series of anthrax letters showed that biological terrorism, which had been largely a theoretical possibility, is a reality. These two developments, as well as several revelations regarding the al-Qai'da terrorist network's interest in weapons of mass destruction, have placed the threat of terrorists causing mass casualties using biological agents squarely before policymakers and an anxious public.

Although the anthrax letters did not appear to have been designed to cause mass casualties, there is now great concern that these or similar perpetrators might employ higher technology delivery systems and affect larger numbers of people in future attacks. The September 11 attacks and the subsequent anthrax letters, combined with evidence of al-Qai'da's interest in toxic agents, have focused renewed attention on the possibility of terrorism involving chemical, biological, radiological, or nuclear weapons, commonly called weapons of mass destruction (WMD). WMD terrorism is not a new phenomenon: in March 1995, the Japanese doomsday cult Aum Shinrikyo released sarin nerve agent in the Tokyo subway, killing 12 and injuring over 1,000. This incident, perpetrated by an apocalyptic group seeking to inflict mass casualties, demonstrated that at least some terrorist groups are capable of acquiring and using chemical weapons.

Mass casualty terrorism is also not new to the United States. In April 1995, a truck bomb destroyed the Alfred P. Murrah Federal Building in Oklahoma City, killing 168 and injuring more than 700. Perpetrated by a lone actor influenced by right-wing ideology, this unprecedented attack brought the threat of mass casualty terrorism albeit with conventional explosives to the American heartland. In the aftermath of these events, some analysts declared that a new era of terrorism had emerged, one involving a sea change in terrorist tactics and goals. With religion arguably replacing politics as the primary ideological motivation for terrorist groups, it was possible to envision terrorist groups, relatively unconstrained by societal norms, seeking to perpetrate more extreme acts of violence than more "traditional" terrorist organizations.

For example, Usama bin Laden, the alleged mastermind of the September 11 attacks, the 1999 bombing of the USS Cole in Yemen, and the 1998 near simultaneous bombings of the U.S. embassies in Kenya and Tanzania, openly declared an interest in acquiring WMD for attacks against American targets; more recently, alleged members of his organization have been apprehended with dangerous poisons. At the same time, the spread of dual use technologies and WMD relevant materials to state sponsors of terrorism and the lack of controls on weapons materials and know-how in the former Soviet Union have raised serious concerns about the increasing threat of terrorists acquiring and using WMD. This is especially relevant in the context of increasing tensions and possible conflict between the United States and countries that have developed WMD and have supported terrorist groups in the past, such as Iraq and North Korea.

The Anthrax Attacks and Bioterrorism

The anthrax letters of 2001 were an entirely new phenomenon. They moved the threat of bioterrorism, which had previously been mostly theoretical, closer to reality. Despite hundreds of anthrax hoaxes in the few years prior to October 2001, the anthrax letters represented the first time that actual, virulent anthrax spores were sent through the mail. The attacks were scattered, isolated incidents targeted at prominent media and political figures, but also resulted in a number of people, notably postal workers and congressional staff, suffering from collateral exposure. One of the most significant aspects is that, thus far, the perpetrator remains at large.

There have been conflicting reports from various government agencies regarding the quality of the anthrax used in the attacks. It may have been highly sophisticated: milled to a fine powder and treated with chemical additives to keep the spores from clumping and becoming weighed down by humidity, so that they aerosolize more readily.

The Perpetrators

The fact that the anthrax may have been milled to a fine powder and mixed with chemicals techniques involving specialized military knowledge unlikely to be available to laboratory microbiologists suggests that the perpetrator(s) may have been involved at one point in time with the biological weapons program of a state perhaps even a scientist who worked on the former U.S. biological weapons program. Although the chemical additives are readily available, the critical skill is to know which additives to use, and how and when to use them.

These findings are consistent with a number of

hypotheses: the perpetrators were aided by a foreign state, were assisted by scientists who once worked in a state-level bioweapons program, or purchased the anthrax on the international black market. The FBI has released only a vague profile of the perpetrator(s), as most probably male, with a scientific background and an intimate knowledge of Trenton, New Jersey.

The fact that the same strain of anthrax appears to have been used in the letter attacks directed against individuals in Florida, New York, and Washington, D.C. also suggests that this is a coordinated effort by a single individual (i.e., a biological Unabomber), a small domestic group, or a large network such as al-Qai'da. Still, the identity of the perpetrator or perpetrators remains unclear. Some evidence, such as the quality of the anthrax, points to an international source, but other evidence points in the direction of domestic terrorists.

Mass Casualty Terrorism

According to terrorism scholar Bruce Hoffman, until September 11, 2001, fewer than 1,000 Americans had been killed in terrorist attacks in the United States or abroad since 1968. The quantum leap in casualties with more than 3,000 dead is particularly alarming in terms of terrorist motivations. Terrorist trends have suggested an increase in casualties per incident, and the September 11 attacks appear to conform to this pattern. However, the anthrax incidents have been small in scale, with the apparent intent of frightening rather than killing large numbers of people.

It is possible that the perpetrators of the anthrax attacks had only a limited amount of powdered anthrax spores enough to deliver in small amounts through the mail, but not enough to disseminate through the air as an aerosol cloud that could infect large numbers of people. They may also not have been motivated to inflict mass casualties, even if they could. Critics have also pointed out the significant technical hurdles to the use of chemical or biological weapons to cause massive numbers of casualties. Despite Aum Shinrikyo's vast financial resources and scientific expertise, it was unable to perpetrate mass casualty attacks with either chemical or biological weapons. In any case, large numbers of casualties can be caused by terrorists without resorting to WMD. The September 11 terrorists did not require advanced weaponry to cause mass casualties and mass destruction. They used a low technology operation and returned to decades old terrorist tactics hijacking planes to achieve their goals.

One thing that the 2001 anthrax attacks made abundantly clear is that public health is a key component of U.S. national security. The anthrax attacks revealed serious gaps in the public health system, particularly at the state and local levels. Fortunately, alert physicians diagnosed the early cases correctly. One would hope that the attacks served as a lesson to public health officials by putting them on guard for the possibility of a covert bioterrorist attack, thus lessening the impact of any future attack. Yet many other doctors and health departments in other cities and towns around the country are not prepared to recognize or contain a bioterrorist attack. These gaps must be remedied immediately if the country is to be prepared for more serious threats. Indeed, improving the public health infrastructure will help address the threat posed by bioterrorism as well as the arguably much greater threat from emerging infectious diseases.

The silver lining of the current dark cloud is that there is a window of opportunity to improve our preparedness for a larger scale biological attack. It is important, however, to address these vulnerabilities in a systematic and determined way, rather than continuing to ride the sine wave of alarmism and complacency that has plagued earlier efforts to improve domestic preparedness. U.S. policymakers must also be prepared for an entirely different type of attack. If terrorists have access to a significant manufacturing capability, the United States must be prepared for the possibility of an escalation from targeted attacks to mass casualty attacks with powdered anthrax or some other agent. The most ominous, but not the most likely, threat would involve the deliberate release of a contagious agent, such as pneumonic plague or smallpox. The health system would then have to detect and contain the outbreak before it spread widely. Concerns about mass casualty bioterrorism have again been raised in connection with Usama bin Laden's al-Qai'da group.

Uncorroborated testimony in a high-profile Egyptian trial in 1999 indicated that al-Qai'da had acquired dangerous biological agents such as the anthrax bacterium, the Ebola virus, salmonella, and botulinum toxin, while other reports mentioned plague and ricin. Al-Qai'da's purported research efforts were focused on weaponizing anthrax and U.S. forces discovered a partially built biological weapons lab near Kandahar that was designed to produce anthrax even though no actual agents were found. There is still no conclusive evidence that al-Qai'da succeeded in weaponizing any of these agents. However, in January 2003, traces of the toxin ricin were found in an apartment in London used by a group of men potentially linked to al-Qai'da. At the same time, there are fears that potential conflict with Iraq could result in Saddam Hussein becoming desperate enough to hand over some of his suspected remaining biological weapons arsenal to terrorists in the hopes that they will use the weapons against the United States.

Preparations and Consequence Management

Preventing mass casualty terrorism with WMD agents and, if prevention fails, managing the consequences of an attack, is an enormously demanding task. Since 1995, the United States has allocated enormous resources to combating WMD terrorism. Numerous government programs have been created in an effort to prevent and deter terrorism or to mitigate the effects of a major attack. These efforts have focused on enhancing the ability of local first responders to decontaminate and treat survivors, augmented by additional capabilities at the state and federal levels. But analysts have criticized the significant overlap and redundancy among various federal counterterrorism programs, as well as the lack of a clear strategy for integrating these diverse elements into a coherent whole. The events of September 11 and the subsequent anthrax attacks have also contributed to these efforts. President Bush, together with Congress, created a new government agency, the Department of Homeland Security, in an effort to ensure greater coordination in response and intelligence collaboration.

Planning domestic preparedness requires coordinating not only some 40 federal agencies, but also a large number of state and local agencies, as well as important elements of the private sector. The creation of the Department of Homeland Security is a useful first step, but the department's head, Tom Ridge, will have to overcome budgetary bottlenecks and chronic turf battles among rival federal bureaucracies. In order to be prepared for a range of contingencies, the first line of defense is to train doctors to recognize the effects of a variety of biological threat agents, and to establish clear channels of communication among primary care physicians and local health departments, as well as among local, state, and federal public health officials.

These various levels must be integrated by e-mail and other communications networks into a seamless web. Diagnostic laboratories around the country also need to have the appropriate tests to identify exotic disease agents such as anthrax in patient specimens. Finally, national distribution mechanisms for drugs and vaccines must be developed so that an outbreak of disease can be contained rapidly. The private sector, such as the U.S. chemical industry, transportation, energy, telecommunications infrastructure, and food companies, will also need to spend more to ensure the safety and security of their products and services. The optimal approach to WMD terrorism is prevention, rather than consequence mitigation. U.S. counterterrorism efforts designed to address this threat have generally been developed in the absence of a realistic assessment of terrorist motivations and technical capabilities for using WMD.

To the extent possible, intelligence collection and analysis capabilities must be strengthened to assess the ability of terrorists to acquire, produce, and deliver biological and chemical agents. Improved capabilities are needed to distinguish between natural and deliberate outbreaks of disease. These new challenges will require the intelligence community to improve its depth of expertise in microbiology, chemistry, and epidemiology. The threat of bioterrorism has not receded since the anthrax attacks of 2001, especially since the perpetrator or perpetrators of those attacks remains unidentified. Recent reports concerning al-Qai'da's efforts to develop biological weapons and the possibility of conflict in Iraq have only increased fears. Despite some empirically based studies and the rich literature on terrorism and WMD issues, the threat of escalation to WMD terrorism remains poorly understood. Continued threat assessments, evaluations and reevaluations of current policies, and heightened vigilance on the part of intelligence agencies will be essential to prepare for the future.

9

Assessing the Threat of Bioterrorism

The specter of terrorists enhancing their already formidable arsenals by acquiring these weapons of mass destruction is truly a horrendous one, one that we all must do our best to prevent. So, how may prevention best be accomplished? A good start is to try to understand the threat of bioterrorism, use that understanding to craft appropriate barriers, and, should barriers be breached, craft effective means for alleviating ill effects resulting from an attack and the apprehending of the perpetrators. To accomplish this objective, it has following parts:

- It provides a brief background of work in arms control.
- Second, findings from an ongoing project to assess applications of advanced biotechnologies for terrorist and criminal purposes and
- Lastly the thoughts on what the major biological threats to our society are and what might be done to meet them are presented.

Much of the activities in the medical sciences are focussed on trying to affect the components of this triangle for the benefit of the host. Thus, from the aspect of the host, some research seeks to devise methods whereby microbial invasions can be prevented or the host's ability to resist infection may be augmented. As to the parasite, the prevention of infectious diseases is sought through vaccine and anti-toxin R&D, while therapeutics, such as antibiotics, germicides, and other agents, weaken or kill the pathogen. Perhaps most important, the characteristics of the "natural" environmental that support the growth of pathogens past a certain critical threshold, or favor the dissemination or transmission of pathogens, may be affected by public health measures, such as proper waste disposal, water treatment, and air filtration.

The biological weapons, either when being developed in the laboratory or when actually used in the field, have the potential to upset the intricate balances that exist within the pestilence triangle by either altering the environment or upsetting parasite-host interactions. In either case, the host will suffer damage or death.

The Possible Applications for Terrorism and Criminality

The NDU/MIIS terrorism project aims to assess the impact of recent and anticipated advances in biotechnology on R&D undertaken for the purpose of perfecting biological weapons. In general, it is exceedingly difficult to forecast developments that can be expected in the future from rapidly evolving and growing scientific fields. Because of its proven value for identifying areas of consensus or disagreement on issues presented to the involved experts, the focus group approach was selected for forecasting. Accordingly, the principal investigators established a focus group constituted by 16 natural and social scientists who possess a wide variety of expertises.

The scientific disciplines represented in the focus group include aerobiology, biotechnology, bioprocessing, human medicine, meteorology, microbiology, molecular biology, phytology, toxincology, veterinary medicine, and virology.

Specialists in criminality, industrial practices, and terrorism also participated.

The focus group was asked to analyze a number of newly developed and emerging biotechnology techniques in terms of their utility in R&D that aims to produce microorganisms of enhanced military or terrorist utility. However, lessons from the history of the pre-1969 U.S. BW program and the Soviet BW program (this program supposedly was terminated in 1992, but some analysts believe it continues in some form in present-day Russia) indicate that research, development, and production to weaponize pathogens and toxins is only a small part of the total process of acquiring biological weapons. The most important parts of the acquisition process are developing "formulations," merging formulations and munitions to produce an efficient weapon system, and designing and producing a mechanism for dispersing pathogens or toxins over a target.

This being so, the NDU/MIIS focus group was also asked to examine whether advanced biotechnologies may be used to enhance the ability of agents to withstand stress brought about by storage, dispersal, and physical and chemical environmental factors. This, in turn, necessitated giving thought to how agents may be used and for what purposes. The focus group was asked to limit its consideration to the next five years; i.e., up to and including 2005. The focus group was not to consider "classical" microbiology except to provide background or for the sake of comparison.

This being the case, the descriptions, opinions, thinking, and conclusions set forth below are mine and do not necessarily represent those of either the NDU or any of the members of the focus group. Biological weapons can be designed and used to injure and kill not only humans, but also animals and plants. Some security analysts believe that the greatest biological threat facing the U.S. is, in fact, the possible use of biological weapons by terrorists or criminals to wage economic warfare by destroying animal and/or plant populations important in agriculture. However, the expertise of the present NDU/MIIS focus group is such that it is best capable of analyzing scientific/technical advances pertinent to BW as waged against humans, so the possible uses of biological weapons by criminals and terrorists against animals, plants, and materials will be the subject of a subsequent NDU/MIIS study.

My analysis of focus group proceedings, as well as of information derived from other sources, leads me to draw certain conclusions about the types of biological attacks terrorists can mount, the most likely scenarios for biological attacks in the immediate future, less likely but still possible scenarios for biological attacks in the immediate future, the possible applications of advanced biotechnologies for terrorist or criminal purposes in the next five years, and the possibilities that advanced biotechnologies offer to terrorists and criminals in the more distant future.

Types of Biological Attacks

In general, terrorists or criminals can carry out three types of biological attacks. First, the pathogen or toxin may be injected. This method is best used when the terrorist or criminal wishes to assassinate an individual. Since individual assassinations are not likely to stress our emergency response and health delivery systems, they are not considered further in this paper.

Second, a quantity of pathogens or toxins may be used to contaminate or poison foods, beverages, or fomites (such as food supplements and medicines taken by mouth). If done skillfully, this method could cause hundreds of casualties. Third, pathogens or toxins may be suspended in a wet or dry formulation and dispersed over a target area as aerosolized particles.

This type of attack could produce thousands of casualties, if three conditions were met:

- The formulation was well designed for aerosol dispersal;
- The aerosol particles produced by the dispersal mechanism were of optimal size and could withstand environmental stresses; and
- Meteorological conditions were just right for blanketing the target area with aerosol particles.

Scenario of Likely Biological Attacks

It is highly probable that biological attacks by terrorists or criminals utilizing foodborne and waterborne pathogens or toxic chemicals will occur in the next five years. Much like what has taken place in the past, these attacks are likely to cause casualties ranging in number from a few to hundreds. Examples of past attacks include the contamination of 10 salad bars by members of the Rajneeshee cult in Oregon in 1984, which caused 751 casualtie, and intentional food contamination in Texas in 1996, which harmed approximately 15 persons.

Events such as these likely will take place with increasing frequency in the years ahead for two main reasons; unprotected, unmonitored salad bars and other food displays have become ubiquitous throughout the U.S. and the number of persons with at least a modicum of training in microbiology is ever increasing (although the population constituted by microbiologists probably is no more or less dishonest or unethical than other populations of professionals, a small proportion of it should be assumed to be willing to lend or sell its skills for terrorist or criminal purposes).

Scenario of Low Probability Biological Attack

The probability that terrorists or criminals will carry out airborne attacks with pathogens in the next five years is low. The reasons are that it is technically difficult to formulate pathogens and toxins for airborne dispersal, to operate dispersal mechanisms successfully, and to ensure proper meteorological conditions for effective aerosol dispersal. For these reasons, this type of attack is too difficult for most terrorist and criminal groups to attempt. The example of the Japanese sect Aum Shinrikyo is illuminative in regard to both pathogens and toxic chemicals. In the biological field, despite having evil intent, a membership that included highly trained bioscientists and chemists, ample funding, and ample time to carry out appropriate R&D, the sect failed utterly to produce effective biological and toxin weapons. It appears that there are two explanations for this failure.

First, the sect used an avirulent strain of *Bacillus anthracis* (the causative agent of the disease anthrax) in their weapons and, second, they used a formulation of pathogens and substrate that clogged up the nozzles of their sprayers. The problem of formulation, especially formulations for airborne attacks, is a difficult one to overcome. Briefly, after they have been produced, pathogens and toxins must be suspended in formulations in preparation for storage or attack. Possibly the major remaining secret of both the pre-1969 U.S. and pre-1992 Soviet BW programs pertains to the formulation of BW agents. After much empirical experimentation, both programs were able to develop methodologies for suspending or dissolving optimal quantities of weaponized pathogens and toxins in special solutions containing preservatives, adjuvants, and anti-static chemicals.

The final emulsion or mixture is what is commonly called formulation. A specific formulation is required for every weaponized pathogen and toxin. Without properly constituted formulation, pathogens or toxins in storage or being transported are likely to loose their virulence or toxicity after a relatively short time (days to weeks); during spraying, solutions containing pathogens or toxins might foul nozzles so that no aerosol is emitted; after being emitted through the spray nozzle, electrostatic attraction between partiçles made up of pathogens or toxins can cause them to clump (bacteria as colloidal particles have electric charges), after which the clumps will fall ineffectually to the ground; and/or environmental stresses, such as UV light and desiccation, will kill or inactivate the aerosolized pathogens or toxins.

Possible Applications for Terrorism in the Next Five Years

After having examined the panoply of advanced biotechnologies, two of them appear to hold the most promise for applications by scientists and technicians intent on weaponizing pathogens and toxins — DNA technologies and genetic and protein engineering. There is a precedent. Scientists who worked for the Soviet Union's BW program are alleged to have used recombinant DNA to combine certain features of the smallpox and Ebola viruses. The result might have been a new type of virus, one that combined the virulence of the Ebola virus with the hardiness and contagiousness via aerosol of the smallpox virus. Soviet scientists also worked at recovering the influenza virus from the corpses of persons who died of influenza in 1918 - 1919 and were buried in permafrost ground. If they were successful, they might have been able to insert this material in influenza viruses circulating in our time, to produce a new variant useful for BW.

Site-directed mutagenesis may be employed in order to change the structure of proteins constituting a bacterium's cell wall so that the modified organism is more difficult to identify or will no longer be recognized by an immune system primed to defend against the parent organism. Protein engineering might be used by a scientist to stabilize toxin molecules so they better resist the action of, for example, chlorine, do not dissociate if placed in water, or resist heat. Further, as many toxins consist of two subunits (one subunit that ferries the toxin molecule to the cell and/or anchors the molecule to the cell membrane and a second subunit that kills the host cell), the possibility exists that protein engineering could be applied to alter a toxin's chemical structure for the purpose of increasing the efficiency of one or both subunits.

The foregoing are examples of what could be done, but I believe it is highly unlikely that any of them will be utilized in laboratories operated by, or working on the behest of, domestic terrorist groups or criminals to weaponize pathogens or operate production systems in the next five years. There are two reasons for this conclusion. First, complex research undertaken to weaponize pathogens is risky because it is more likely to fail than achieve its objectives. The problem of pleomorphic effects is particularly daunting. Pleomorphic effects are manifested as undesirable characteristics that appear in a genetically engineered organism simultaneously to sought after positive characteristics. Thus, even if a laboratory succeeded in genetically engineering a pathogen so it exhibited a new or enhanced characteristic desirable for weapons use, such as antibiotic resistance or added toxin production, the newly developed organism might simultaneously present a weakness to environmental stresses and/or decreased virulence.

If so, a new cycle of research, development, and field testing would have to be done to remove the pleomorphic effects while retaining the sought-after characteristics. If the researcher was unskilled and/or unlucky, he or she might have to undertake several subsequent research, development, and testing cycles before being able to field a strain of pathogen that had improved weapons capabilities over the parent strain. As a consequence of potential difficulties with pleomorphic effects, it is likely that in the next five years or more only well supported, long-term national BW programs would attempt genetic engineering projects for the purpose of weaponizing pathogens.

Second, science's understanding of many natural phenomena, such as infectivity, pathogenesis, host-parasite relationships, and others, is rudimentary. Lack of fundamental information about these phenomena prevents the undertaking of much applied research to, for example, enhance the ability of organisms to infect target hosts, cause severe damage to host systems, and be more specific as to preferred hosts. Further, some important phenomena, such as virulence factors and the ability of a pathogen to penetrate the host's skin or intestinal wall, are controlled by several or many genes; however, the present level of scientific capability allows bioscientists to transfer or modify only single genes. It therefore is impossible to modify phenomena controlled by multiple genes, thus severely circumscribing approaches to weaponizing pathogens.

Possible Applications for Terrorism in the More Distant Future

As a corollary to the preceding finding, the likelihood of advanced biotechnologies being applied successfully for terrorist or criminal purposes will increase substantially during the time 2006 – 2010. The reason is that much basic research is currently being undertaken pertaining to mechanisms of pathogenesis, including pathogenicity islands; histocompatability complexes; retroviral control and ecology; and bacterial genomics.

Information generated by this research will fill many of the gaps discussed in Section A, thereby providing markedly increased opportunities for research to weaponize pathogens. Further, the Human Genome Project will be completed in or shortly after 2003; when this occurs, the human genome constituted by 80,000 – 100,000 genes will have been mapped. As the human genome is being mapped, a new field called functional genomics is growing; functional genomics aims to clarify the functions of identified genes.

It is probable that some of the findings generated by functional genomics could be applied for such purposes as disrupting or destroying physiological functions by designing pathogens, toxins, and naked DNA that will target genes controlling these functions. It has been suggested that functional genomics some day will generate data that may be used to identify genetic markers peculiar to specific human populations. If this was done, pathogens and toxins might be developed that mainly affect persons of populations possessing specified genetic markers. This type of weapons has been called "ethnic" weapons; i.e., weapons that preferentially harm or kill designated national or ethnic populations. While stories about ethnic weapons make for exciting reading, the research required to develop an ethnic weapon would be extremely difficult, have a high probability of failing, take a long time to carry out, and be expensive.

Realistically, the probability of such research being undertaken at all is low; and even if it were to be done by, for example, a well-supported national program, it would probably take more than 25 years to realize findings meaningful for biological weapons development. To conclude this section, there are six reasons why biological and toxin weapons are likely to become ever more attractive to criminals and terrorists as we move into the 21st century. First, as the biotechnology, pharmacology, environmental, and health delivery industries grow, the number of persons possessing expertise in microbiology and the biosciences will increase greatly. It is reasonable to expect that a small proportion of this population will be willing for reasons of greed, ideology, or fear to apply techniques in these disciplines for criminal or terrorist purposes. Second, information on how to produce and disseminate pathogens and toxins is readily available in open sources.

Someone with a modicum of education and training in the microbiological and biotechnological sciences can easily access this information and probably would be able to adapt it for the purpose of weaponizing agents. Third, a tiny quantity of a pathogens or toxin delivered effectively can cause many persons to become ill and die. Fourth, tactical weapons utilizing pathogens or toxins can be designed so that they are easily hidden. Therefore, it would be unlikely that a terrorist or criminal transporting and using a biological weapon would be discovered by either police or nearby citizens. Fifth, the delivery and use of pathogens and toxins do not necessarily require sophisticated methods. In particular, it is not technically difficult to contaminate food or beverages, which could cause hundreds of casualties. Due to significant technical difficulties, it is unlikely that terrorists or criminals will be able to deliver pathogens by aerosol, so a biological attack utilizing the airborne method is unlikely to occur in the next five years. Sixth, there are no defensive technologies available that are, or could be, deployed at civilian facilities to detect and identify deliberately disseminated pathogens or toxins in real or near real time. The fact that a biological attack has occurred would therefore not become known until some time later, when the pathogen's incubation period has passed and many individuals become ill nearly at once.

Comprehensive Threat and Risk Assessment of Chemical and Biological Attacks

Specifically, although much is made of the need to perform a risk assessment of domestic terrorists deploying biological and chemical weapons, there is nothing said about how such a risk assessment should be performed?

To begin, the Report states:

"To perform a sound risk assessment, a multidisciplinary team of experts would use valid, current, documented threat information, including NIEs [National Intelligence Estimates], to develop valid threat scenarios, rank the likelihood of a successful attack, and assure that program countermeasures are not based solely on worst case scenarios."

At first glance, this reads fairly well. However, when examined, the statement raises several questions in the reader's mind. The authors do not define key words, such as "valid" and "sound." They do not explain NIEs and how they are derived. Without this information, the statement becomes at best unclear and at worst meaningless. Unfortunately, its contents are hopelessly muddled, jumping from risk assessment to threat assessment, then to risk management, and back to risk assessment. Regard the following sentence: "A threat analysis – the first step in determining risk – identifies and evaluates each threat on the basis of various factors such as its capability and intent to attack an asset and the likelihood and the severity of the consequences of a successful attack." Can a "threat" has capability and intent? Can it attack? Do the authors equate "threat" with a terrorist group? Or a biological or chemical weapon? What in civilian-speak is an "asset"? Are populations, individuals, police, and/or cows assets?

After assuring the reader for the third time that "Risk assessments are widely recognized as valid decision-making support tools to establish and prioritize program requirements" (there is that word "valid" again; would anyone use "invalid" tools for decision-making?), the authors suggest the use of a multidisciplinary team of experts to: "

- Generate valid attack scenarios;
- Assess and rank the risks (likelihood and severity of consequences) of attack scenarios; and
- Decide on actions and programs focused on reducing or otherwise dealing with risks as assessed." Continuing, the authors state "Risk assessment should include sound inputs and information, such as the best available intelligence and law enforcement information

and analysis, including NIEs and Intelligence Community Assessments. Soundly established requirements could help ensure that specific programs and initiatives and related expenditures are justified and targeted, given the threat and risk of validated terrorist attack scenarios."

As can be realized, the authors of the GAO report argue for the performing of a "sound" risk assessment (versus an "unsound" risk assessment?) of possible future terrorist events that would generate more than 1,000 casualties using "valid" information from various trustworthy sources they name. However, nowhere in the report do they offer suggestions or advice on how such a risk assessment ought to be done. It would seem that some of these experts could have provided concrete guidance on how to conduct the type of risk assessment recommended in the report, but that is not done.

Could it be that a "sound" risk assessment as recommended in the report would be extremely difficult or impossible to perform? I now take the opportunity to explore difficulties inherent to performing risk assessments.

In science, the formula for estimating risk is as follows:

RISK = HAZARD x EXPOSURE

Some risk assessments are relatively straightforward. For example, the estimating of risk associated with adding lead to gasoline would not be difficult for a trained, experienced risk assessor. Hazard can determined because the harm done by various concentrations of lead on humans is known and the amount of lead emitted in exhaust gases of automobiles can be measured. Similarly, exposure can be determined by counting the number of automobiles traversing a locale of interest during a measured time, the half-time of lead in the environment is known, historic meteorological data may be consulted to determine dispersal patterns of gases over the local of interest, and demographic data may be mined for information on the population of the local of interest.

Estimating possible risks attendant to the introduction of a genetically engineered microorganism into the open terrestrial environment was at one time very difficult to do. When the first such introduction was proposed, the U.S. Department of Agriculture (USDA) and the U.S. Environmental Protection Agency (EPA) had great difficulty developing a protocol for appropriate risk assessment that should be done before a decision could be made whether the proposed introduction would be forbidden or allowed to proceed. Eventually, the EPA was given the authority to regulate proposed introduction of genetically engineered microorganisms into the environment, while the USDA has authority over proposed introductions of genetically engineered plants. Both agencies developed risk assessment protocols for proposed introductions that have been followed by researchers and industrialists for over 10 years.

As this is written, over 3,000 genetically introductions of genetically engineered plants and microorganisms have taken place in the U.S., with no apparent harm (hundreds of introductions have also taken place in many other countries of the world). Thus, it would appear as if the risk assessment protocols developed and used by the EPA and USDA has done what they were supposed to do, namely, they protect human health and the environment while allowing possibly risky but economically beneficial activities to proceed under specified conditions.

In 1990, the EPA developed "21 Points to Consider" (United States Environmental Protection Agency, 1990), which lays the basis for risk assessment. It is unnecessary here to provide a detailed listing of these points; it is sufficient to say that a developer of a genetically engineered microorganism must provide information that satisfy five criteria – familiarity with the organism donating genetic material, familiarity with the organism receiving genetic material, familiarity with the environment of the site onto which the proposed introduction will take place, ability to contain the introduced organism to the designated site and, should containment fail, knowledge of the damage that the escaped organism would cause to human health and/or the environment. If information can be provided that satisfies these familiarity and containment criteria, the EPA is able to perform an adequate and appropriate risk assessment of the proposed action.

When I attempted to determine the risks that might attend or result from the introduction of genetically engineered marine microorganisms into the open marine environment, I found that EPA's 21 Points to consider could not be satisfied. The main reasons had to do with lack of familiarity with the marine environment; the inability to contain microorganisms to the site of application because of currents eddies, and other natural forces; and the lack of knowledge about possible damaging actions by escaped microorganisms. In other words, although the EPA's 21 Points to consider appear to provide a satisfactory basis for risk assessment in the marine environment, the lack of fundamental scientific information about marine organisms and the marine environment precludes the performing of an adequate risk assessment of a proposed action involving an application of genetically engineered microorganisms in oceans.

The point of the foregoing is that it is not possible to perform a meaningful or adequate risk assessment in all cases because the information to do so is not available. If solid information is lacking, the tendency might be to substitute assumptions for information. The more assumptions that are made while performing a risk assessment, the less rigorous will be the analysis. For illustrative purposes, it is worthwhile considering how one might go about trying to assess whether a domestic terrorist group is likely to use biological weapons capable of causing more than 1,000 casualties. The first question that would be answered is, which terrorist groups in the U.S. possess the necessary expertise to acquire and deploy biological weapons that depend on aerosol dispersion of pathogens for effect? I do not know how many terrorist groups exist in the U.S., but it may be a sizeable number. Perhaps the FBI and/or local police have information on each of these groups' membership, including whether microbiologists, biotechnologists, or other technical people belong to them. However, since relevant expertise is the key ingredient to any endeavor in applied microbiology, be it peaceful or ill willed, without this basic information, one cannot perform a risk assessment of terrorist capabilities in applied microbiology.

To get around this stumbling block, let us assume that a certain proportion, say a conservative 0.1%, of any population of workers will consist of bad persons; i.e., individuals who would be willing to use their skills for nefarious purposes. The population of scientists and technicians trained in microbiology probably numbers approximately 100,000; based on the foregoing assumption about 100 of them would be willing to apply microbiology for terrorist or criminal purposes. We do not know how many of these individuals belong to terrorist or criminal groups and how many of them would prefer to be lone operators. Let us make another assumption; fifty belong to groups that might wish to mount biological attacks and 50 are potential microbiology equivalents to the Unabomber.

Assuming even distribution of ill-willed microbiologists, then 50 groups in the U.S. each has one microbiologist and thereby possesses the requisite capability to acquire biological weapons. This brings up the next difficult problem to the risk assessor; which of these groups have leaders that intend to deploy biological weapons? This problem may be illustrated by referring to the microbiology technician Larry Wayne Harris. During an interview conducted in

September 1999 by a German reporter, Harris was asked whether he would use biological weapons. He replied "If God tells me to do it, I will." No risk assessor would be in a position to determine if and when God gives Harris, or others of his ilk, the requisite command.

The intentions of others have proven equally difficult to ascertain. For instance, no outsider, as far as is known, was able to divine the intent of the Aum Shinrikyo to use biological and chemical weapons before it actually deployed a chemical weapon in 1993 in Tokyo. No one outside Iraq knows why Saddam Hussein, who possessed sizeable BW and CW programs, decided not to arm saboteurs or terrorists with biological and chemical weapons before and during Desert Shield and Desert Storm. Might he decide to do so in the future? Might Fidel Castro attempt to strike back at the U.S. with biological weapons in retribution for the many biological attacks he perceives Cuba has experienced? A risk assessor cannot know the answer to questions such as these.

Whatever the weapons system, the question whether or not it will be used depends on the intent of the leader or leadership controlling it. No risk assessor will be in a position to know the intent of the leadership of microbiologically capable domestic terrorist groups. Therefore, more assumptions have to be made when assessing the risk these groups pose to our society. The easiest would be to say that if a group has the capability; it should be assumed that it will acquire biological weapons. It follows that if a group possesses biological weapons, it should be assumed that it will use them.

It can be seen from the discussion presented above that fundamental information about capabilities and intent of domestic terrorist groups is lacking and probably cannot be obtained. This being the case, the analyst would have to make a series of assumptions if he or she wished to perform a threat or risk assessment of any one group. The product of such a threat or risk assessment would, to my mind, be worthless. If our government cannot use results from risk assessment to guide decision-making, what might it do to meet the so far theoretical threat of bioterrorism?

The major biological threat facing U.S. society is infectious diseases of natural origin, in particular, emerging infectious diseases, reemerging infectious diseases, and transported infectious diseases. An example of the first was AIDS in the early 1980s and the Hantavirus outbreak in Four Corners in 1993. These types of diseases typically seem to appear out of nowhere and may cause tremendous damage and untold suffering among a susceptible population. Examples of the second type include the reemergence of cholera in South America after an absence in that continent since the early 1900s. There could be many reasons why diseases that have not been seen for a long time reemerge. In the case of cholera, a combination of factors probably was responsible, including an unusual El Niño condition and a breakdown in sanitary systems. An outbreak of Marburg hemorrhagic virus disease outbreak in Germany earlier this year and the just concluded outbreak of West Nile fever in the New York area are examples of the third type.

In these cases, the causative infectious agents are transported from an area where they are endemic to a new site where they have never been detected previously. With the emerging infectious diseases, transported infectious diseases are likely to come into contact with a population that is immunologically naïve, and therefore eminently susceptible. In comparison to the real and enormous threat of emerging, reemerging, and transported infectious diseases, the problem of deliberately caused disease is almost insignificant. From a public policy perspective, it would make sense to pay much more attention to the larger problem while not neglecting the smaller one. However, that is not the situation at present in the U.S.; the overwhelming attention of executive agencies, the legislative branch, and the concerned public is affixed on the theoretical problem of bioterrorism and not on natural infectious diseases. Fortunately, this is not necessarily a bad development.

When a disease outbreak is first detected, no one is in a position to know if it has a natural or laboratory etiology. Thus, the initial public health and medical response to a disease outbreak remains the same whatever its etiology. Public health practitioners get busy trying to determine the etiology of the disease of concern by applying classical and molecular epidemiological techniques, while health providers treat those who have taken ill and try to prevent secondary spread of disease.

Our society's response to a natural versus deliberately caused disease outbreak would differ only after there are clear signs that the disease of concern might be the result of a terrorist or criminal attack. An explosive outbreak of a disease striking hundreds or thousands of persons and whose etiological agent normally is spread by aerosol would be one such sign. Another, more subtle sign, would be a cluster of cases where the causative agent is a foodborne or waterborne pathogen and a specific food or beverage source seems to be its likely source. Once the suspicion arises among public health and/or health delivery personnel that the disease of concern was deliberately caused, and then law enforcement officials will also become involved, gathering evidence that might lead to the arrest and prosecution of the perpetrators.

Since the initial response by the public health and health delivery systems would be the same to an outbreak of disease whatever its origin, it follows that if the ability of these systems to respond effectively and appropriately to any medical disaster were enhanced, our society's ability to cope with both natural disease outbreaks and the aftermath of terrorist attacks would increase. If the following three steps were taken, I believe a significant increase in the ability of public health and health delivery systems to respond to disease outbreaks would result.

First, there seems to be a general agreement among emergency responders that no municipality in the U.S. is prepared to deal with the aftermath of a massive outbreak of disease; i.e., one that generates thousands of casualties within a few days. I suggest that assessments be made by each major city and state to determine what it would take for the city or state in question to prepare for dealing with the aftermath of such a health disaster.

The assessment might be conducted in phases. Thus the first phase, or the generic phase, might determine what is needed to process, treat, and house a thousand casualties whatever the cause of their illness. A second phase might do the same, but would consider 10,000 casualties. A third phase might consider the special conditions that would have to be taken into account if a contagious disease agent caused the 1,000 or 10,000 cases of illness. After that, the special situations brought about by individual diseases might be clarified.

Second, each municipality should perform a study that includes assessing its ability to respond to disease outbreaks of lesser magnitude than what is discussed in the preceding paragraph and clarify possibilities for receiving assistance should its response ability be surpassed. The purpose of each assessment would be to determine the maximum numbers of casualties that the municipality in question could handle without outside assistance, make known the assistance that it could count on to receive from the state should the maximum be exceeded and, should a massive disaster strike, set up procedures for requesting federal assistance, including necessary military forces. The federal government might consider providing funding and expert assistance to those municipalities who need them in order to conduct these studies.

Third, the reporting system in the U.S. for infectious diseases needs to be significantly improved. During the last three years, significant improvements have been made to this system as a result of the current bioterrorism threat. However, this is still not a high priority item; out of the approximately $ 10 billion being spent annually on countering the threat of terrorism, less than $ 200 million is earmarked for public health surveillance and reporting. The reporting system should be sufficiently build up so that it would generate information that could be quickly analyzed for indications of emerging, reemerging, transported, and deliberately caused infectious diseases. To do this, more intensive training on how to detect and report unusual disease outbreaks must be given to local public health personnel and emergency medical personnel.

Further, a certain proportion of law enforcement people should be given training in public health to the extent that they could spot indications of deliberately caused diseases and know what evidence they need to collect to verify the cause of these diseased and to track down and apprehend perpetrators. The possibility of establishing a detection system for automatically and continually surveying the entire Internet for information indicative of suspicious and unusual disease outbreaks should be considered. The Canadian government has set up an Internet-based surveillance system to track influenza on a worldwide basis; this experience should prove useful when setting up the surveillance system proposed here.

To conclude, it is not likely that rigorous risk assessments can be done of threats posed by terrorists or criminals armed with biological and chemical weapons. This being the case, risk management of the terrorist threat has to be undertaken on an empirical basis. Some steps to this end are suggested in this paper, such as improving the ability of federal, state, and local police to analyze information indicative of illicit biological activity, improving the ability of public health and health delivery personnel to deal with the aftermath of disease outbreaks, and improving the national system for detecting, surveying, and monitoring disease outbreaks. What is not so obvious and what I try to make clear in this paper is that there is need for placing the threat of bioterrorism in perspective – the greater biological threat facing the U.S. is not terrorists armed with biological weapons, it is, as it always has been, diseases of natural origin. If we can successfully meet and defeat the real threat of emerging, reemerging, and transported infectious diseases, then we have also gone a long way towards being able to handle whatever manifestation of bioterrorism that will occur.

10

The Global Partnership and Biological Weapons

Although the G-8 pronouncement at the Kananaskis Summit in June 2002 pledged to raise and expend $20 billion to prevent terrorists, or those that harbor them, from acquiring or developing nuclear, chemical, radiological and biological weapons; missiles; and related materials, equipment, and technology, very little work has been accomplished in the biological weapons (BW) area. Indeed, as best I can discern, practically nothing is being done on biological security issues except by the United States. France is making a very modest contribution while Canada, the United Kingdom, and Sweden are providing or have pledged small amounts to the International Science and Technology Center (and the STCU) for work that may include biosecurity issues.

To be more specific, of the 750 million Euros pledged to the Global Partnership, France has committed 5 million Euros for work on biological issues (cryptically identified in the public accounts I could find as funds for "security renovations at highly sensitive Russian laboratories"). According to the *2003 First Annual Report by the United Kingdom on the G-8 Global Partnership*, the UK had expended 20,000 pounds in 2002-2003 for preparation of its first BW project proposal involving a plant health institute in Georgia, and projected expenditures for another 200,000 pounds for the project in 2003-2004. I have been told by a colleague at CSIS that this money subsequently has been redirected to the ISTC. For its part, Sweden has committed 950,000 Swedish Krones (or about $130,000) to bio-safety and biosecurity projects out of a total Global Partnership pledge of 10 million Euros, while Canada has pledged 18 million Canadian dollars/year for five years to the ISTC, some portion of which is likely to be directed to BW projects. Finally, of its ten-year $10 billion pledge to the Global Partnership, the United States has committed approximately $55 million to enhance the protection of biological facilities in the former Soviet Union, and an additional $10 million to redirect former BW scientists.

It is possible that my figures are not perfectly up to date and that there may be a slow but positive trend in Global Partnership commitments to and expenditures for BW-related issues. Nevertheless, to date, far less than one percent of the funds pledged to the Global Partnership have been committed to BW issues, and one must ask what accounts for this unsatisfactory situation. One can identify at least six reasons why so little money has been pledged and so few activities have been undertaken. I would group them into the categories of "high politics," "low politics," limited expertise, the low salience of the issue, a fixation on Russia, and a lack of creativity. The most obvious obstacle to more assistance and the one most often cited by Western analysts involves the politics of BW programs, the secrecy surrounding them, and suspicions about the degree to which Russia, in particular, has been forthcoming about its past activities and is in compliance with its obligations under the Biological and Toxin Weapons Convention (BWC).

These suspicions are not eased by Russian refusal to allow Western access to biological institutes run by the Ministry of Defense, Ministry of Health, and Ministry of

Agriculture. In addition to these so-called problems of "high-politics," efforts to expand cooperation in the biosecurity sector have been impeded by bureaucratic inertia and the force of standard operating procedures - typical features of organizations when they confront circumstances with which they are not familiar. And, indeed, for most countries, the issue of biological weapons is a remote and esoteric topic understood by few government experts, commanding little attention by senior policymakers, and perceived by the political leadership as having little, if any, domestic political impact or constituency. Given the low salience of the issue and the limited body of experts, even among the nonproliferation community within and outside of governments, it is not surprising that funding for BW nonproliferation activities lags well behind that for nuclear nonproliferation projects.

Also contributing to this funding picture is the tendency for the participants in the Global Partnership to pledge funds for activities they already were undertaking or had planned. Since little work was being done on biosecurity issues before the creation of the Global Partnership, it is understandable, although unfortunate, why little work has been initiated since its creation. An additional, less obvious reason for the low expenditure of Global Partnership funds on BW projects is the fixation by most Global Partners on Russia to the exclusion of other post-Soviet republics. This is exceptionally unfortunate and dangerous from the standpoint of weapons proliferation, brain drain, and bioterrorism given the large numbers of highly trained BW scientists and large stock of BW pathogens currently residing in a number of the non-Russian successor states. To date, only the United States has taken much interest in this problem, and its intervention, although significant, is both late and inadequate.

Finally, for purposes of my list, I would argue that almost all parties have been very rigid in how they have defined the nature of the BW problem and uncreative in selecting tools and strategies to ameliorate it. In particular, we have tended not to place enough emphasis on the relationship between disease surveillance, epidemiological response and bioterrorism preparedness; to invest adequately in enhancing public health as a cost-effective bioterrorism prevention strategy; and to utilize nonproliferation education and training as powerful tools to combat the spread and use of biological weapons. It is, of course, easier to call attention to the many facets of the problem than to propose recommendations that are both innovative and practical. I will limit my suggestions for next steps to four, which I believe at least meet the test of practicality.

Emphasize Consolidation

My favourite mantra or principle in the realm of nuclear material protection, control, and accountability is secure, consolidate, and eliminate. I believe at least the first two parts of this nonproliferation formula are equally relevant to the BW realm. The formula, however, is not being implemented in a timely or systematic fashion, and far too many sites in too many countries possess inadequately protected dangerous pathogens. A good example is the Belarus Research Institute of Epidemiology and Microbiology in Minsk, which holds - precariously - some of the world's most dangerous viral agents. Rather than invest heavily in providing biosecurity upgrades at this site, the material should be removed to a more secure facility elsewhere. Given the political difficulties the Untied States is likely to have in directly facilitating this removal effort, it would be of enormous value were an EU member such as Sweden to cooperate with Russia in arranging for the safe shipment of the pathogens from Belarus to Russia.

As an incentive for Belarus to give up its deadly pathogens, the EU, Sweden, or a pair of Global Partnership countries might offer to re-equip the Belarus lab as a CDC-like public health diagnostic laboratory. This kind of approach would serve the dual purpose of consolidating dangerous pathogens and enhancing disease surveillance and public health capabilities in Belarus. This approach, which could usefully be applied to many other sites throughout the former Soviet Union and beyond, also could help to realize the promise of nonproliferation cooperation implied, but too often unfulfilled, by the phrase "Global Partnership."

Greater Focus on Central Asia and the Caucasus

As with the case in the nuclear sector, international attention to the proliferation risks posed by BW expertise and pathogens in the non-Russian republics came too little too late. As a consequence, although the United States has begun to implement various biosecurity and biosafety projects in Kazakhstan and Uzbekistan, and has plans to expand these activities to Georgia and Ukraine, there is tremendous room for greater Global Partnership involvement in these efforts and also comparable activities in countries such as Tajikistan, Belarus, Armenia, Azerbaijan, Kyrgyzstan, and Turkmenistan. Although the size and nature of BW expertise, infrastructure, and stocks of pathogens vary widely across these states, each of them hosts a variety of biomedical facilities that were connected to the network of Soviet Anti-Plague system. This system in the late 1980s encompassed six institutes and approximately 200 regional and field stations scattered throughout the southern and south-eastern parts of the Soviet Union. Among the specific tasks that other Global Partnership states might undertake at these sites outside of Russia, in addition to consolidating dangerous pathogens at fewer sites in fewer countries as much as possible, are:

- Upgrading the biosafety and biosecurity of microbial collections and research facilities to reduce the risk of accidental infections and the potential for theft or diversion of dangerous pathogens;

- Strengthening systems for epidemiological surveillance of both human and veterinary infectious diseases at the Anti-Plague Institutes and stations;
- Exploring the feasibility of better integrating the disparate disease surveillance systems operated by the Anti-Plague Institutes, the military, and other agencies, which are poorly, if at all, coordinated; and
- Computerizing the voluminous paper archives at the Anti-Plague Institutes that contain historical data on past disease outbreaks in order to create searchable databases that could serve as valuable epidemiological research tools.

Greater Access in Russia

As noted previously, concerns on the part of some Western states about Russian compliance with the BWC have been a very contentious issue that has impeded cooperative nonproliferation activities in the biosecurity sphere in Russia. Most unfortunately, these impediments - most importantly a lack of transparency - extend to the five Anti-Plague Institutes in Russia, some of which have been described collectively as a "biosecurity nightmare waiting to happen." As a consequence, unlike the sister institutes in Central Asia, no U.S. Cooperative Threat Reduction or ISTC activities have been planned with Russian Anti-Plague Institutes.

That being said, there are institutional advocates within the Russian government for cooperation in this sphere and it is possible that the Russian Ministry of Health may emerge as a supporter following the recent government reorganization, although I an unaware of changes in its perspective. Until now, however, there have been too many entities involved in deliberations about biosecurity cooperation and pathogen collection consolidation (no institute wants to part with its collection). What is badly needed is a focal point within the Russian government for biosecurity cooperation.

Nonproliferation Education and Training

On November 22, 2002, the United Nations General Assembly adopted without a vote Resolution 57/60 entitled "United Nations Study on Disarmament and Non-Proliferation Education," and conveyed the recommendations of the study for implementation, as appropriate, by member states and other entities. As key principle underlying the UN study is that education is an underutilized tool for promoting both disarmament and nonproliferation. Although a number of Global Partnership states including Japan and Sweden were key proponents of the UN study and helped to draft its recommendations, and despite the fact that all Global Partnership members supported the recommendations of the UN study, a nonproliferation education and training initiative has yet to be launched under the auspices of the Global Partnership.

While one can imagine numerous ways in which nonproliferation education could be employed to promote the objectives of the Global Partnership, a good starting point for such an initiative might be to provide nonproliferation training to former BW scientists, researchers working with pathogens generally, and epidemiologists in Central Asia and the Caucasus. The Anti-Plague Institutes and the field stations in the region are in various states of disrepair and insolvency, but the staffs of these facilities include scientists and technicians who are knowledgeable about some of the world's deadliest pathogens and possess unique collections of pathogenic bacterial, fungal, and viral strains. Accordingly, today the anti-plague systems in the post-Soviet states have the potential for spawning both harmful and beneficial applications. A Global Partnership nonproliferation education initiative might make the difference in steering this potential in a positive direction.

A possible model for this kind of training program is one the Center for Nonproliferation Studies (CNS) in Monterey has employed over the past 13 years, and is also being used to good effect by the PIR Center. In the past year, for example, with the support of the Nuclear Threat Initiative (NTI), CNS organized a nonproliferation training session in Almaty for anti-plague scientists and technicians from Armenia, Azerbaijan, Belarus, Georgia, Kazakhstan, Kyrgyzstan, Tajikistan, Ukraine, and Uzbekistan. It also hosted two scientists from Anti-Plague Institutes in Kazakhstan and Uzbekistan for three months of in-depth nonproliferation training in Monterey. Four more are to receive such training this year.

The potential impact of such nonproliferation training is evident today in the role played by the PIR Center in Russia. NGOs, however, cannot do the work alone. It is now time for the members of the Global Partnership to take the lead in promoting nonproliferation education as a means to enhance biological security and prevent the spread and use of biological weapons.

Biological Weapons and Bioterrorism

Of the three regimes of weapons of mass destruction-nuclear, chemical and biological, it is the last one that is most potent, accessible and the weakest regime in the global efforts to prohibit and prevent. With India having a well-developed bio technology infra structure that includes numerous pharmaceutical production facilities, bio-containment laboratories for working with lethal pathogens, it is very necessary for the government to ensure that the biological agents do not fall into wrong hands.

While the Geneva Protocol of 1925 and the Biological and Toxin weapons convention (BTWC) 1972 are in place which prohibits research, development and production of offensive biological weapons, the latter does allow defensive research. The importance and seriousness of bioterrorism has not been understood or felt until the September 11 WTC attacks and occurrence of anthrax cases reported across USA.

In India too, two cases of anthrax incidence have been reported in the states of Karnataka, and earlier in Tamil Nadu and Andhra Pradesh. More cases are likely to be reported in the coming weeks. The government of India has rightly cautioned the people to be on high alert on the possibility of biological and chemical warfare attacks by terrorists in India following such incidents in USA. The DRDO Scientists are emphatic that anthrax is endemic to India and it is learnt that the Defence ministry and the Home ministry are getting "rapid response teams" to combat threats of such terrorist attacks. Biological weapons pose the greatest threat as these are ideal for bioterrorism for the following reasons:

- Have a delayed response thus preventing immediate detection
- The easiest to acquire
- Less expensive
- Not easily detected
- Even a small quantity can be fatal affecting masses
- Have potential for major public health impact
- Might cause public panic and social disruption
- Require special action for public health preparedness

Biological Agents are grouped under three categories based on the potency and ease of dispersion. Anthrax comes under the top category for its powerful effect and easy availability. One redeeming feature is that it can be cured with antibiotics if detected in time.

Category A: High-priority agents include organisms

that pose a risk to national security because they can be easily disseminated or transmitted person-to-person; cause high mortality, with potential for major public health impact; might cause public panic and social disruption; and require special action for public health preparedness.

Agents include variola major (smallpox); *Bacillus anthracis* (anthrax); *Yersinia pestis* (plague); *Clostridium botulinum toxin* (botulism); *Francisella tularensis* (tularaemia); filoviruses; Ebola hemorrhagic fever, Marburg hemorrhagic fever, and arenaviruses; Lassa (Lassa fever), Junin (Argentine hemorrhagic fever) and related viruses.

Category B: The second highest priority agents include those that are moderately easy to disseminate; cause moderate morbidity and low mortality; and require specific enhancements of CDC's diagnostic capacity and enhanced disease surveillance.

Agents are *Coxiella burnetti* (Q fever); *Brucella* species (brucellosis); *Burkholderia mallei* (glanders); alpha viruses, Venezuelan encephalomyelitis, eastern and western equine encephalomyelitis; ricin toxin from *Ricinus communis* (castor beans); epsilon toxin of *Clostridium perfringens;* and *Staphylococcus enterotoxin B.*

A subset of List B agents includes pathogens that are food or waterborne. These pathogens include but are not limited to *Salmonella* species, *Shigella dysenteriae, Escherichia coli O157:H7, Vibrio cholerae,* and *Cryptosporidium parvum.*

Category C: The third priorities agents include emerging pathogens that could be engineered for mass dissemination in the future because of availability; ease of production and dissemination; and potential for high morbidity and mortality and major health impact.

Category C agents include Nipah virus, Hantaviruses, tickborne hemorrhagic fever viruses, tickborne encephalitis viruses, yellow fever and multi drug resistant tuberculosis.

In the past there have been only two known cases of Bioterrorism which have been extensively researched and analysed. The incidents involving the Rajneesh cult and Aum Shinrikyo are well known. Aum's chief microbiologist died under mysterious circumstances, perhaps felled by one of his own experiments with biological agents. History shows that terrorists are prone to copy each other. Since terrorist groups often strike without warning, we really do not know when and where a terrorist organization might strike after taking inspiration from the previous cases and the recent incidents relating to anthrax.

CIA director George Tenet on February 2, 1999 is said to have made a statement that Bin Laden, was trying to acquire chemical, biological and nuclear weapons. His operatives are trained to conduct such attacks with toxic chemicals or biological toxins and there are indications he is seeking to obtain chemical, biological, radiological, or nuclear weapons.

The points made includes:

- The ISI had established well fortified facilities in Kandahar in Afghanistan for production of chemical, bacteriological and radiological weapon (perhaps) too. This set-up was established in May 1998 with the acquisition of plant and machinery from Yugoslavia. This plant arrived via Pakistan with assistance of ISI
- The first WMD base at Kandahar commenced training of terrorist operatives for biological and chemical weapons from Pakistan, Bangladesh, Afghanistan, Egypt and the Gulf states there after.
- The second WMD base is reported to have been established at Zenica in Bosnia-Herzegovina. Terrorist operative training here was being imparted to first generation European Muslims convertees and second generation emigres from the Muslim world. Sources claim that chemical and biological weapons materials/

samples have been obtained or purchased for relatively small amounts of money.

Russian sources indicate that the network members (Bin Laden) have allegedly purchased pedals of anthrax from an East Asian country for $3695 and the lethal viral agent botulinum from a laboratory in the Czech Republic for $7500 a sample. Representatives of the Moro National Liberation Front in the Philippines, having close links to Al Qaida are also understood to have obtained anthrax from an Indonesian pharmaceutical company. Plague and Anthrax viruses have also been bought from arms dealers in Kazakhstan.

The question that would arise- why Anthrax is being chosen for bioterrorism whereas equally potent agents are available? The reasons are -It is dangerous, easily available with its low cost of production. It does not need advanced technology. Knowledge about anthrax relating to source, culturing, transportation and dispersion are widely available. It is easy to produce in large quantities and easy to weaponise. The most important feature is that it is extremely stable and can be stored almost indefinitely as a dry powder and the bacteria can multiply even in its dormant stage.

Anthrax bacteria *(Bacillus anthracis)* remain in a dormant state as spores and when it come in contact with skin lesion, or inhaled or in intestine, are activated as rod shaped bacteria, which cause cutaneous, pulmonary, intestinal anthrax disease. It mainly affects the hooved animals but a human being can also become its victim. With the advance in technology (genetic engineered and drug resistant strains of the biological agents) and the increase interest of the terrorists in biological weapons, there is need to pay greater attention to Bioterrorism and steps taken to prevent attacks of biological agents.

11

Strategies to Prevent the Misuse of Dangerous Pathogens

As shown by the anthrax letter attacks of fall 2001, terrorist acquisition of dangerous biological pathogens is a serious threat. Is the international community doing enough to prevent a bioterrorist attack? On June 18 the Institute hosted a presentation by senior fellow Jonathan Tucker on "Biosecurity: Assessing Strategies to Prevent the Misuse of Dangerous Pathogens." A former United Nations Special Commission (UNSCOM) biological weapons inspector in Iraq, Tucker directed the Chemical and Biological Weapons Nonproliferation Program at the Monterey Institute of International Studies before coming to the Institute in 2002. He has also served as a specialist on chemical and biological arms control at the United States Arms Control and Disarmament Agency and the Congressional Office of Technology Assessment.

The director of the Chemical and Biological Weapons Nonproliferation Program at the Center for Nonproliferation Studies at the Monterey Institute since 1996, Tucker has worked on a wide array of security issues regarding chemical and biological weapons. In 1995, he served on the Presidential

Advisory Committee on Gulf War Veterans' Illnesses and investigated alleged chemical and biological weapons exposures during the 1991 Persian Gulf War. He is also a member of the Board of Editors for *Scientific American.*

Tucker has done numerous radios and television interviews regarding biosecurity and authored an assortment of articles, op-eds, and books on the subject. His most recent book, *Scourge: The Once and Future Threat of Smallpox* (Atlantic Monthly Press, 2001), was selected as a Washington Post Best book of the year. During his tenure at the Institute, Tucker has been investigating prevention-oriented strategies for countering bioterrorism.

Bioterrorism, long a hypothetical threat, became a harsh reality in the fall of 2001, when letters containing a refined preparation of dried anthrax spores were sent through the U.S. mail, infecting more than twenty people and killing five. Although the October 2001 anthrax attack was fortunately limited in scale, it hinted at the mayhem that could result from the deliberate release of "weaponized" disease agents. In his project report, "Biosecurity: Assessing Strategies to Prevent the Misuse of Dangerous Pathogens," Institute senior fellow Jonathan B. Tucker explored current national and international efforts to prevent terrorists from acquiring dangerous pathogens and argued for the establishment of a set of global biosecurity standards.

To date, most of the emphasis in countering bioterrorism has been on the medical and public health response to an attack, rather than on prevention. Tucker noted that while improved disease surveillance and medical countermeasures such as new drugs and vaccines are important, it is also desirable to invest in reducing the risk of an attack. He then distinguished between the concepts of biosafety and biosecurity. Whereas biosafety refers to measures to prevent the accidental release of pathogens, biosecurity involves measures that guard against the deliberate release of pathogens for malicious purposes.

However, most national and international legislation to date has focused on biosafety and not biosecurity. In a belated effort to improve security at microbiological laboratories and biological suppliers, the U.S. Congress passed a bioterrorism bill in 2002 that tightened controls over dangerous pathogens and toxins stored, used, and transferred within the United States. Nevertheless, according to Tucker, the international dimension of the biosecurity problem remains to be addressed. No uniform global standards for laboratory security currently exist on which individual states can base national legislation and regulatory structures. This lack of harmonization, Tucker said, has given rise to gaps and vulnerabilities that must be addressed as part of a coordinated global strategy to prevent bioterrorism.

The United States is only one of many countries that conduct research on infectious disease agents and maintain collections of dangerous pathogens. According to Tucker, one area of particular concern is the legacy of the Soviet offensive biological warfare program. Today, many former bioweapons-related facilities—now located in the independent states of Russia, Kazakhstan, Uzbekistan, and Georgia—have been converted to civilian activities. Nevertheless, they continue to possess collections of highly dangerous pathogens that could potentially be stolen or diverted for military, terrorist, or criminal purposes. Although improved security for collections of dangerous pathogens in the former Soviet Union is urgently needed, many laboratories—such as those associated with the network of Anti-Plague Institutes and field stations—lack the necessary financial and technical resources to implement these measures.

Tucker cautioned that the former Soviet Union is not the only area of concern. Several countries now operate maximum containment laboratories designed for work with the most dangerous and incurable pathogens. Security risks are also associated with roughly a third of the 1,500 state-owned and commercial culture collections worldwide that possess, exchange, and sell samples of microorganisms and toxins for legitimate scientific and biomedical research. Culture collections vary widely in size and content, ranging from large organizations such as the non-profit American Type Culture Collection (ATCC) in Virginia and the U.S. Department of Agriculture's collection of plant and animal pathogens in Ames, Iowa, to small "boutique" collections of microbial strains at universities, federal agencies, and private companies. Numerous culture collections outside the United States are not adequately secured and controlled, making them potentially vulnerable to theft by proliferators and terrorists.

In addition, trade in microbial cultures is poorly regulated, both within countries and among them. In order to address this problem, several countries in addition to the United States have passed legislation relating to laboratory security. Nevertheless, Tucker argued, national biosecurity regulations must be reasonably uniform to prevent terrorists from stealing deadly pathogens from poorly protected facilities in those countries where laws or enforcement are lax. Relying exclusively on uncoordinated national standards would lead to a patchwork quilt of regulations, creating pockets of weak implementation or enforcement that terrorists could exploit as targets of opportunity. Only global biosecurity standards, Tucker stressed, would place significant obstacles in their path.

Recently, a few international organizations have launched initiatives in the biosecurity field, including the World Federation for Culture Collections, the Organization for Economic Cooperation and Development, the European Union, and health ministers from the Group of Seven plus Mexico. While these initiatives are useful steps in the right direction, they remain uncoordinated and incomplete. Tucker stressed that truly global biosecurity standards would reduce the risk that terrorists could obtain dangerous pathogens from foreign sources, and would facilitate collaborative research to develop protective vaccines and drugs. For this reason, the international scientific community and the security community should work closely together to develop practical and cost-effective approaches to biosecurity.

Tucker offered a roadmap for the negotiation of global biosecurity standards, suggesting that they should include the following basic elements:

- Registration and licensing of facilities that work with dangerous pathogens,
- Guidelines for the physical security of these facilities,
- Measures for the accountability of dangerous pathogens and other biohazardous materials,
- Background investigations to ensure the suitability and reliability of laboratory personnel, and
- An emergency response plan in case of breaches in biosecurity. Given that model legislation is problematic because countries have incompatible legal systems, Tucker suggested that a technical working group be established under the auspices of the Biological Weapons Convention (BWC) to develop detailed guidelines for national legislation. In addition to representatives of BWC member-states, this group might include experts from the World Health Organization, the Food and Agriculture Organization, and the World Organization for Animal Health.

To ensure a degree of uniformity and accountability in national implementation of the voluntary standards, Tucker also proposed that an international oversight mechanism be created. This mechanism, which might be coordinated by a small secretariat, would invite the participating states to submit written reports on implementation of the biosecurity standards and to attend annual meetings at which they can raise concerns about possible gaps in biosecurity in other countries and apply political pressure to ensure their correction. Tucker concluded his report by stating that the negotiation of global biosecurity standards would provide a concrete means of reducing the risk of bioterrorism, while strengthening the international legal norm against the acquisition and use of biological weapons by both states and terrorist organizations.

Countermeasures against Biological Terrorism

Bioterrorism is terrorism which utilizes pathogenic microorganisms or toxins. The Federal Bureau of Investigation (FBI) of the USA defines bioterrorism as "the intentional use of microorganisms or toxins derived from living organisms to produce death or disease in humans, animals, or plants". After the September 11, 2001 attack on the World Trade Center in New York City, a succession of acts of anthrax terrorism were committed in the USA and public concern about bioterrorism was raised. USA officials, however, have studied countermeasures against bioterrorism for a long time, especially since the Aum Shinrikyo act of terrorism in 1995 in Tokyo. At that time Aum Shinrikyo used a chemical agent, sarin gas, but the cult had also previously attempted 3 unsuccessful bioterrorism acts using anthrax and botulinum toxin. They had also tried to obtain Ebola virus from Zaire.

Attempts to use infectious materials to attack an enemy have a long history before the prior to the establishment of pathogenic microbiology. From the late 19th to the early 20th century, many pathogenic microorganisms were identified, and research on biological weapons using those pathogens was carried out secretly in many countries. Japan also has a shameful memory of inhumane research on biological weapons conducted by Unit 731 in Manchuria, Northeastern China during World War II. Biological weapons have been called low-priced weapons of mass destruction. Usual microbiology laboratories are adequate for their production and expenses are low. Furthermore, recent progress in biotechnology has made it possible to construct more potent pathogens by manipulating those using genetic engineering methods. Biological warfare between nations has not obtained the desired results in history, but use of biological weapons for terrorism has proven effective to induce panic in the general public. Now we are in danger of terrorism acts of various types: biological, chemical or even cyber terrorism since the end of the Cold War. To confront such acts, we must know our opponent. The present paper briefly reviews the history and the present situation of biological weapons and countermeasures against them.

Recognition of biological materials as tools for killing or wounding humans and animals has a long history. Infectious diseases were recognized for their potential impact on people since before Christ. Phyto- and zoo-toxins were used for poisoned arrows, and knowledge of the action of these toxins stimulated the development of medical drugs. The plague (pest) pandemic spread through Europe in the 14th century, to which more than one third or one fourth of Europeans were thought to have fallen victims. The Tartar forces which experienced an epidemic of plague in 1346 converted their misfortune into a military operation by hurling the cadavers of their deceased into the opponent's city to spread the disease.

Although they had no knowledge of the pathogen of plague, because the discovery of pest bacilli did not occur until the 19th century, they had recognized person to person transmission of plague. Smallpox was also used as an effective biological weapon. In the 15th century, Pizarro, a leader of a Spanish troop is thought to have presented South American natives with variola-contaminated clothing. In North America, the deliberate use of small-pox against the native Indian population in the French-India war is suggested. These historical attempts to use diseases in biological warfare are thought to be based on the difficulty of differentiating between a naturally occurring endemic and an alleged biological warfare attack. The progress of pathogenic bacteriology by bacteriologists represented by Louis Pasteur and Robert Koch in the late 19th century made possible the isolation and stocking of specific pathogens and those used for biological weapons.

Actual attempts by German troops in World War I to ship horses and cattle inoculated with pathogens such as *Bacillus anthracis* (anthrax bacilli) or *Pseudomonas pseudomallei* (melioidosis bacilli) to the USA and other countries are suspected. However, these attempts were not targeting humans, but live-stock damage: so-called "agro-terrorism". On the other hand, many chemical weapons including chlorine and phosgene were frequently used in World War I. In the aftermath of World War I, international diplomatic directives were made to limit the proliferation and use of weapons of mass destruction including biological and chemical weapons. On June 17, 1925, the "Protocol for the Prohibition of the Use in War of Asphyxiating, Poisonous or Other Gases and of Bacteriological Methods of Warfare," commonly called the Geneva Protocol of 1925, was signed. A total of 108 nations, including eventually the 5 permanent members of the United Nations (UN) Security Council, signed the agreement.

The USA, however, did not ratify the Geneva Protocol until 1975. Therefore, the Geneva Protocol did not produce satisfactory results, because several countries including Belgium, Canada, France, Great Britain, Italy, Japan, the Netherlands, Poland, and the Soviet Union began to develop biological weapons soon after its ratification. Especially, the center of the Japanese biological warfare program known as "Unit 731" commanded by Shiro Ishii is infamous for its experiments against humanity. The unit started as the Laboratory of Prevention of Epidemics, Army

Medical School in 1932 in Tokyo, and then the Department of Prevention of Epidemics, Japanese Kantong gun Army in Manchuria, in northeastern China, was established in 1936. The apparent objective of the unit was hygienic control of the troops, but the concealed and actual objective of the research was the development of chemical and biological weapons which continued until 1945, the end of World War II. Various pathogenic bacteria including *B. anthracis, Neisseria meningitidis, Vibrio cholerae, Shigella* spp, and *Yersinia pestis* were tested as candidates for biological weapons.

Many prisoners including Chinese, Mongolian, Soviet, American, British, and Australian soldiers are believed to have died as a result of experimental infection during the program. The group also tried to instigate a plague epidemic by spreading laboratory fleas which were fed plague infected rats. An attack on the city of Changteh in 1941 was believed to have led to approximately 10,000 casualties, but 1,700 deaths were also reported among Japanese troops during this incident. Thus biological warfare also has the risk of causing disaster on the offensive side, a so-called "boomerang effect", if proper preparation, training and equipment for preventing infection are not completely in place. At the end of World War II, most of the experimental data of Unit 731 was incinerated to hide proof of what had occurred, although some documents were believed to have been transferred to American and Soviet troops.

In the USA, a biological warfare program was begun in 1942 under the direction of a civilian agency, the War Reserve Service. The program included a research and development facility at Camp Detrick (Fort Detrick), Maryland, which is known today as the US Army Medical Research Institute of Infectious Diseases (USAMRIID). The British army conducted a test to use *B. anthracis* spores as an agro-terrorism mechanism in Gruinard Island, Scotland in World War II, but the experiments led to heavy contamination of the island by the bacterial spores. In 1986, the island was finally decontaminated by treatment with formaldehyde. After World War II, research on developing biological weapons was continued by many countries. The 1925 Geneva Protocol still existed but was ineffective in controlling the proliferation of biological weapons. Because of public concerns about biological weapons, UK submitted a proposal to prohibit the development, production and stockpiling of biological weapons to the UN Committee on Disarmament in 1969.

In the same year the World Health Organization issued a report regarding the possible consequences of the use of biological warfare agents. In 1970 President Nixon terminated the offensive biological weapons program of the USA, although research for developing counter measures, including vaccines and antisera were still continued. The entire arsenal of biological weapons was destroyed by February 1973. Thereafter USAMRIID was established to continue research and develop medical defenses for the US military against a potential attack with biological weapons. Subsequently, the 1972 "Convention on the Prohibition of the Development, Production, and Stockpiling of Bacteriological (Biological) and Toxin Weapons and on Their Destruction," known as the BWC, was developed. The BWC went into effect in March 1975 with agreement of 103 cosigning nations. The number of states which are parties to the BWC as of 2006 is 155, and 16 countries have signed but not ratified the document.

The Japanese Government signed it in 1972 and ratified and established a law for enforcing BWC in 1982. However, effectiveness of the BWC is low because it does not provide firm guidelines for inspections and control of disarmament and adherence to the protocol or for dealing with violations. Several of the signatory nations of the BWC have continued their development of banned items. A typical episode is an epidemic of anthrax which occurred among citizens of

Sverlvoask (now Ekaterinburg), Russia in April 1979. The epidemic spread among people who lived and worked near a Soviet military microbiology facility (Compound 19) in Sverdlovsk, and many livestock died of anthrax in the same area.

Perception of Risk of Terrorist Attacks

An overwhelming and fairly consistent majority believes that there is a significant likelihood of further terrorist attacks on US soil. A New York Times poll taken October 25-28 found that 88% believed it very likely (53%) or somewhat likely (35%) that there would be "another terrorist attack on the United States within the next few months." Belief in the likelihood of an attack does not appear to have subsided over the past few weeks. The same question was posed in a CBS News poll conducted October 8, when 85% believed another attack in the next few months was very likely (46%) or somewhat likely (39%). Similarly, in an October 7 NBC News poll (taken the day of the initial strikes against Afghanistan), 91 % said that in the next several months it is very likely (65%) or fairly likely (26%) that "terrorists will retaliate and strike again in America."

Responding to a more specific question on October 11-12, 85% told Newsweek that it is likely (48% very likely) that "more terrorist attacks will be carried out against major US cities, buildings or national landmarks in the near future." When Newsweek asked the same question September 13-14, 82% thought it likely (43% very) that such attacks would occur. Asked to think about the next ten years, 75% thought it very (41%) or somewhat (34%) likely that "the US will be attacked by terrorists in a similar way that it was attacked this week" (NBC/Wall Street Journal, September 15-16). However, only, a minority feels that "terrorist acts like the ones we just experienced" will be "very common" (8%) or "somewhat common" (31%) in the future. Fifty-three percent think they will be "not too common" (39%) or "not at all common" (14%).

Large majorities continue to express concern or worry about the prospect of future attacks, though the intensity of that worry has declined somewhat. An October 15 ABC News/Washington Post poll indicated that 78% worried a great deal (35%) or somewhat (43%) about "the possibility there will be more major terrorist attacks in the United States." Only 23% said it worried about them "not too much" (14%) or "not at all" (9%). Between September 27 and October 7, three other ABC/Washington Post polls asked the same question, and each found about four in five saying they were at least somewhat worried. When the question was asked on September 11, over 90% expressed worry. As time has passed the percentage saying they worry about the possibility of more major attacks a "great deal" has declined from 49% on September 11 to 35% on October 15. The Pew Research Center, in a poll conducted October 10-14, asked how much respondents worried that there will "soon be another terrorist attack on the United States" (emphasis added). In this case, a smaller but still robust majority of 67% said they were at least somewhat worried (37% very worried). On September 20, - an NBC News poll also asked about worry - that the United States will experience another major terrorist attack.

Using a slightly different set of response options, it found 30% very worried, 29% somewhat worried, 40% only slightly worried, and 26% not really worried. About half say they worry about the possibility that a family member might "become a victim of a terrorist attack." An October 11-14 Gallup poll found 51% worried (18% very), and an October 10-14 Pew poll found 50% worried (again, 18% very worried). On October 8, when ABC News gave respondents just two options, an even smaller percentage (44%) expressed worry that "a close relative or friend might be the victim of a further terrorist attack." In the September

20 NBC poll, only about one in four worried that they or someone they love would "be the victim of a terrorist attack," while 71% were not worried. However, as above, the NBC poll is not quite comparable because respondents tend to gravitate to "slightly worried" when it is the third option, rather than "not too worried", which is the third option in the other polls.

A clear minority of Americans are worried that a terror attack will occur in their community and few report avoiding certain areas because of fear of terrorism. On October 17-18, only 43% told Fox News that they are very (12%) or somewhat (31%) worried that "terrorist attacks might take place where [they] live or work." A majority of 56% said they were not very (28%) or not at all (28%) worried about this. Similarly, on October 8, 30% said they personally worried about "a terrorist attack in the area where [they] live" (CBS News). According to an October 11-13 Zogby poll, even fewer (27%) felt it was likely that their "hometown" would be the "target of a terrorist attack." In an October 12 Harris poll, just 32% said they "personally worry" about terrorism when they are in "public places". And a Pew poll taken October 11-12 found that only about 1 in 10 (12%) reported "avoiding certain buildings or landmarks" as a result of the New York and Washington attacks.

When asked specifically about the linkage between the current military action in Afghanistan and the likelihood of future terror attacks, the public shows a level of worry similar to its worries about future terrorist incidents in general. But, interestingly, smaller majorities believe the war will make future attacks more likely. In the October 11-12 Newsweek poll, 80% said they were worried (41% very worried) that "the military action will lead to... more terrorism against US citizens at home." In the same survey, 83% were worried (44% very) that our action in Afghanistan would result in "more terrorism against US citizens abroad." These results mirror questions mentioned above that found 4 in 5 worried about future terror attacks overall. (When asked by Zogby in an October 11-13 survey if they were "afraid" that US military action in Afghanistan would "lead to more terrorism aimed at the US", a smaller majority of 57% said they were and 40% said they were not.) An intriguing finding, however, is that while polls from mid-October find more than 4 in 5 feel that future terror attacks against the US are "likely", a substantially smaller majority (66%) told Harris Interactive that "the military action in Afghanistan had made a terrorist attack in the US" more likely (October 12).

As noted elsewhere in this report, while a majority of Americans think military action will probably lead to future attacks, they believe doing nothing is even more likely to lead to future incidents.

Finally, when asked in the Harris Interactive survey whether the action in Afghanistan would make an attack on "the community in which you live" more likely, just 23% felt that would be the case.

A modest to very strong majority thinks that a whole range of terrorist incidents are likely to occur in the US. A Harris Interactive survey conducted October 12 asked respondents about several types of terror attacks and asked whether they were "likely or not likely to occur in the United States in the next 12 months." All but one on the list were deemed to be likely by a majority, including:

- A bomb carried in a car or truck — 83% likely
- A chemical or biological weapon other than anthrax — 70% likely
- At a major public event like a concert or athletic event — 67% likely
- On some part of the nation's water supply - 64% likely
- Against the Internet - 59% likely
- On a nuclear power plant - 58% likely

Interestingly the only type of attack not seen as likely by a majority was one "against another skyscraper like the Empire State Building or Sears Tower in Chicago." Forty-seven percent considered such an attack likely, while 50% thought it unlikely.

Terrorist Use of Weapons of Mass Destruction

A majority believes that terrorists have access to weapons of mass destruction and are likely to use them at some point in the future. In a Fox News survey (September 19-20) nearly two-thirds (63%) agreed that it is "likely that terrorist groups like bin Laden's currently have access to nuclear weapons." Just 23% did not think so, with 14% unsure.

Additionally, an NBC/Wall Street Journal poll (September 15-16) that asked respondents to think about threats the US "might face in the next ten years" found substantial majorities believing that weapons of mass destruction will be used. A strong majority (68%) said the US was likely to "be attacked within its borders by terrorists possessing nuclear or biological weapons." When asked about nuclear threats only, a somewhat smaller majority (57%) believed the US "will face an attack by a single nuclear missile from a terrorist or nation."

Probably as a result of the anthrax attacks, biological and chemical weapons are becoming a larger concern. As noted above, the October 12 Harris Interactive poll found 70% saying it is likely that a "chemical or biological weapon other than anthrax" will be used in the US in the next twelve months. Similarly, on October 8-9, four in five (80%) told ABC News they were at least somewhat concerned (37% very concerned) "about the possibility of a terrorist attack in the United States using biological or chemical weapons." That level of concern is much higher than in an NBC poll completed October 7 — just after the first anthrax victim but before the second. In that poll, a bare majority of 51%

thought that such an attack in the near future was very (23%) or fairly (28%) likely. At that point, the level of concern was not substantially higher than in an April 1997 Pew poll. Asked how much they worried "about the chance that terrorists could use a nuclear, chemical, or biological weapon to attack a US city," about half (48%) said they were worried "a great deal" or "somewhat," and the other half (51%) said they were "not at all" or "not much."

When asked about nuclear threats only, a somewhat smaller majority (57%) believed the US "will face an attack by a single nuclear missile from a terrorist or nation." The public clearly perceives chemical and biological weapons to be a greater danger than nuclear weapons at this time. Given a list of four potential kinds of terrorist strikes in an October 18 Fox News poll, a strong majority (62%) chose "chemical or biological" weapons as the "biggest threat." Only 9% chose "tactical nuclear weapons" while 14% chose "truck or car bombs" and just 5% thought the biggest threat would be "planes being hijacked and crashed." Likewise, a September 19-20 Fox poll also found lower concern about nuclear weapons than chemical or biological weapons.

Asked whether they believed "nuclear weapons or chemical and biological weapons" were "more of a real danger right now", the vast majority said chemical and biological weapons (75% to 13%). Past data suggest a low level of confidence that the government is prepared for terrorism with biological weapons. According to a February 1998 Newsweek survey just 35% believed the US to be "well prepared to deal with the threat of terrorists armed with biological weapons." A slim majority (52%) felt the US was not well prepared.

Long-Standing Pessimism

While recent events appear to have increased worries, past data show a long-standing pessimism about the prospect of eliminating terrorism. In an October 1998 Gallup survey, just 23% felt the "threat of terrorism" would be better by 2025. Seven in ten (70%) thought it would be worse, and 4% volunteered that it would be about the same. An April 1995 Pew poll taken just prior to the Oklahoma City bombing found that only a small minority (19%) felt the US was "making progress" on the "problem of international terrorism." An overwhelming majority felt the US was either "losing ground" (36%) or that the situation was staying "about the same" (40%). This question also received virtually identical results in March 1994. Also in April 1995, 76% said it was very likely (48%) or somewhat likely (38%) that "an act of terrorism will occur somewhere in the United States in the next twelve months" - only moderately less than the perceived likelihood today.

However, there is some evidence that concerns may have been moderating somewhat prior to the New York and Washington attacks. For example, when asked in January 2000 whether "in the next century...acts of terrorism would increase, decrease, or remain about the same," 45% felt they would increase and 43% thought they would stay the same. Just 5% thought they would decrease (CBS News). While this response is quite consistent with the overall pessimism about terrorism, it is a good deal more optimistic than the response to the same question two years earlier, in March 1998. At that time, a strong majority (61%) thought acts of terrorism would increase, 29% felt they would remain about the same, and 7% thought they would decrease.

The foiled plots surrounding the millennium celebrations may partly explain the difference. Yet a similar shift took place between March 1997 and November 1999 in a Time/CNN question about air transport issues. When asked about "the threat of terrorism...making it less safe to fly on commercial airplanes these days," 43% said it was a "big problem." A slim majority (51%) felt it was a "not so big a problem." This was a far more optimistic response than in early 1997, when nearly two in three (62%) thought it to be a big problem, and just 34% saw it as not a big problem.

Criminology

As a subdivision of the larger field of sociology, criminology draws on psychology, economics, anthropology, psychiatry, biology, statistics, and other disciplines to explain the causes and prevention of criminal behaviour. Subdivisions of criminology include penology, the study of prisons and prison systems; biocriminology, the study of the biological basis of criminal behaviour; feminist criminology, the study of women and crime; and criminalistics, the study of crime detection, which is related to the field of Forensic Science.

Criminology has historically played a reforming role in relation to Criminal Law and the criminal justice system. As an applied discipline, it has produced findings that have influenced legislators, judges, prosecutors, lawyers, Probation officers, and prison officials, prompting them to better understand crime and criminals and to develop better and more humane sentences and treatments for criminal behaviour. The origins of criminology are usually located in the late-eighteenth-century writings of those who sought to reform criminal justice and penal systems that they perceived as cruel, inhumane, and Arbitrary. These old systems applied the law unequally, were subject to great corruption, and often used torture and the death penalty indiscriminately.

The leading theorist of this classical school of criminology, the Italian Cesare BONESANO BECCARIA (1738–94), argued that the law must apply equally to all, and that punishments for specific crimes should be standardized by legislatures, thus avoiding judicial abuses of power. Both Beccaria and another classical theorist, the Englishman Jeremy Bentham (1748–1832), argued that people are rational beings who exercise free will in making choices. Beccaria and Bentham understood the dominant motive in making choices to be the seeking of pleasure and the avoidance of pain. Thus, they argued that a punishment should fit the crime in such a way that the pain involved in potential punishment would be greater than any pleasure derived from committing the crime. The writings of these theorists led to greater Codification and standardization of European and U.S. laws.

Criminologists of the early nineteenth century argued that legal punishments that had been created under the guidance of the classical school did not sufficiently consider the widely varying circumstances of those who found themselves in the gears of the criminal justice system. Accordingly, they proposed that those who could not distinguish right from wrong, particularly children and mentally ill persons, should be exempted from the punishments that were normally meted out to mentally capable adults who had committed the same crimes. Along with the contributions of a later generation of criminologists, known as the positivists, such writers argued that the punishment should fit the criminal, not the crime.

Later in the nineteenth century, the positivist school of criminology brought a scientific approach to criminology, including findings from biology and medicine. The leading figure of this school was the Italian Cesare Lombroso (1836–1909). Influenced by Charles R. Darwin's theory of evolution, Lombroso measured the physical features of prison inmates and concluded that criminal behaviour correlated with specific bodily characteristics, particularly cranial, skeletal, and neurological malformations. According to Lombroso, biology created a criminal class among the human population. Subsequent generations of criminologists have disagreed harshly with Lombroso's conclusions on this matter. However, Lombroso had a more lasting effect on criminology with other findings that emphasized the multiple causes of crime, including environmental causes that were not biologically determined. He was also a pioneer of the case-study approach to criminology.

Other late-nineteenth-century developments in criminology included the work of statisticians of the cartographic school, who analyzed data on population and crime. These included Lambert Adolphe Quetelet, (1796–1874) of France and André Michel Guerry, of Belgium. Both of these researchers compiled detailed, statistical information relating to crime and also attempted to identify the circumstances that predisposed people to commit crimes. The writings of French sociologist Emile Durkheim (1858–1917) also exerted a great influence on criminology. Durkheim advanced the hypothesis that criminal behaviour is a normal part of all societies. No society, he argued, can ever have complete uniformity of moral consciousness. All societies must permit some deviancy, including criminal deviancy, or they will stagnate. He saw the criminal as an acceptable human being and one of the prices that a society pays for freedom.

Durkheim also theorized about the ways in which modern, industrial societies differ from nonindustrial ones. Industrial societies are not as effective at producing what Durkheim called a collective conscience that effectively controls the behaviour of individuals. Individuals in industrial societies are more likely to exhibit what Durkheim called *anomie*—a Greek word meaning "without norms." Consequently, modern societies have had to develop specialized laws and criminal justice systems that were not necessary in early societies to control behaviour.

Early efforts to organize criminologists in the United States attracted law enforcement officials and others who were interested in the criminal justice system. In 1941, a group of individuals in California organized for the purpose of improving police training and the standardization of police-training curricula. In 1946, this movement developed into the establishment of the Society for the Advancement of Criminology, which changed its name to the American Society of Criminology in 1957. Initial efforts of this organization focused upon scientific crime detection, investigation, and identification; crime prevention, public safety, and security; law enforcement administration; administration of criminal justice; traffic administration; and probation.

The American Society of Criminology has since attracted thousands of members, including academics, practitioners, and students of the criminal justice system. Studies of criminology include both the theoretical and the pragmatic, and some combine elements of both. Although some aspects of criminology as a science are still considered radical, others have developed as standards in the study of crime and criminal justice.

Sociology and Criminology

During the twentieth century, the sociological approach to criminology became the most influential approach. Sociology is the study of social behaviour, systems, and structures. In relation to criminology, it may be divided into social-structural and social-process approaches. Social-Structural Criminology Social-structural approaches to criminology examine the way in which social situations and structures influence or relate to criminal behaviour. An early example of this approach, the ecological school of criminology, was developed in the 1920s and 1930s at the University of Chicago.

It seeks to explain crime's relationship to social and environmental change. For example, it attempts to describe why certain areas of a city will have a tendency to attract crime and also have less-vigorous police enforcement. Researchers have found that urban areas in transition from residential to business uses are most often targeted by criminals. Such communities often have disorganized social networks that foster a weaker sense of social standards.

Another social-structural approach is the conflict school of criminology. It traces its roots to Marxist theories that saw crime as ultimately a product of conflict between different classes under the system of capitalism. Criminology conflict theory suggests that the laws of society emerge out of conflict rather than out of consensus. It holds that laws are made by the group that is in power, to control those who are not in power. Conflict theorists propose, as do other theorists, that those who commit crimes are not fundamentally different from the rest of the population. They call the idea that society may be clearly divided into criminals and noncriminals a dualistic fallacy, or a misguided notion. These theorists maintain, instead, that the determination of whether someone is a criminal or not often depends on the way society reacts to those who deviate from accepted norms. Many conflict theorists and others argue that minorities and poor people are more quickly labeled as criminals than are members of the majority and wealthy individuals.

Critical criminology, also called radical criminology, shares with conflict criminology a debt to Marxism. It came into prominence in the early 1970s and attempted to explain contemporary social upheavals. Critical criminology relies on economic explanations of behaviour and argues that economic and social inequalities cause criminal behaviour. It focuses less on the study of individual criminals, and advances the belief that existing crime cannot be eliminated within the capitalist system. It also asserts, like the conflict school, that law has an inherent bias in favor of the upper or ruling class, and that the state and its legal system exist to advance the interests of the ruling class. Critical criminologists argue that corporate, political, and environmental crime are underreported and inadequately addressed in the current criminal justice system.

Feminist criminology emphasizes the subordinate position of women in society. According to feminist criminologists, women remain in a position of inferiority that has not been fully rectified by changes in the law during the late twentieth century. Feminist criminology also explores the ways in which women's criminal behaviour is related to their objectification as commodities in the sex industry. Others using the social-structural approach have studied Gangs, juvenile delinquency, and the relationship between family structure and criminal behaviour.

Social-process criminology theories attempt to explain how people become criminals. These theories developed through recognition of the fact that not all people who are exposed to the same social-structural conditions become criminals. They focus on criminal behaviour as learned behaviour. Edwin H. Sutherland (1883–1950), a U.S. sociologist and criminologist who first presented his ideas in the 1920s and 1930s, advanced the theory of differential association to explain criminal behaviour. He emphasized that criminal behaviour is learned in interaction with others, usually in small groups, and that criminals learn to favor criminal behaviour over noncriminal behaviour through association with both forms of behaviour in different degrees. As Sutherland wrote, "When persons become criminal, they do so because of contacts with criminal patterns and also because of isolation from anticriminal patterns." Although his theory has been greatly influential, Sutherland himself admitted that it did not satisfactorily explain all criminal behaviour. Later theorists have modified his approach in an attempt to correct its shortcomings.

Control theory, developed in the 1960s and 1970s, attempts to explain ways to train people to engage in law-abiding behaviour. Although there are different approaches within control theory, they share the view that humans require nurturing in order to develop attachments or bonds to people and those personal bonds are the key in producing internal controls such as conscience and guilt and external controls such as shame. According to this view, crime is the result of insufficient attachment and commitment to others.

Walter C. Reckless developed one version of control theory, called containment. He argued that a combination of internal psychological containments and external social containments prevents people from deviating from social norms. In simple communities, social pressure to conform to community standards, usually enforced by social ostracism, was sufficient to control behaviour. As societies became more complex, internal containments played a more crucial role in determining whether people behaved according to public laws. Furthermore, containment theorists have found that internal containments require a positive self-image. All too often, a sense of alienation from society and its norms forms in modern individuals, who, as a result, do not develop internal containment mechanisms.

The sociologist Travis Hirschi has developed his own control theory that attempts to explain conforming, or lawful, rather than deviant, or unlawful, behaviour. He stresses the importance of the individual's bond to society in determining conforming behaviour. His research has found that socioeconomic class has little to do with determining delinquent behaviour, and that young people who are not very attached to their parents or to school are more likely to be delinquent than those who are strongly attached. He also found that youths who have a strongly positive view of their own accomplishments are more likely to view society's laws as valid constraints on their behaviour.

Political criminology is similar to the other camps in this area. It involves study into the forces that determine how, why, and with what consequences societies chose to address criminals and crime in general. Those who are involved with political criminology focus on the causes of crime, the nature of crime, the social and political meanings that attach to crime, and crime-control policies, including the study of the bases upon which crime and punishment is committed and the choices made by the principals in criminal justice.

Although the theories of political criminology and conflict criminology overlap to some extent, political criminologists deny that the terms are interchangeable. The primary focus points in the new movement of political criminology similarly overlap with other theories, including the concerns and ramifications of street crime and the distribution of power in crime-control strategies. This movement has largely been a loose, academic effort. Criminologists also study a host of other issues related to crime and the law. These include studies of the Victims of Crime, focusing upon their relations to the criminal, and their role as potential causal agents in crime; juvenile delinquency and its correction; and the media and their relation to crime, including the influence of Pornography. Much research related to criminology has focused on the biological basis of criminal behaviour. In fact, a field of study called biocriminology, which attempts to explore the biological basis of criminal behaviour, has emerged. Research in this area has focused on chromosomal abnormalities, hormonal and brain chemical imbalances, diet, neurological conditions, drugs, and alcohol as variables that contribute to criminal behaviour.

The true effect of criminology upon practices in the criminal justice system is still subject to question. Although a number of commentators have noted that studies in criminology have led to significant changes among criminal laws in the various states, other critics have suggested that studies in criminology have not directly led to a reduction of crime.

In *McCleskey v. Kemp,* an individual who had been sentenced to death for a murder in Georgia demonstrated to the U.S. Supreme Court that a criminologist's study showed that the race of individuals in that state impacted whether the defendant was sentenced to life or to death. The study demonstrated that a black defendant who had killed a white victim was four times more likely to be sentenced to death than was a defendant who had killed a black victim. The defendant claimed that the study demonstrated that the state of Georgia had violated his rights under the *equal protection clause* of the Fourteenth Amendment, as well as under the Eighth Amendment's protection against Cruel and Unusual Punishment.

The high court disagreed. Although the majority did question the validity of the study's findings, it held that the study did not establish that officials in Georgia had acted with discriminatory purpose, and that it did not establish that racial bias had affected the officials' decisions with respect to the death sentence. Accordingly, the death sentence violated neither the Fourteenth Amendment nor the Eighth Amendment.

Criminology has had more of an effect when states and the federal government consider new criminal laws and sentencing provisions. Criminologists' theories are also often debated in the context of the death penalty and crime control acts among legislators and policymakers. In this light, criminology is perhaps not at the forefront of the development of the criminal justice system, but it most certainly works in the background in the determination of criminal justice policies.

12

Biological Warfare

Despite the end of the Cold War, the United States still faces a range of serious national security issues. One at the forefront is the issue of the proliferation of biological weapons, and the accelerated development of the capabilities to design and produce biological weapons on the part of many Third World nations.

The Committee on Armed Services of the U.S. House of Representatives, in their Special Inquiry into the Chemical and Biological Threat, concluded that despite the demise of the Soviet Union, with its sizable chemical and biological arsenal, the threat has increased in terms of widespread proliferation, technological diversity, and the probability of use.

Of the nations currently believed to have an offensive biological warfare program, only a few are candidates for a direct armed conflict with the United States. The most likely route for the United States or our allies to become involved in a biological conflict would be as third parties in regional conflicts, whether as members of a United Nations peacekeeping force or through an act of terrorism. This is due to our increased participation in low intensity operations, however, and does not diminish the threat that biological warfare poses to our forces fighting a conventional war.

North Korea and China

During the 1990s, hostilities have mounted in North Korea over allegations that evidence of nuclear weapons activities is being hidden from international inspectors. This is the kind of future conflict that could involve the United States. In 1993, the Russian Foreign Intelligence Service, successor to the Soviet Union's KGB, released a statement that said, in part:

North Korea is performing applied military-biological research in a whole number of universities, medical institutes and specialized research institutes. Work is being performed in these research centers with inducers of malignant anthrax, cholera, bubonic plague and smallpox. Biological weapons are being tested on the island territories belonging to the DPRK (Democratic Peoples Republic of Korea).

Mr. Gordon Oehler, director of the CIA's Non-Proliferation Center, confirmed this Russian report. The use of smallpox in a weapon, whether the use be tactical or strategic, would have disastrous effects, as the military and civilians are not immunized against this disease nor have they been for many years.

In his last message to congressional leaders on January 19, 1993, outgoing President George Bush revealed intelligence reports (previously highly classified) that China still has an active biological warfare program — despite their having signed the international treaty banning such weapons. Even as recently as May 1994, a reporter investigating China's military-industrial complex stated that arms sales, especially unreported sales and transfers of weapons of mass destruction to some of the most dangerous governments in the world, are part of the dark side of China's commercial activities. The newspaper report went on to state: "China has violated every non-proliferation pledge it has ever made, including its pledge not to engage in an offensive biological warfare program." This is alarming, especially as we consider the close relationship between China and North Korea.

Iraq

As reported by the Department of Defense in 1992, by the time Iraq invaded Kuwait, Iraq had developed the most extensive biological warfare program in the Arab world (despite having been a signatory to the 1972 Biological Weapons Convention outlawing such endeavors). After the Persian Gulf War (1990-1991), Iraqi authorities admitted the program included anthrax bacteria and botulinum toxin. Then in August 1995, Iraq revealed to United Nations inspectors that it had had a far more extensive and aggressive biological warfare program prior to the Persian Gulf War than had previously been admitted. The Iraqi authorities claimed production of thousands of liters of botulinum toxin and of *Bacillus anthracis*. Additionally, they stated that unspecified amounts of both agents were loaded on Scud missile warheads and aerial bombs. In this same revelation to United Nations inspectors, the Iraqis claimed to have destroyed the agents during the January-February 1991 time frame, but they have yet to produce evidence to support their claim.

Iraq's biological capabilities, described as "a sizable stockpile," by William Webster, former Director of Central Intelligence, caused the coalition forces to procure large quantities of special biological warfare vaccines (against anthrax and botulinum) for their military personnel. These vaccines were in extremely limited supplies, forcing commanders to allocate vaccine only to troops they believed were at greatest risk to the use of these agents. Situations like this require commanders to make ethical decisions, as it was not known definitively who was at greatest risk.

The anthrax vaccine, which is licensed by the FDA, was given to approximately 150,000 military personnel (25%-30% of the deployed U.S. forces). The botulinum toxoid vaccine was given to approximately 8,000 military personnel (1% of deployed U.S. forces). The biological weapons threat posed by Iraq during this crisis has been characterized as the most serious such threat faced by U.S. forces since World War I.

During January 1991, the image of a scared, shaking television reporter wearing a gas mask and the trembling of his voice as he reported the detonation of an incoming Iraqi Scud missile near Tel Aviv, Israel, brought home to all a frightening view of the increasing sophistication of the chemical and biological threat and the apparent vulnerability of soldiers and civilians alike.

The reasons why Iraq did not use these weapons during the Persian Gulf War, the subject of much speculation, will probably never be known with certainty. However, this Iraqi threat highlighted the problems posed by the proliferation of weapons of mass destruction among Third World nations and the potential threat posed to U.S. forces as well as other nations. On April 3, 1991, the United Nations Security Council passed Resolution 687, which required that:

- Iraq's chemical, biological, and nuclear weapons are registered;
- These weapons and all production and research facilities be destroyed, rendered unusable, or removed;
- Iraq disclose all its holdings and programs and allow unhindered on-site inspections, and destroy the weapons-making potential on its territory itself or permit those weapons to be destroyed.

In conjunction with a longer-term verification regime established by United Nations Resolution 715, Iraq was also required to renounce the possession of any weapons of mass destruction. On April 6, 1991, Iraq accepted the terms of Resolution 687. However, the Iraqi government has steadfastly refused to accept Resolution 715 and regards the resolution as an unwarranted infringement on its sovereignty.

The Security Council entrusted implementation of the resolution to a special commission known as *UNSCOM* (*United Nations Special Commission*), which was set up by the United Nations Secretary General in May 1991. UNSCOM has carried out a series of inspections of Iraqi facilities, but relations with Iraq have been marked by frequent instances of misinformation, concealment, lack of cooperation, and obstruction and harassment of the inspection teams. Before the 1995 admission by Iraq of having weaponized biological agents, inspections into two suspected key Iraqi biological warfare facilities — Salmon Pak and Al Hakam — found no conclusive evidence of an Iraqi offensive biological program. However, evidence (such as Iraq's inability to explain the use of tons of growth media suitable for biological agent production) strongly pointed to the existence of a program. Furthermore, the inspection teams had only obtained an admission by Iraqi officials that Iraq had carried out a program of biological research for military purposes. The UNSCOM experience underscores the difficulty of monitoring compliance with the Biological Weapons Convention.

Foreign and Domestic Terrorism

Although biological warfare is most often discussed in terms of weapons of mass destruction, usually in the context of war, terrorist use of biological agents cannot be excluded. Biological warfare agents are, for the most part, inexpensive and readily obtainable, and "cookbook" approaches are readily available. One such book is *Silent Death*, by an author who calls himself Uncle Fester. Other titles from the same publisher include *The Poisoner's Handbook* and *Crimes Involving Poisons*.

Unfortunately, recent examples of possible intent to use are not difficult to find. A laboratory in a safe house of the Red Army Faction in Paris, France, was found to have made quantities of botulinum toxin; it is believed that none was used. More alarming were the actions of the Aum Shinrikyo cult in Japan in early 1995. In addition to releasing the nerve agent sarin in the Tokyo subway on March 18, 1995, cult members were preparing vast quantities of *Clostridium difficile* bacterial spores for terrorist use. Although possibly not producing large numbers of casualties, the use of even small amounts of such an agent would almost assuredly create major panic.

In March 1989, the most intensive food safety investigation in FDA history took place when a terrorist threatened to poison this nation's fresh fruit supply, to focus attention on the living conditions of the lower classes in Chile. The terrorist made good on his phone call to the FDA, as two grapes were found laced with small amounts of cyanide. Fortunately no one was poisoned, but the incident cost millions of dollars to investigate in this country, and had a significant impact on Chile's national economy, where fruit and vegetable exports are second in importance only to copper. A biological toxin could have been used just as easily as cyanide in this instance.

The amounts of toxin needed to obtain the desired effect are exceedingly small. "For example, about 30 grams of the toxin ricin, easily concealed in a pocket, would be sufficient to lethally poison one batch of 150 pounds of meat, enough to produce 1,500 hot dogs." The threat is real. And the knowledge required is not esoteric:

> *To engage in bioterrorism requires only the type of knowledge that Kateuas found in his herbals - that is, a sophisticated understanding of the properties of various edible plants, medicinal herbs, toxins and venoms, and infectious and pharmaceutical agents.*

The use of biological agents in domestic terrorism has been attempted on several occasions in recent years, causing alarm and illustrating the ease of obtaining these agents. In May 1995, the American Type Culture Collection (ATCC), a nonprofit organization in Rockville, Maryland, that supplies biological specimens to scientists all over the world, shipped a package containing three vials of *Yersinia pestis* to the home of a white supremacist in Ohio. (This organism causes plague and killed one quarter of the population when it struck Europe in the 14th century and wreaked havoc in India as recently in 1994.) The American Type Culture Collection has tightened its controls on which it will provide hazardous materials to, but even terrorists can produce legitimate request documents: the white supremacist is a qualified microbiologist. When his house was searched, police reported finding hand grenade triggers, homemade explosive devices, and detonating fuzes. Fortunately, he was caught prior to any intentional use.

Two members of the Minnesota Patriots Council were convicted in 1995 for planning to use a lethal biological agent against U.S. marshals and Internal Revenue Service agents. According to trial testimony, they planned to poison U.S. agents by placing ricin toxin on doorknobs. Lastly, in March 1992, a Tyson's Corner, Virginia, man was arrested and charged with malicious wounding in a hoax in which he sprayed his roommates with a fluid that he claimed contained anthrax bacteria. The house was placed under quarantine immediately after the incident, and while awaiting test results, 20 people — one a pregnant woman — were treated for possible exposure to anthrax. The threat that terrorists will use biological agents cannot be ignored and we have to remain strong, vigilant, and determined to defeat this form of terrorism as we do every other act of terrorism.

International proliferation of biological warfare programs broadens the range of agents that members of the U.S. armed forces may encounter. Ironically, the modernization of many Third World nations — with the subsequent development of industrial, medical, pharmaceutical, and agricultural facilities needed to support these advancing societies — provides the basis for development of a biological weapons program, should a nation decide to pursue such an endeavor. A biological weapons program can easily be concealed within legitimate research-and-development and industrial programs, even by countries that are signatories to the 1972 Biological Weapons Convention. Actions such as these are grave threats to our national security.

Biological warfare agents may be more potent than the most lethal chemical warfare agents, and provide broader area coverage per pound of payload than any other weapons system. The proliferation of technology and of scientific progress in biochemistry and biotechnology has simplified production requirements and provided the opportunity for the creation of exotic agents. This could involve the tailoring of pathogenic microorganisms capable of creating a novel disease, perhaps on an epidemic scale. Humans need not be the only target of biological weapons. These weapons might be meant to attack a country's revenue or food crop, animal herds, or even a supply of a material that is vital for revenue or defense.

Despite the end of the Cold War, the United States still faces serious national security issues. One at the forefront is the issue of the proliferation of biological weapons, especially in Third World nations that have compelling military, technical, economic, and political incentives to pursue this capability. The use of biological agents in future wars and actions by terrorists — foreign and domestic — is a legitimate issue of concern. Resolution of this problem should be given the highest priority.

Terrorist Use of Chemical Weapons

It was calm early morning on the subway train. Many of the passengers were napping on their way to work. The train slowed to a stop to allow more passengers on, then sped along to its destination, the central government district in Tokyo. Many of the passengers found it strange that a man who got on at the last stop was wearing sunglasses, but soon dismissed it remembering how safe the subways and their homeland have always been. Well, they were mistaken. The man with the glasses got off the train before it reached its destination, but wait, had he forgotten something. By the time anyone became suspicious many people on the train were coughing. Those near enough to see the package and the clear liquid seeping from it began feeling dizzy and many were bleeding from the nose and mouth.

This was not the only train car to receive such a dangerous package. This and four similar incidents took place at about the same time in the Tokyo subway system on March 20, 1995. The five packages were disguised to look like lunch boxes or soda containers and it was reported that the chemical agent used was an impure or dilute solution of sarin, a nerve agent developed by Nazi Germany during the '30's. This was the beginning of a frightening future for the modern world. "Organized and indiscriminate murder" (Tokyo, A1) on a large scale is clearly possible and chemical weapons are likely to be a terrorist's vehicle for mass destruction. The threat of terrorist use of chemical weapons is now quickly forcing its way into the thoughts of people all around the world. The attack in Japan, "says Israeli terrorism expert Yonah Alexander, 'has global implications. It's a quantum leap to terrorism by mass destruction" (Strasser, 36). There is such broad selection of chemical weapons exhibiting such diverse characteristics that the very nature of these substances makes them quite suitable for terrorist use.

There are many more advantages for terrorists to use chemical weapons rather than conventional ones, and the disadvantages that do exist seem quite small. In general it seems that the chemical weapons may become a key component in the terrorist arsenal. If this threat is left unchecked the world's population may soon live under a dark cloud of constant fear. This would be the fear that any crazy person, terrorist, or activist group has the potential to commit random acts of brutal mass murder at low cost and relatively low risk to them.

Classification of Chemical Weapons

The broad spectrum of chemical agents capable of causing damage to living organisms often makes discussion of such compounds difficult. Because of this our discussion shall be limited to substances effecting humans only. There are several different ways to classify such agents but most useful is to classify them by their effects. There are four major categories under which the chemical agents may be classified; these include the blister agents, the choking agents, the blood agents, and the nerve agents. The blister agents are intended to "cause incapacitation rather than death". These agents were used extensively during World War I, and their use by a terrorist group depends largely on the groups objectives and moral standing.

Obviously if the intention of a chemical attack was to injure many people and overload a regions medical facilities while causing as few deaths as possible, then a blister agent such as lewisite or mustard gas may be the best choice. Choking agents were the agents most used during WW I, but have lost much of their usefulness since the advent of the nerve agents. These substances are intended to cause death and offer their greatest advantage to terrorists by being easily obtained. Phosgene or CG as it is designated by the military, is a common industrial chemical with a moderate lethal dose, and is a choking agent. Cyanide based compounds are the main components of the blood agents. Hydrogen cyanide (AC) is a blood agent which has a lethal dose slightly higher than that of phosgene but is less effective due to its rapid rate of evapouration. These compounds aren't really suited for use on large numbers of people, so their primary role would most likely be in assassinations.

The newest trend in chemical weapons has been the nerve agents. The original nerve agents were developed by German scientists during the 1930's as insecticides then were developed into chemical weapons by the Nazi military. Since then these agents, sarin, tabun, soman, and others, have been the main weapon stockpiled as chemical weapons. In general they are hundreds to thousands of times more lethal than blister, choking, and blood agents. These chemicals are the most useful to terrorists because of the small quantity needed to inflict a substantial amount of damage. These chemicals, in their most effective form, are more difficult to obtain. VX and sarin, the most toxic of the nerve agents, can be synthesized by "a moderately competent organic chemist, with limited laboratory facilities" (Kupperman, 65).

Advantages

The use of these chemical agents offers many advantages to the terrorists who use them. Many of these advantages are unique, or in other words exhibit qualities which conventional weapons lack. The other advantage is the severity of chemical weapon's effects. These advantages include the limited capability of anti-terrorist groups of detecting such weapons, the low cost and low technology required to develop chemical weapons, their extremely frightening image and the overall efficiency of such weapons. One of the difficulties which has long plagued chemical warfare defense also lends difficulty to counter terrorist capabilities. This is the lack of effective detectors. Very few chemical warfare (CW) agents can be reliably detected when in use.

And these substances are virtually impossible to detect while being stored in a closed container. This lack of available detection technology makes CW agents ideal to transport and conceal due to their clandestine nature. Chemical weapons have long been considered "the poor man's atomic bomb" (Oberdorfer, A1) due to their relative low cost and ease of manufacture. This is supported by a group of experts who said that "for a large-scale operation against a civilian population, casualties might cost $2,000 per square kilometer with conventional weapons, $800 with nuclear weapons, $600 with nerve-gas weapons and $1 with biological weapons" (Anderson).

The argument that chemical weapons are too difficult for most terrorists to manufacture was discredited when a CIA report "concluded that 'clandestine production of [chemical and biological weapons] for multiple casualty attacks raises no greater technical obstacles than does the clandestine production of chemical narcotics or heroin" (Stern, 402). These factors make chemical weapons attainable, not only to well fund terrorist groups, but also to any disgruntled postal employee or other lunatic.

One of the aspects which make chemical weapons such an appropriate weapon for a terrorist is the name terrifying nature of chemical weapons. Ever since the first use of chemical weapons they have been criticized and ridiculed by civilians and soldiers alike. They've been considered unconventional, uncivilized, and even gruesome. These adjectives have also been employed often when describing terrorists. In general terrorists thrive off the shock factor of their activities and chemical warfare exhibits a high degree of shock factor.

Therefore, the use of chemical weapons may "enhance" many terrorist groups' images. The final advantage offered by chemical weapons is their enormous ability to inflict casualties. These weapons are extremely cost effective and 40 times more weight effective than conventional explosive weapons. The overall efficiency of CW agent combined with the entire previously mentioned advantages make a frighteningly inexpensive, undetectable, and efficient weapon.

Disadvantages

As with all methods of terrorism there are disadvantages to the use of chemical weapons. Some of these disadvantages will be encountered by terrorists regardless of their methods, and some are unique to chemical weapons. Two of the major disadvantages of chemical weapons are due to their terrifying and deadly nature, this may have two affects. The first affect may be an increased effort in retaliation from anti-terrorist forces; the second disadvantage is that chemical weapons may hurt the image of some terrorist groups if not used within the terrorist's beliefs. Following the assessment of whether or not to use chemical weapons, the terrorist must now obtain the necessary chemical agents. After acquiring the agents the terrorists would have to decide how they can effectively dispense the agent at as little risk to themselves as possible.

Regardless of the nature of any terrorist action some type of retaliation can be expected from the victimized group. The severity of that group's reaction depends on several factors. The first factor to consider is who the group is, for instance any terrorist activity in the United States is responded to with remarkable force and speed, as was seen with the quick response to bombing of the World Trade Center. The same can be assumed of any attack in any major country. Also the method of the attack will contribute to a victim's response. In general, the more horrible an attack is the retaliation is likely to be or seem to be more severe. However, in reality, the overall impact of this retaliation on the terrorist group is probably going to be about the same. Take the World Trade Center bombing for example, a few radicals filled a van with several thousand pounds of explosives and detonated it in a parking garage below a large building. This killed a few people and injured a few hundred or so. Had those terrorists decided to somehow distributed 100 grams of sarin the ventilation system of the building the only real difference in the operation would be a change in the method of the attack. There would probably be about the same number of casualties, and the offending persons would be in the same place they are now, prison.

Not only must a terrorist group consider the political factors associated with the employment of chemical weapons, but there are also a few minor technical problems to overcome. The most obvious of these technical difficulties is the method of obtaining the necessary chemical agents. This, however, is not as difficult as it may seem. One way to get chemical weapons is to manufacture them. As discussed earlier, small groups or individuals frequently manufacture a variety of narcotic substances secretly. These people easily overcome difficulties similar to those encountered in the manufacture of chemical weapons. So, the answer to the question, of whether or not the development of chemical weapons is within a terrorist's ability, is yes.

Another way for terrorist groups to get chemical weapons would be to purchase them. They can either be purchased from an illegal source, such as from a former Soviet state or from a sympathetic third world country, or deadly industrial chemicals can be legally purchased and employed in a chemical attack. Since the break down of the U.S.S.R. the black market for military goods has increased significantly. The Soviet Union had and possibly still has a large stockpile of chemical weapons. The media and public have overlooked the serious threat of chemical weapons being sold, this is due largely to the overpowering fear of the sale of nuclear material or devices. Even a NATO official said he was "more concerned about chemical weapons" falling into terrorist hands. There is definitely a threat of this type of sale, but if this isn't the route, there are always terrorist groups which have connections with nations sympathetic to their cause who may have better access to such weapons.

Illegal purchase isn't the only way terrorists could acquire a chemical agent with dangerous properties. Many industrial chemicals are closely related to chemical weapons; in fact several industrial chemicals were even employed as chemical weapons during World War I. Chlorine and phosgene were both used extensively by the German, British, and French during the war. Although these substances are far less lethal than the nerve agents, they are quite common and have "many legitimate industrial applications". Even more frightening is that entire classes of industrial chemicals are of a highly toxic nature. These are the organophosphates, in fact this is also the class of chemical to which sarin (GB) and VX belong. These chemicals are commonly used as insecticides and include parathion, an insecticide notorious for the threat it poses to those who use it. The lethal doses for the industrial chemicals of this class are in general ten to fifty times higher than those of the military agents; however they are still very dangerous with lethal doses ranging from 1.05 to 7.0 mcg/kg which translates to.000698 kg for a 220 pound person.

One may realize that many of these industrial agents are well suited for use as a weapon, and that their legitimate uses make it particularly difficult to regulate sales. So, in general chemical compounds suitable for use as a weapon are abundant and easily available, regardless of the method used to acquire them. Once a terrorist group has decided to use chemical weapons and has obtained them the final obstacle is to effectively use them without causing harm to themselves. This is merely an engineering feat, which would pose little trouble to most of the terrorist groups at their current technology level. A government study even reported that "the level of technological sophistication required [for effective use of chemical agents]... may be lower than was the case for some of the sophisticated bombs that have been used against civilian aircraft". In this age of increasing education and booming technology, it is much easier to find the necessary technical and mechanical assistance for any project, legal or otherwise.

The Future

Now that the world has progressed so far that mass destruction is within reach of a far greater percentage of the population, the likeliness of an incident involving weapons of mass destruction, particularly chemical weapons, is much greater. The future holds many developments in store for the civilized world, when it comes to terrorists and chemical weapons the threat is real and deadly. Many things are taking place which will contribute to the spread of this plague. The first two concern chemical weapons alone, these are the development of binary weapons and the further proliferation of chemical weapons to nations sympathetic to terrorists. The next group concerns the nature of terrorism. This includes the simple increase of terrorist activity, the e crackdown by anti-terrorist forces on traditional methods, and the decrease in the reluctance of a terrorist group to use chemical weapons due to the successful incident in Tokyo last month.

Recent events have made chemical weapons even more desirable as a terrorist weapon. The first is the development of the binary weapon. This is a chemical weapon in which the agent is stored as two precursor chemicals which only need to be combined to form the final lethal product. This reduces the risk that a terrorist must face in the storage and transport of their weapons, it also reduces the threat of accidental exposure upon dispersal of the agent. If the chemical device is engineered correctly, with some sort of time delay, the terrorist could be long gone even before the lethal agent is made. Another factor which will contribute to the terrorist use of chemical weapons is the spread of chemical weapons capability to third world countries which may have connections with terrorists. "Iran, Iraq, Libya, N. Korea and Syria a ll listed by the State Department as supporters of terrorism are believed to posses some capability for chemical and biological warfare".

And can be considered possible sources of chemical weapons for terrorists. Although the Chemical Weapons Conference has reduced the proliferation of chemical weapons and, in fact, made it illegal to develop and stockpile chemical weapons, the amount of chemical agent necessary for a terrorist operation would be extremely difficult to detect and can even be justified by claiming it as research material. After considering the chemical weapons themselves, one needs to realize that terrorists haven't been inactive in recent years. Quite the contrary is true; the world has seen an increase in terrorist incidents by 400% from the 1970s to the 1980s. With this increase in terrorism the diversity of terrorist attacks are likely to increase. Within this increase in diversity chemical weapons are more likely to find their way into more incidents, and in general find a wider acceptance as a viable technique available to terrorist groups.

Along with the increase in terrorism there has been an significant increase in anti-terrorism activity and capabilities. As police and government authorities world wide become better prepared to handle terrorist activities, and more anti-terrorist technology is developed, the traditional methods terrorists are accustomed to using become less likely to succeed. With most of the anti-terrorist developments focusing on preventing hi-jackings and bombings, the difficulty encountered by terrorists attempting to use these techniques has increased. With the increase in complications the chances of success are reduced enough to force some terrorists to consider alternate methods. Among the alternates are chemical weapons with all of the advantages they offer.

Lastly, and most important of all, there has been a breech in the invisible barrier which has kept terrorists from using chemical weapons in the past. The CIA has warned that if this barrier were breached by "one successful incident in volving such [lethal] agents [it] would significantly lower the threshold of restraint on their application by other terrorists" (Anderson). This barrier was composed of fear and uncertainty. The terrorists were afraid of the consequences of such a weap on and the danger to themselves, and they were uncertain of the success of such an attack. Now, after the sarin attack in Japan in March, it is obvious how effective a small amount of chemical agent is at tying down a subway system, injuring thousands of people, and enraging people all over the world. This essentially opened the door to a whole new form of terrorism. The only thing now keeping terrorists from using chemical weapons is their lack of knowledge, and once they realize that the production of these weapons is well within the scope of their operations, there will be very little left to stop them.

Solutions

Now, with the threats becoming more and more real every day, one needs to consider what could be done to counter this great danger. To start with, counter terrorist organizations must continue with their information gathering and observations of terrorist organizations. The first specific step is that precursor chemicals or potential chemical weapons must be better regulated. Then response capabilities must be increased and improved to deal with chemical attacks, this should include an improvement in chemical detection capabilities. And finally, the public must be better informed on the subject of chemical attacks, in specific "What to do in an emergency."

Restricting chemicals used to make CW (chemical warfare) agents or used as CW agents, may be the least effective method of preventing terrorists from using chemical weapons. This merely increases the costs for a group to obtain their weapons. It does, however, reduce the chances of "casual" terrorist using chemical weapons. The casual terrorist may not be willing to go through the difficulties of obtaining chemical weapons due to time considerations or a loss in motivation. Another way restrictions would help reduce CW is through the methods outlined in the Chemical Weapons Conference. This prevents the development or sale of chemical weapons by any of the signatory nations, and thus reduces the number of sources from which terrorists can acquire their weapons.

An improvement in preparedness for chemical attacks and the organization of a special team of experts for response to chemical attacks would be more successful than simply a restriction on chemicals. Many emergency agencies (like police, fire departments, and hospitals) aren't adequately supplied and trained to deal with chemical attacks, especially on a large scale. Just a slight increase in instruction on how to identify the signs of a chemical attack and deal with those affected may make quite a difference. Even more important would be the development of a government response team specifically trained to deal with large chemical attacks could improve the United States response capability drastically. This team would be composed of experts in the field of chemical weapons, the effects of those weapons and decontamination people and equipment. The number of capable people in this field is quite large but consists of mainly military personnel. What needs to be established is quick method of deployment of these people and their equipment. Along with this skilled response team there needs to be increased detection capabilities. Most desirable would be a device which could be integrated into current airport x-ray and detection equipment. The increase in a counter terrorist group's capability of detecting chemical weapons has the obvious advantage of preventing an attack before it happens. This should clearly be a priority of government officials.

Increased public knowledge is probably the best defense or response to the new chemical weapon threat. The ideal case would be a public knowledge campaign to teach people what the threats are and how to identify the signs of a chemical weapon attack. It is, of course, impractical to expect such a "Just say no to chemical weapons" campaign to be implicated or even be listened to at this stage. But as soon as the people of the United States realize the threat it might become necessary. For the time being, education can be on the managerial level. Large corporations, schools, and buildings alike may designate a group of people to become educated in what to do in the event of such an emergency. This group could in turn instruct the masses of people in an emergency. Likely targets of chemical attacks could also instruct their personnel and post signs regarding the response to such an emergency. For instance, if subway workers in the March incident, had been able to identify that che mical attack more quickly, their lives as well as the lives of others may have been saved. This increase in awareness would most likely contribute greatly to a reduction of chemical weapon casualties.

These possible solutions could seriously reduce the effectiveness of a terrorist chemical weapon attack. This type of attack has been in the public eye for a month now and has been lingering in the back of terrorist minds for many years. Now with this increase in publicity everybody knows the terrifying effects of chemical weapons and it's really only a matter of time before the United States has to deal with a similarly terrifying event.

13

Biological Threats and Bioterrorism

The use of biological agents as weapons of war has a very long history. As far back as the 7th century, the Assyrians used ergot (a fungal disease found in rye) to poison the water wells of their enemies. The fungus produced a hallucinogenic effect similar to that of LSD.

- In 600 B.C. purgative hellebore was used during a siege of Cirrha to cause violent diarrhea.
- In 400 B.C. the Spartans used arsenic smoke to drive out the enemy during the siege of Plataea and Delium. In one of the more famous ancient cases of biological warfare, the Tartar Army catapulted corpses of plague victims over the walls of the besieged city of Kaffa to spread disease among the defenders.
- In 1767 During the French and Indian War, the English gave blankets laced with smallpox to Indians loyal to the French.
- On June 17, 1925 The Geneva Protocol baned biological weapons. It is the first multilateral agreement that created a prohibition on the use of chemical agents and biological agents. Japan refused to approve the ban.
- In 1932 Japanese troops invaded Manchuria and began experiments using biological agents as weapons.

- In 1936 Japan formed Unit 731, the world's first bio-warfare unit, and begans field tests of biological agents on Chinese and Manchurian populations.
- Between 1936 - 1941 the Japanese systematically used plague as a weapon of war on the populations of China and Manchuria.
- In 1941 the British began experiments with Anthrax.
- In 1941 the US begans a biological warfare program at Camp Detrick, Frederick, MD.
- In 1945 the Japanese destroyed Unit 731 facilities in China and Manchuria.
- In 1946 US announced its involvement in bioweapons research and made a covert deal with Unit 731 officers in which data on research would be shared in return for immunity for war crimes.
- In 1956 the Soviet Union announced that they had the capability of using chemical and biological warfare agents.
- In 1962 the U.S. opened the Desert Test Center at Ft. Douglas, Utah for the purpose of testing biological weapons and defenses to biological weapons.
- In 1969 - 1970 President Nixon limited research on biological weapons research to defense only.
- In 1972 Biological Weapons Convention (a.k.a. Convention on the Prohibition of the Development, Production, and Stockpiling of Bacteriological and Toxin Weapons and on their Destruction) was signed. Eventually 103 nations signed the convention. The U.S. signed the convention in 1975.
- In 1981 and 1985 the deal between the U.S. and officers of Unit 731 was uncovered and released to the public.
- Fall 2001, 18 cases of anthrax occurred after anthrax was sent through the U.S. mail. Of the 18 cases, 11 were inhalation and 7 were cutaneous infections. 5 deaths occurred due to the anthrax incident. The anthrax was weaponized grade.

- With the end of the Cold War and the rise militant Islamism, the threat of biological terrorism is the newest threat to the world. Until recently, the threat of the use of biological weapons was limited to their use in conventional warfare between. The anthrax attack in Fall 2001, the sarin gas attack in Japan by Aum Shinrikyo in 1995 in addition tothe group's failed attempt to release anthrax in 1993 and its failure to secure the Ebola virus in 1992 demonstrates that the use of biological weapons is not limited to Middle Eastern terrorist or rogue nations.
- The U.S. took the threat of biological weapons attack seriously after the gulf war and fears that such weapons would be used in the war against Iraq. American troops were given anthrax vaccinations and weapons inspectors tried to detect and destroy the weapons in Iraq after the war.
- In addition to nations like Iraq who are listed in the State Department Patterns of Global Terrorism 2001 and 2002 reports as suspected of manufacturing of biological weapons, the fall of the Soviet Union and the discovery of their advanced biological weapons industry has been a major issue in American anti-terrorism assessments. The Soviets during the 1980's manufactured various types of biological weapons for use against the West. Their program made significant advances in gene engineering creating new strains of viruses and bacteria for biological weapons. They conducted experiments with ebola and Marburg, which cause hemorrhagic fever - the vascular system dissolves, as well as smallpox. After the fall of the Soviet Union, the U.S. has been concerned with preventing:
    - The biological weapon materials,
    - The expertise in making the weapons, and
    - The equipment used to make biological weapons from being secured by terrorist groups and rogue

nations. This is one of the reasons many of the Russian scientists that were involved in the biological weapons programs are being hired at biological research facilities in the United States and in the West. The goal is to keep these scientist in employment (something that is in short supply in Russia) so they are not recruited by terrorist groups or countries like Iraq and Iran.

- The Soviet Union was not the only country that developed biological weapons. The following countries are believed to have biological weapons and/or in the process of developing them:

Libya	Pakistan
Iran	Syria
Iraq	North Korea
Israel	Egypt
Russia	Sudan
China	Taiwan
Vietnam	Bulgaria
Laos	South Korea
Cuba	Romania
South Africa	Bulgaria

- All of the above nations with the exception of Israel, Syria and Egypt signed the 1972 convention against the manufacturing of these weapons. Syria and Egypt signed the convention but did not ratify it.

Basics of Biological Weapon Design

There are two basic categories of biological warfare agents - microorganisms and toxins. Microorganisms are living organic germs, such as anthrax. The three types of microorganisms are bacteria, viruses and rickettsiae. Bacteria cause sickness by invading the tissues or through the toxins they release. Sickness occurs because the body is overwhelmed by the fast reproduction of the bacteria. Bacteria can divide every six minutes. Viruses are parasites that can only live within the cells of another organism. Viruses enter the cell of a host and use the cell to replicate. The new viruses then break out of the host cell (killing the cell) and then impregnate other cells to replicate again. Viruses cause sickness due to the cell damage to the host organism. Rickettsiae are intracellular bacteria that have the characteristics of both bacteria and viruses.

Like bacteria they are susceptible to antibiotics but like viruses they can only survive inside of living cells. Rickettsiae are spread through infected insects and not from human contact. Toxins are poisons produced by the metabolic activities of the bacteria. Biological weapon development is about the selection, manufacturing, and improvement of viruses, bacteria, rickettsiae and toxins. Biological warfare research attempts to make bacteria resistant to antibiotic treatment, viruses resistant to vaccination and toxins more potent.

Bacteria	Small Pox
Anthrax	Venezuelan Equine
Plague	Encephalitis (VEE)
Tularema	Ebola
Brucellosis	Toxins
Salmonella	Botulinum
Viruses	Ricin

Modern research on biological weapons began during the first half of the 20th century and despite treaties to the contrary, research on the development of biological weapons continued through the second half of the 20th century. After the second World War, the United States and the Soviet Union became the two leading powers in the research of biological weapons. The reason biological weapons were studied and developed was due to fear that "the other side" was working on them and that in the event of their use, the U.S. needed to have an appropriate response - i.e., use of non-nuclear weapons. Additionally, the development of these weapons was in line with basic U.S.-Soviet military balance theory; neither side would use such weapons because each knew the other had the weapons ready to use in response. Thus the Mutually Assured Destruction (MAD) theory that kept nuclear weapons under control worked as well with biological weapons.

Weaponized Biological Agents Biological agents are divided into two general types: contagious agents and non-contagious agents. U.S. research focused on non-contagious agents because contagious biological weapons proved not to be useful tactical weapons. The reason being that once used, the impact and effect of the weapons can't be contained. Non-contagious agents are better tactical weapons because the impact of the attack and the targeting of victims can be contained. Although the threat of rogue nations and transnational terrorist groups developing biological weapons is a serious threat, it is not a simple process to make a biological weapon. Weaponizing biological agents requires the following:

Securing and using a virulent strain of a bacteria, virus or toxin. Having a stable electrical source to maintain very sophisticated equipment. High level of manufacturing knowledge and ability in handling biological agents make a biological agent to make it free floating. Knowledge of turning the biological material into material has primary and secondary aerosolization and ability to make the biological material small enough (between 1 to 5 microns) to be useful as a weapon. Thus the nature of biological weapons requires a high level of sophistication of manufacturing. A useful biological weapon must be airborne and be made of the right biological agent. Aum

Shinrikyo attempted to manufacture an anthrax biological weapon in 1993 but used a non virulent strain of anthrax so the attack failed.

EMS and Terrorism

Although present in various forms and locations for countless years, terrorism has increasingly been the focus of public concern. Emergency Medical Services (EMS) plays a vital role in responding to, evaluating, and intervening in potentially catastrophic events. EMS often co-manages initial scenes in many medium- to large-scale incidents involving large numbers of casualties. EMS may also manage the scene until state or federal agencies arrive. Americans will never forget the tragic events of September 11, 2001. More than 3350 people were killed, and more than 10,000 people were injured in an incredibly complicated and choreographed attack. However, not all remember the WorldTradeCenter bombing in 1993 that killed 6 people and injured more than 1000. In April 1995, the federal building in Oklahoma City was bombed, killing 168 people. A pipe bomb was detonated in Centennial Park during the 1996 Olympic Games in Atlanta, Georgia, killing 2 people and wounding 110.

The bombing of 4 commuter trains in March 2004 claimed the lives of 190 and injured more than 1800 people in Madrid, Spain. Such events emphasize the potential loss of life and property caused by terrorist activities. Many authorities consider the United States a continuing high-profile target. For all Americans, the attack on the World Trade Center on September 11, 2001, brought home the tragic realization that America is not immune to terrorism. Philip Stern, an expert on terrorism with the Fairfax Group, said, "As an open society and a democracy, this country is particularly vulnerable. We have free passage, coast-to-coast, anyone can apply for a visa to visit and the population is enormous and diversified."

Such an inviting atmosphere and free society may make terrorist activity inevitable. Many of the terrorist groups of today appear more and more willing to use weapons of mass destruction. Perhaps even more disturbing is the potential for terrorists to utilize more technologically advanced weapons and communications. Access to the Internet and information on the World Wide Web facilitates tremendous technological advancement in destructive potential.

All of these issues underscore the importance of proper education in EMS and advance planning. Terrorist activity may have various mechanisms, including chemical or biological weapons and explosives, as well as new and unanticipated methods of destruction. Full response to a terrorist incident requires in-depth interagency planning involving police; fire; EMS; regional, state, and national emergency organizations; as well as a wide array of ancillary community services. Each agency should be assigned respective roles as soon as possible, well in advance of potential terrorist acts.

Aspects of Terrorism

Weapons of mass destruction (WMD) hold great attraction to terrorists: they have great potential to create fear, both in victims and in the public at large; can be created inexpensively; may be difficult to detect even when being sought; and can be engineered for a delayed onset of symptoms—nerve agents within minutes, vesicants within hours, and biological agents within days. Protecting large populations from exposure to WMD is problematic at best and impossible at worst. The drawbacks of WMD use are largely ignored by terrorists: contempt for users, retaliation, and prohibition treaties are not priorities for terrorist organizations. Deployment dangers, including injury or even death of deploying persons, are rarely considered risks sufficient to prevent use.

Determining the actual extent of the terrorist threat in the United States is difficult, as it is poorly defined and rapidly changing. James Alan Fox, Dean of Northeastern University's Criminal Justice Program in Boston, believes the 2 current motivations for terrorism are revenge and attention. Either motivation can be justification for exposing large numbers of the populace to a wide variety of dangerous or deadly toxins. The *Morbidity and Mortality Weekly Report,* April 21, 2000 states "The public health infrastructure must be prepared to prevent illness and injury that would result from biological and chemical terrorism, especially a covert terrorist attack. As with emerging infectious diseases, early detection and control of biological and chemical attacks depends on a strong and flexible public health system at the local, state, and federal levels."

Preplanning

Effective response to a terrorist incident hinges on comprehensive planning and interagency cooperation. Agencies must address and resolve jurisdictional issues well in advance. After a plan has been devised, it must be updated regularly to reflect changes in resources, population, terrorist activities, or potential targets. Local police, fire, EMS, and Disaster & Emergency Services (DES) agencies should form the first line of response. Other agencies that may be included are as follows:

- Secret Service
- Bureau of Alcohol, Tobacco, and Firearms (BATF)
- State disaster agencies
- Military or reserve units, including National Guard
- Specialized medical units

Depending on the circumstances, state or federal response agencies, such as the Emergency Broadcast System, Federal Aviation Administration, or National Weather

Service, may need to become involved. The Federal Bureau of Investigation (FBI) has been designated as lead agency in crisis management response, and Federal Emergency Management Agency (FEMA) is designated as lead agency in consequence management response. The Defense Against Weapons of Mass Destruction Act (Nunn-Lugar-Domenici Bill) of 1996 required the Secretary of Defense to establish a program to advise and train federal, state, and local officials until 1999 and allows the President or Attorney General to request military support for local authorities in chemical/biological incidents.

An act of terrorism in a metropolitan area may cause major health and medical consequences that could easily overwhelm all local health facilities; thus, ongoing contact with state and national agencies is recommended for the additional resources they can provide. The FBI is the federally designated lead agency in a confirmed domestic terrorist event. Depending on location, however, some federal agencies may not be on-site for 24 hours or more.

On a national level, the US Government has established the National Disaster Medical System (NDMS). This organization assists in providing medical care and transportation for disaster victims. The NDMS comprises sections of the Department of Health and Human Resources, the Department of Veterans Affairs, the Department of Defense, and the FEMA. Any state can enlist the services of NDMS, which provides assistance at the disaster site, evacuates patients, and finds beds for evacuated patients. Congress also has established a Domestic Preparedness Program that provides enhanced training for local first responders and forms metropolitan medical strike teams in major cities.

In evaluating sites of potential terrorist activity, the release of chemical or biological agents into crowded and contained areas, such as sports stadiums, office or public buildings, and transportation systems (eg, the Tokyo subway Sarin incident) should be considered. Such places provide tempting targets despite on-site security. Rapid identification of the chemical or biological agent is critical to proper disposition of patients and to management of affected areas. Disasters involving hazardous materials (HAZMATs), radioactive materials, or chemical agents may produce unfamiliar medical problems that cannot be identified rapidly in. the readily available emergency medicine literature. All possible resources should be used early in the incident to ensure proper identification of the agent and prompt initiation of proper protocols.

Incident Management

Most of the principles of terrorist incident management are similar to the principles in the management of mass casualty incidents. The primary concern in potential terrorist incidents is to secure the area and to ascertain the severity and the nature of the threat. Delayed explosives or materials intended to harm rescue workers may have been planted at the site. A safe scene must be obtained to avoid further endangering survivors and health care workers. Primary and secondary perimeters must be established and secured. It should also be determined if a cleared, downwind perimeter is needed, and one should be established if required.

The Acronym ASBESTOS can be used to remember the important aspects of exposure:

A - Agent(s) - Type and amount of doses

S - State - Liquid, solids, or aerosolized

B - Body sites - Areas of exposure, lungs, skin, or other

E - Effects - Area of effects; local or systemic

S - Severity, of symptoms

T - Timing of events

O - Other diagnoses to consider

S - Synergism - Interaction between multiple agents or coexisting disease

Early involvement of support and ancillary services, mutual aid agencies, and local agencies in the planning process is prudent. After identifying the potential threat, it should be determined which type of protective equipment is necessary. Emphasis must be placed on protection and decontamination of rescuers and victims.

After establishing a decontamination and triage area, rescuers should put on appropriate protective clothing before entering the affected area and beginning rescue efforts. The first focus is on supportive care with emphasis on aggressive airway control and decontamination. Issues associated with simultaneous containment, neutralization, and/or decontamination may be addressed by ancillary agencies. Following initial triage, patients are given primary or aggressive aid depending on their presentation and the resources available. The patients should be decontaminated and transported to a facility that has been informed about the etiology of the incident as soon as feasible. A secure and clean area completes the physical response. Record keeping, analysis of the incident, and investigations conclude the complete response.

Conventional Explosives

While lacking the cachet of nuclear, biological, or chemical weapons, conventional explosives are more likely to be the instrument of a terrorist attack. Ease of obtaining materials and knowledge make conventional explosives more likely a vehicle than other, more difficult to obtain or manufacture agents. Historical analysis consistently demonstrates that the most likely terrorist weapon causing a mass casualty event is a standard explosive device detonated in a crowded area. An explosive is a normally stable material that, when introduced into a chemical reaction, converts rapidly from a solid or a liquid to an expanding gas. Explosives cause damage primarily through tremendous increases in atmospheric pressure. The initial shock, called the positive pressure wave, is the almost instantaneous increase of pressure from a blast, and the negative pressure wave immediately follows, as the displaced air rushes in to fill the void caused by the initial pressure wave.

Explosives are categorized as either low grade or high grade. Low-grade explosives burn rapidly. Black powder, the original low-grade explosive, served as the basis for the development of smokeless gunpowder and some rocket propellants. Other examples of low-grade explosives are nitrostarch, nitrocellulose, and commercial fireworks. High-grade explosives, also termed detonating explosives, are more stable than low-grade explosives, frequently requiring trauma or shock for detonation. Nitroglycerin is the original high-grade explosive. Ammonium nitrate is another example of the early types of detonating explosives. Composition B, C-3, C-4, and TNT were developed later. Other examples include Amatol 80/20, RDX, PETN, and dynamite. Initiating high-grade explosives are a separate class of very sensitive high-grade explosives, such as lead styphnate and lead azide.

Explosions in confined spaces are often associated with much higher mortality. Solid surfaces act to reflect and compound the shock waves, causing magnification of the destructive forces. Similarly, blasts that are channeled by alleyways or hallways can have profound impact far outside the normal blast radius because the forces are focused on a smaller area of effect.

Blast injuries can often be categorized as primary, secondary, or tertiary. Primary blast damage is seen as a result of the tremendous pressure changes associated with explosives, in particular high explosives. Bowel, nervous system, cardiovascular system, ears, and lungs are most often affected by the primary blast. Cardiac contusion, esophageal rupture, hemothoraces or pneumothoraces, perforated bowel, arterial gas embolism, or immediate or delayed GI injuries should be suspected as clinically indicated. Burns are also possible, depending on the proximity to the blast.

Secondary blast injuries occur when victims are struck with shrapnel or objects sent airborne during the primary blast. Shrapnel can be the result of environmental objects as innocuous as sticks or rocks, or as malevolent as screws and nuts packed within the primary explosive. Tertiary blast injuries occur when victims themselves are thrown due to the incredible pressures from the blast. These injuries can include a wide variety of traumatic etiologies similar to a fall of significant magnitude.

"Suicide bombers" often carry a small amount (5-40 lb) of high explosives with an associated detonating device in a clandestine manner seeking to detonate the explosives near a large group of victims. Typical sites include sporting events, restaurants, nightclubs, or other public functions. Shrapnel can serve to extend the injury area, and a suspicion for projectile injuries should be maintained. Extreme care should be exercised in approaching a potential suicide bomber, even if incapacitated. Suspected perpetrators should be evaluated by experienced bomb squad personnel before EMS intervention to ensure a safe environment.

Chemical Agents

Chemical agents were first used extensively in World War I with dramatic results against unprepared troops. Although far less lethal than conventional explosives, chemical weapons can affect and incapacitate large numbers of troops in a short time. Chemical warfare agents were defined by the United Nations in 1969 as "chemical substances, whether gaseous, liquid or solid, which may be employed because of their direct toxic effects on man, animals, or plants."

The ready availability of precursors of modern chemical weapons and copious documentation on their preparation make the use of chemical weapons for terrorist actions far more likely than use of nuclear or biological weapons. In addition, potential terrorists could easily locate a chemical production facility, sabotage it using chemical or conventional explosives, and allow ambient winds to spread the toxins. The resultant environmental contamination would fulfill many terrorists' objectives of generating fear, trepidation, and panic among the population. Chemical agents are separated into 2 broad categories: lethal and nonlethal. Lethal agents include cyanides, nerve agents, vesicants, and choking agents. Nonlethal agents include lacrimating, emesis-inducing, and incapacitating agents.

Lethal Chemical Agents

Cyanide Compounds

Although they have been used since World War I, cyanide compounds are highly volatile, rendering them less useful than chlorine. The military designates hydrogen cyanide (AC) and cyanogen chloride (CK) as the substances used in warfare. Cyanide and its compounds are among the most rapidly acting chemical agents. Cyanide may be one of the most likely asphyxiant agents used in a terrorist action. Signs and symptoms include air hunger, hyperpnea, apnea, seizures, coma, and death. Cyanide poisoning is treated with a combination of nitrites and thiosulfates. A commercial kit is available, called a Cyanokit. Protective masks, gowns, and gloves are necessary until the patient is completely decontaminated.

Nerve Agents

Nerve agents are chemicals that inhibit acetylcholinesterase irreversibly. They combine with acetylcholine (ACH) to prevent transmission at the neuromuscular junction and affect both the sympathetic and parasympathetic nervous systems. Salivation, lacrimation, urination, defecation, and emesis (SLUDGE) are common signs. Muscarinic effects may cause the most serious complications, including bronchoconstriction, laryngospasm, and respiratory depression or arrest. These nerve agents may be delivered by droplet, vapour, or both. Symptoms of skin exposure appear much more slowly than those from inhalation. Onset of symptoms varies from 1 minute to a few hours. If cyanide compounds are inhaled or absorbed through the mucus membranes, death can occur in 1-10 minutes.

Therapy includes atropine sulfate, with as much as 10-40 mg required in some instances. Currently, the US Army uses 2-PAM (pralidoxime chloride), although it is not completely effective. It is least effective against Soman (GD). Pretreatment with pyridostigmine competitively inhibits the nerve agent. Pyridostigmine combines reversibly with ACH, which can resume neurotransmission after disassociation. However, such pretreatment does not protect against seizures.

Current nerve agents include tabun (GA), sarin (GB), soman (GD), and VX. These more potent agents may be the most likely nerve agents to be used in terrorism. Exposure to these agents can cause dramatic and sudden symptoms, especially when vapours or aerosolized agents are used. Transdermal exposure can produce delayed symptoms, as can exposure to limited amounts of either aerosolized or liquid agents. Local decontamination of these agents includes washing with soap and water. Health care providers should wear full protective gear until the patient is cleared by an environmental health specialist. VX, considered the most toxic of the nerve agents, is also the most difficult to decontaminate because of its low volatility.

Choking Agents

Causing pronounced irritation to the upper and lower

respiratory tracts, these agents are potentially dangerous because of a period of latency. A victim with dyspnea and mild chest discomfort may deteriorate after several hours to apnea and subsequent death. Chlorine is a widely used chemical that falls into the choking agent class. Chlorine causes upper- and lower-respiratory irritation, lacrimation, chest pain, dyspnea, coughing, laryngeal edema, pulmonary damage, and pulmonary edema.

Treatment is symptomatic with nebulized sodium bicarbonate. Decontaminate by copious flushing of affected areas with water. Medical providers need no special protection from chlorine-exposed patients.

Vesicant Agents

Vesicant agents, also termed blistering agents, may be toxic to the lungs, eyes, and mucous membranes. They are named for their tendency to cause blisters. Mustard gas is the best-known vesicant, originally used in World War I. It is a primary tissue irritant and has no significant allergenic component. Lesions are primarily cutaneous, but respiratory, ocular, and GI manifestations may occur, as well as cough, bloody sputum, and dyspnea. Areas of exposure become erythematous and progress to bullae, similar to toxic epidermal necrolysis. Symptoms may not occur for several hours after exposure. No antidote is available. Medical providers require protective masks and clothing for patient management. They should decontaminate by blotting and cleansing with soap and water and avoid scrubbing and hot water.

Nonlethal Chemical Agents

Lacrimator Agents

Lacrimator agents (tear gases) are widely used by law enforcement and the military. The most common effects are nasal and ocular discharges, photophobia, and burning sensations in the mucous membranes. Prolonged exposure may produce tightness in the chest, shortness of breath, and malaise and may cause vesiculations or bullae. Physical injuries may be observed from explosive discharge or kinetic effects of projectiles. At least 1 death has been attributed to lacrimator agents.

Most patients can be decontaminated fully by undressing, showering, and washing with soap and water. Medical personnel should use protective masks, gowns, and gloves, since lacrimator agents are transmitted by physical contact.

Types of lacrimator agents include bromobenzyl cyanide (CA), ortho-chlorobenzylidenemalonitrile (CS), dibenzoxazepine (CR), 2-chloroacetophenone (CN), chloroacetophenone in chloroform (CNC), and chloroacetophenone and chloropicrin in chloroform (CNS).

Emesis-inducing Agents

Emesis agents, also termed nausea gases, are not used routinely in the United States. They produce respiratory and skin irritation effects similar to those of lacrimator agents, as well as profound nausea. Examples of such compounds include adamsite (DM), diphenylcyanoarsine (DC), and diphenylchloroarsine (DA).

No decontamination is required in the field, and diluted bleach solution has proven effective for definitive cleaning. Ordinary clothing protects against these agents; chemical insert masks and standard gloves are adequate.

Incapacitating Agents

The possibility of a nonlethal incapacitating agent has long intrigued military commanders. Several agents have been tested, including lysergic acid diethylamide (LSD), mescaline, psilocybin, and psilocin. The only successful agent in production is benzilate (BZ).

BZ is a delayed-onset (1-4 h) agent causing tachycardia,

dizziness, vomiting, blurred vision, stupor, confusion, and random activity. Affected persons may be docile, belligerent, stuporous, or confused. They may appear intoxicated.

Decontaminate by washing with soap and water or with dilute bleach solution. Protective masks with charcoal filters provide adequate protection. Gloves are not necessary, since the agent is not absorbed through the skin.

Biological Agents

The Biological and Toxin Weapons Convention of 1972 banned the development, production, and stockpiling of biological weapons not required for peaceful intentions. The United States, United Kingdom, Soviet Union, and 67 other nations signed this document. Despite the fact that no biological agents have been used officially in warfare to date but the prospect of their use raises many concerns. Terrorism's history suggests the potential for the use of biological agents. Many authorities fear the use of biological agents more than the use of chemical agents because antidotes and specific countermeasures are available for some chemical weapons. Use of biological agents in terrorist acts potentially could cause tens of thousands of casualties and cost the US economy billions of dollars.

Various scenarios involving use of biological weapons are possible, from a sudden epidemic to a subacute, prolonged pandemic. Pathogens might be disseminated without anyone's realizing it until after the incubation period ends, by then exposing hundreds or thousands of civilians. Anticipating and controlling the dissemination of biological weapons may be difficult, causing complications for terrorists and intended victims. The effects of a biological agent also could evolve as a slowly developing, hard-to-categorize cluster of widely scattered cases, inadvertently allowing further dissemination of the pathogen until the connection is recognized. Certain aspects of a disease outbreak may combine to prompt suspicion of terrorist activity, including temporal patterns of illness, selected populations of victims, clinical presentation of illness, certain strains or species of pathogens, geographic location, morbidity or mortality patterns, antimicrobial resistance patterns, residual infectivity, route of exposure, weather or climate conditions, incubation period, or concurrence with other terrorist activities.

Biological agents could prove to be a devastating vector; a release of only 30 kg of anthrax spores could cause as many as 30,000-100,000 deaths; in comparison a 1,000-kg atomic bomb would result in approximately 23,000-80,000 deaths. The number of potential biological agents is nearly impossible to estimate. '

Agents range from simple viruses to bacteria and compounds derived from vertebrate animals. Biological agents are classified into 2 broad groups: infectious and noninfectious.

Infectious Agents

This group includes viruses, bacteria, protozoa, and fungi. The list of potential pathogens is extremely long, although an abbreviated list of agents can be considered that is based on previous use as agents during wartime. The synopsis presented for each disease is meant only as an overview. Consult definitive texts for complete information.

Anthrax

Bacillus anthracis, the causative organism of anthrax occurs naturally, is relatively easy to access, is very durable; it may live for up to 50 years in soil. Even a small number of anthrax spores, enough to fit on the head of a pin (5,000-8,000 spores), is sufficient to cause the inhalational form of anthrax. The inhalational form of anthrax can be difficult to diagnose in the earliest stages and may be very difficult to treat once clinical signs become apparent.

Cutaneous clues are necrotic lesions that spontaneously heal, and inhalation can produce a 1- to 3-day incubation period with fever, dyspnea, necrotizing hemorrhagic mediastinitis, and hypotension leading to death. Death usually occurs in 24-36 hours but may be as long as 7 days. Mortality can reach as high as 95% of inhalational exposures. Standard precautions, including masks, gowns, gloves, and isolation are sufficient. Vaccine is available.

Brucellosis

Highly infectious *Brucella* species are less commonly fatal than anthrax. Fever, malaise, osteomyelitis, and genitourinary (GU) infections may occur. Endocarditis is typically the cause of death. Standard precautions are sufficient. Precautions against direct contact should be included if draining lesions are present.

Encephalitis Viruses

Venezuelan, Eastern, and Western equine encephalitis viruses are likely to be used in weapons. Fever, headache, confusion, obtundation, dysphasia, seizures, paresis, and death may be observed. The Eastern variety has the highest mortality rate at 50-75%. A vaccine for Venezuelan equine encephalitis (VEE) is available, and effective vaccines for the others are currently in development. Standard precautions are sufficient; however, mosquito control is suggested, since mosquitoes are a vector.

Clostridium botulinum

An epidemic of descending and progressive bulbar and skeletal paralysis in afebrile patients may suggest botulinum poisoning. Respiratory failure is the most frequent cause of death. Since an antitoxin is available, standard precautions are sufficient.

Yersinia Pestis (Plague)

Plague usually manifests as pneumonia, culminating in respiratory failure and shock. A vaccine is available, yet precautions are required against pulmonary and droplet exposure.

Coxiella Burnetii (Q Fever)

A zoonotic disease with domestic livestock as vectors, Q fever varies in its manifestations. Fever, chills, and headache are the most common symptoms, although malaise, diaphoresis, and myalgia often are observed. Mortality rate is low, even when the disease is untreated. A vaccine is under investigation. Standard precautions are sufficient.

Rift Valley Fever

A hemorrhagic virus infection, Rift valley fever manifests with symptoms such as malaise, fever, prostration, generalized vascular permeability, and abnormal circulatory regulation. Several different varieties of hemorrhagic viruses are documented, including Ebola. Most are highly infectious and cause morbidity. Some carry high mortality rates. Depending on the strain, a vaccine may be available. Precautions against direct contact are recommended. Additional precautions may be necessary if massive hemorrhage is present.

Smallpox Virus

Smallpox may be a viable biological weapon, since the last natural case occurred in 1977 and the smallpox vaccine no longer is produced. Aerosol exposure causes viremia, malaise, fever, headache, delirium, and prolonged rash. Morbidity is caused primarily by secondary bacterial pneumonia. Precautions against aerosol infection are necessary.

***Francisella Tularensis* (Tularemia)**

Tularemia, a zoonotic disease, occurs in ulceroglandular

or typhoidal form. Typhoidal form manifests as fever, prostration, and respiratory symptoms. Mortality rate in typhoidal tularemia is approximately 35%. Standard precautions are sufficient. A vaccine is available as an investigational drug.

Noninfectious Agents

Allergic agents come from a variety of sources, including mite and insect particles, feathers, epithelium, hair, urine, feces, and powdered enzymes. Problems caused by these agents may include respiratory symptoms, conjunctivitis, and/or dermatitis.

Responding to a terrorist event can represent a considerable drain on resources for all agencies involved. The potential for death and destruction is tremendous. Agencies responsible for responding to terrorist events can only ensure that appropriate preparations are in place should unforeseen circumstances arise. Extensive preplanning and interagency cooperation is essential in mitigating the effects of terrorist attacks. A prepared and determined populace makes a less inviting target for potential terrorists.

14

Botulinum Toxin as a Biological Weapon

Botulinum toxin poses a major bioweapon threat because of its extreme potency and lethality; its ease of production, transport, and misuse; and the need for prolonged intensive care among affected persons. An outbreak of botulism constitutes a medical emergency that requires prompt provision of botulinum antitoxin and, often, mechanical ventilation, and it constitutes a public health emergency that requires immediate intervention to prevent additional cases. Timely recognition of a botulism outbreak begins with an astute clinician who quickly notifies public health officials.

Botulinum toxin is the most poisonous substance known. A single gram of crystalline toxin, evenly dispersed and inhaled, would kill more than 1 million people, although technical factors would make such dissemination difficult. The basis of the phenomenal potency of botulinum toxin is enzymatic; the toxin is a zinc proteinase that cleaves 1 or more of the fusion proteins by which neuronal vesicles release acetylcholine into the neuromuscular junction.

It is regrettable that botulinum toxin still needs to be considered as a bioweapon at the historic moment when it has become the first biological toxin to become licensed for treatment of human disease. In the United States, botulinum toxin is currently licensed for treatment of cervical torticollis, strabismus, and blepharospasm associated with dystonia. It is also used "off label" for a variety of more prevalent conditions that include migraine headache, chronic low back pain, stroke, traumatic brain injury, cerebral palsy, achalasia, and various dystonias.

Consensus Methods

The working group included 23 representatives from academic, government, and private institutions with expertise in public health, emergency management, and clinical medicine. The 2 primary authors (S.S.A. and R.S.) conducted a literature search on use of botulinum toxin as a bioweapon. The OLD MEDLINE and MEDLINE databases were queried for all articles published between January 1960 and March 1999 that contained words referring to biological warfare (*bioterrorism, biowarfare, terrorism, war, warfare,* and *weapon*) in combination with terms related to *Clostridium botulinum* (*bacillus, botulin, botulinal, botulinum, botulinus, botulism, clostridia, clostridial,* and *clostridium*). In addition, published and unpublished articles, books, monographs, and special reports in the primary authors' collections were reviewed. Additional MEDLINE searches were conducted through April 2000 during the review and revisions of the consensus statement.

The first draft of the consensus statement was a synthesis of information obtained in the formal evidence-gathering process. Members of the working group provided written and oral comments about the first draft at their meeting in May 1999. Working group members then reviewed subsequent drafts and suggested additional revisions. The final statement incorporates all relevant evidence obtained in the literature search in conjunction with final consensus recommendations supported by all working group members. The assessment and recommendations provided herein represent the best professional judgment of the working group based on currently available data and expertise. These conclusions and recommendations should be regularly reassessed as new information becomes available.

Terrorists have already attempted to use botulinum toxin as a bioweapon. Aerosols were dispersed at multiple sites in downtown Tokyo, Japan and at US military installations in Japan on at least 3 occasions between 1990 and 1995 by the Japanese cult Aum Shinriky. These attacks failed, apparently because of faulty microbiological technique, deficient aerosol-generating equipment, or internal sabotage. The perpetrators obtained their C *botulinum* from soil that they had collected in northern Japan. Development and use of botulinum toxin as a possible bioweapon began at least 60 years ago. The head of the Japanese biological warfare group (Unit 731) admitted to feeding cultures of C *botulinum* to prisoners with lethal effect during that country's occupation of Manchuria, which began in the 1930s.

The US biological weapons program first produced botulinum toxin during World War II. Because of concerns that Germany had weaponized botulinum toxin, more than 1 million doses of botulinum toxoid vaccine were made for Allied troops preparing to invade Normandy on D-Day. The US biological weapons program was ended in 1969-1970 by executive orders of Richard M. Nixon, then president. Research pertaining to biowarfare use of botulinum toxin took place in other countries as well.

Although the 1972 Biological and Toxin Weapons Convention prohibited offensive research and production of biological weapons, signatories Iraq and the Soviet Union subsequently produced botulinum toxin for use as a weapon. Botulinum toxin was 1 of several agents tested at the Soviet site Aralsk-7 on Vozrozhdeniye Island in the Aral Sea. A former senior scientist of the Russian civilian bioweapons program reported that the Soviets had attempted splicing the botulinum toxin gene from C *botulinum* into other bacteria. With the economic difficulties in Russia after the demise of the Soviet Union, some of the thousands of scientists formerly employed by its bioweapons program have been recruited by nations attempting to develop biological weapons.

Four of the countries listed by the US government as "state sponsors of terrorism" (Iran, Iraq, North Korea, and Syria) have developed, or are believed to be developing, botulinum toxin as a weapon. After the 1991 Persian Gulf War, Iraq admitted to the United Nations inspection team to having produced 19 000 L of concentrated botulinum toxin, of which approximately 10 000 L were loaded into military weapons. These 19 000 L of concentrated toxin are not fully accounted for and constitute approximately 3 times the amount needed to kill the entire current human population by inhalation. In 1990, Iraq deployed specially designed missiles with a 600-km range; 13 of these were filled with botulinum toxin, 10 with aflatoxin, and 2 with anthrax spores. Iraq also deployed special 400-lb (180-kg) bombs for immediate use; 100 bombs contained botulinum toxin, 50 contained anthrax spores, and 7 contained aflatoxin.

It is noteworthy that Iraq chose to weaponize more botulinum toxin than any other of its known biological agents. Some contemporary analyses discount the potential of botulinum toxin as a bioweapon because of constraints in concentrating and stabilizing the toxin for aerosol dissemination. However, these analyses pertain to military uses of botulinum toxin to immobilize an opponent. In contrast, deliberate release of botulinum toxin in a civilian population would be able to cause substantial disruption and distress. For example, it is estimated that a point-source aerosol release of botulinum toxin could incapacitate or kill 10% of persons within 0.5 km downwind. In addition, terrorist use of botulinum toxin might be manifested as deliberate contamination of food. Misuse of toxin in this manner could produce either a large botulism outbreak from a single meal or episodic, widely separated outbreaks. In the United States, the Centers for Disease Control and Prevention (CDC) maintains a well-established surveillance system for human botulism based on clinician reporting that would promptly detect such events.

Microbiology and Virulence Factors

Clostridium botulinum is a spore-forming, obligate anaerobe whose natural habitat is soil, from which it can be isolated without undue difficulty. The species *C botulinum* consists of 4 genetically diverse groups that would not otherwise be designated as a single species except for their common characteristic of producing botulinum toxin. Botulinum toxin exists in 7 distinct antigenic types that have been assigned the letters A through G. The toxin types are defined by their absence of cross-neutralization (eg, anti-A antitoxin does not neutralize toxin types B-G). The toxin types also serve as convenient epidemiological markers. In addition to *C botulinum*, unique strains of *Clostridium baratii* and *Clostridium butyricum* have the capacity to produce botulinum toxin.

Botulinum toxin is a simple dichain polypeptide that consists of a 100-kd "heavy" chain joined by a single disulfide bond to a 50-kd "light" chain; its 3-dimensional structure was recently resolved to 3.3 A. The toxin's light chain is a Zn^{++}-containing endopeptidase that blocks acetylcholine-containing vesicles from fusing with the terminal membrane of the motor neuron, resulting in flaccid muscle paralysis. The lethal dose of botulinum toxin for humans is not known but can be estimated from primate studies. By extrapolation, the lethal amounts of crystalline type A toxin for a 70-kg human would be approximately 0.09-0.15 μg intravenously or intramuscularly, 0.70-0.90 μg inhalationally, and 70 μg orally. Therapeutic botulinum toxin represents an impractical bioterrorist weapon because a vial of the type A preparation currently licensed in the United States contains only about 0.3% of the estimated human lethal inhalational dose and 0.005% of the estimated lethal oral dose.

Pathogenesis and Clinical Manifestations

Three forms of naturally occurring human botulism exist: foodborne, wound, and intestinal (infant and adult). Fewer than 200 cases of all forms of botulism are reported annually in the United States. All forms of botulism result from absorption of botulinum toxin into the circulation from either a mucosal surface (gut, lung) or a wound. Botulinum toxin does not penetrate intact skin. Wound botulism and intestinal botulism are infectious diseases that result from production of botulinum toxin by *C botulinum* either in devitalized (i.e., anaerobic) tissue or in the intestinal lumen, respectively. Neither would result from bioterrorist use ot botulinum toxin.

A fourth, man-made form that results from aerosolized botulinum toxin is inhalational botulism. This mode of transmission has been demonstrated experimentally in primates, has been attempted by bioterrorists, and has been the intended outcome of at least 1 country's specially designed missiles and artillery shells. Inhalational botulism has occurred accidentally in humans. A brief report from West Germany in 1962 described 3 veterinary personnel who were exposed to reaerosolize botulinum toxin while disposing of rabbits and guinea pigs whose fur was coated with aerosolized type A botulinum toxin. Type A botulinum toxin was detected in serum samples from all 3 affected individuals.

Once botulinum toxin is absorbed, the bloodstream carries it to peripheral cholinergic synapses, principally, the neuromuscular junction, where it binds irreversibly. The toxin is then internalized and enzymatically blocks acetylcholine release. Accordingly, all forms of human botulism display virtually identical neurologic signs. However, the neurologic signs in naturally occurring foodborne botulism may be preceded by abdominal cramps, nausea, vomiting, or diarrhea. These gastrointestinal symptoms are thought to be caused by other bacterial metabolites also present in the food and may not occur if purified botulinum toxin is intentionally placed in foods or aerosols.

Botulism is an acute, afebrile, symmetric, descending flaccid paralysis that always begins in bulbar musculature. It is not possible to have botulism without having multiple cranial nerve palsies. Disease manifestations are similar regardless of botulinum toxin type. However, the extent and pace of paralysis may vary considerably among patients. Some patients may be mildly affected, while others may be so paralyzed that they appear comatose and require months of ventilatory support. The rapidity of onset and the severity of paralysis depend on the amount of toxin absorbed into the circulation. Recovery results from new motor axon twigs that sprout to reinnervate paralyzed muscle fibers, a process that, in adults, may take weeks or months to complete.

Patients with botulism typically present with difficulty seeing, speaking, and/or swallowing. Prominent neurologic findings in all forms of botulism include ptosis, diplopia, blurred vision, often enlarged or sluggishly reactive pupils, dysarthria, dysphonia, and dysphagia. The mouth may appear dry and the pharynx injected because of peripheral parasympathetic cholinergic blockade. Sensory changes are not observed except for infrequent circumoral and peripheral paresthesias from hyperventilation as a patient becomes frightened by onset of paralysis.

As paralysis extends beyond bulbar musculature, loss of head control, hypotonia, and generalized weakness become prominent. Dysphagia and loss of the protective gag reflex may require intubation and, usually, mechanical ventilation. Deep tendon reflexes may be present initially but diminish or disappear in the ensuing days, and constipation may occur. In untreated persons, death results from airway obstruction (pharyngeal and upper airway muscle paralysis) and inadequate tidal volume (diaphragmatic and accessory respiratory muscle paralysis).

Because botulism is intoxication, patients remain afebrile unless they also have acquired a secondary infection (eg, aspiration pneumonia). The toxin does not penetrate brain parenchyma, so patients are not confused or obtunded. However, they often appear lethargic and have communication difficulties because of bulbar palsies. Botulism may be recognized by its classic triad: symmetric, descending flaccid paralysis with prominent bulbar palsies in an afebrile patient with a clear sensorium. The prominent bulbar palsies can be summarized in part as "4 Ds": diplopia, dysarthria, dysphonia, and dysphagia.

Epidemiology

Early recognition of outbreaks of botulism, whether natural or intentional, depends on heightened clinical suspicion. Aerosol dissemination may not be difficult to recognize because a large number of cases will share a common temporal and geographical exposure and will lack a common dietary exposure. However, identification of the common exposure site initially may be difficult because of the mobility of persons exposed during the incubation period. Botulism and botulinum toxin are not contagious and cannot be transmitted from person to person. In contrast, a microbe intentionally modified to produce botulinum toxin might be contagious.

No instances of waterborne botulism have ever been reported. Although the potency of botulinum toxin has led to speculation that it might be used to contaminate a municipal water supply, this scenario is unlikely for at least 2 reasons. First, botulinum toxin is rapidly inactivated by standard potable water treatments (eg, chlorination, aeration). Second, because of the slow turnover time of large-capacity reservoirs, a comparably large (and technically difficult to produce and deliver) inoculum of botulinum toxin would be needed. In contrast with treated water, botulinum toxin may be stable for several days in untreated water or beverages. Hence, such items should be investigated in a botulism outbreak if no other vehicle for toxin can be identified.

If food were deliberately used as a vehicle for the toxin, the outbreak would need to be distinguished from naturally occurring foodborne botulism. During the past 20 years, the epidemiology of foodborne botulism has expanded beyond its traditional association with home-preserved foods and now includes nonpreserved foods and public eating places, features that could make terrorist use of botulinum toxin more difficult to detect. Characteristics of outbreaks of botulism include:

Incubation Period

The rapidity of onset and severity of botulism depend on the rate and amount of toxin absorption. Symptoms of foodborne botulism may begin as early as 2 hours or as long as 8 days after ingestion of toxin. Typically, cases present 12 to 72 hours after the implicated meal. In 1 large foodborne outbreak, new cases presented during the ensuing 3 days at a fairly even rate before decreasing. The time to onset of inhalational botulism cannot be stated with certainty because so few cases are known. Monkeys showed signs of botulism 12 to 80 hours after aerosol exposure to 4 to 7 multiples of the monkey median lethal dose. The 3 known human cases of inhalational botulism had onset of symptoms approximately 72 hours after exposure to an unknown but probably small amount of reaerosolized toxin.

Age and Sex

Persons of all ages are potentially susceptible to botulism. There are no sex differences in susceptibility.

Agent and Vehicles

Botulinum toxin in solution is colorless, odorless, and, as far as is known, tasteless. The toxin is readily inactivated by heat (85°C for 5 minutes). Thus, foodborne botulism is always transmitted by foods that are not heated, or not heated thoroughly, before eating. Almost every type of food has been associated with outbreaks of botulism, but the most commonly implicated foods in the United States are vegetables, particularly "low-acid" (i.e., higher pH) vegetables such as beans, peppers, carrots, and corn.

A novel epidemiological development is the occurrence of foodborne botulism after eating various nonpreserved foods in restaurants or delicatessens. Foil-wrapped baked potatoes are now known to be capable of causing restaurant-associated foodborne botulism when held at room temperature after baking and then served plain, as potato salad, or as a Mediterranean-style dip. Other outbreaks that originated in restaurants resulted from contaminated condiments such as sautéed onions, garlic in oil, and commercial cheese sauce. Additional examples of notable commercial foods that have caused botulism outbreaks include inadequately eviscerated fish, yogurt, cream cheese, and jarred peanuts.

Incidence and Outbreak Size

Naturally occurring foodborne botulism is a rare disease. Approximately 9 outbreaks of foodborne botulism and a median of 24 cases occur annually in the United States. The mean outbreak size has remained constant over the years at approximately 2.5 cases per outbreak. The largest outbreak of foodborne botulism in the United States in the last 100 years occurred in Michigan in 1977; 59 cases resulted from eating home-preserved jalapeño peppers at a restaurant. However, only 45 of the 59 patients had clinically evident weakness and hypotonia.

Toxin Types

Of the 135 foodborne outbreaks in the 16 years from 1980 to 1996 in the United States, the toxin types represented were: type A, 54.1%; type B, 14.8%; type E, 26.7%; type F, 1.5%; and unknown, 3.0%. Type F foodborne outbreaks are rare in the United States; a 1962 outbreak resulted from homemade venison jerky, while other type F cases actually may have had intestinal botulism. Toxin types C and D cause botulism in wildlife and domestic animals but have not caused human foodborne disease. However, humans are thought to be susceptible to these toxin types because they have caused botulism in primates when ingested. Toxin type G is produced by a bacteria species discovered in South American soil in 1969 that has never caused recognized foodborne botulism. Aerosol challenge studies in monkeys have established the susceptibility of primates to inhaled botulinum toxin types C, D, and G.

Distribution

Although outbreaks of foodborne botulism have occurred in almost all states, more than half (53.8%) of the US outbreaks have occurred in just 5 western states (California, Washington, Oregon, Colorado, and Alaska). East of the Mississippi River, 60% of the foodborne outbreaks have resulted from type B toxin, while west of the Mississippi River, 85% have resulted from type A toxin. In the 46 years between 1950 and 1996, 20 states, mainly in the eastern United States, did not report any type A botulism outbreaks, while 24 states, mostly in the western United States, did not report any type B outbreaks. In Canada and Alaska, most foodborne outbreaks resulted from type E toxin associated with native Inuit and Eskimo foods.

Bioterrorism Considerations

Any outbreak of botulism should bring to mind the possibility of bioterrorism, but certain features would be particularly suggestive. The availability and speed of air transportation mandate that a careful travel and activity history, as well as a careful dietary history, be taken. Patients should also be asked whether they know of other persons with similar symptoms.

Absence of a common dietary exposure among temporally clustered patients should suggest the possibility of inhalational botulism.

Diagnosis and Differential Diagnosis

Clinical diagnosis of botulism is confirmed by specialized laboratory testing that often requires days to complete. Routine laboratory test .results are usually unremarkable. Therefore, clinical diagnosis is the foundation for early recognition of and response to a bioterrorist attack with botulinum toxin.

Any case of suspected botulism represents a potential public health emergency because of the possibility that a contaminated food remains available to others or that botulinum toxin has been deliberately released. In these settings, prompt intervention by civil authorities is needed to prevent additional cases. Consequently, clinicians caring for patients with suspected botulism should notify their local public health department and hospital epidemiologist immediately to coordinate shipment of therapeutic antitoxin, laboratory diagnostic testing, and epidemiological investigation.

In most jurisdictions of the United States, botulism suspected on clinical grounds alone by law must be reported immediately by telephone to local public health authorities. The attending clinician needs to be both prompt and persistent in accomplishing this notification.

Differential Diagnosis

Botulism is frequently misdiagnosed, most often as a polyradiculoneuropathy (Guillain-Barré or Miller-Fisher syndrome), myasthenia gravis, or a disease of the central nervous system. In the United States, botulism is more likely than Guillain-Barré syndrome, intoxication, or poliomyelitis to cause a cluster of cases of acute flaccid paralysis. Botulism differs from other flaccid paralyses in its prominent cranial nerve palsies disproportionate to milder weakness and hypotonia below the neck, in its symmetry, and in its absence of sensory nerve damage. A large, unintentional outbreak of foodborne botulism caused by a restaurant condiment in Canada provides a cautionary lesson about the potential difficulties in recognizing a covert, intentional contamination of food.

During a 6-week period in which the condiment was served, 28 persons in 2 countries became ill, but all were misdiagnosed. The 28 were identified retrospectively only after correct diagnoses in a mother and her 2 daughters who had returned to their home more than 2000 miles away from the restaurant. Four (14%) of the cases had been misdiagnosed as having psychiatric disease, including "factitious" symptoms. It is possible that hysterical paralysis might occur as a conversion reaction in the anxiety that would follow a deliberate release of botulinum toxin.

Diagnostic Testing

At present, laboratory diagnostic testing for botulism in the United States is available only at the CDC and approximately 20 state and municipal public health laboratories. The laboratory should be consulted prospectively about specimen collection and processing. Samples used in diagnosis of botulism include serum (30 mL of blood in "tiger"-top or red-top tubes from adults, less from children), stool, gastric aspirate, and, if available, vomitus and suspect foods. Serum samples must be obtained before therapy with antitoxin, which nullifies the diagnostic mouse bioassay. An enema may be required to obtain an adequate fecal sample if the patient is constipated. Sterile water should be used for this procedure because saline enema solution can confound the mouse bioassay. Gastric aspirates and, perhaps, stool may be useful for detecting inhaled aerosolized botulinum toxin released in a bioterrorist attack.

A list of the patient's medications should accompany the diagnostic samples because anticholinesterases, such as pyridostigmine bromide, and other medicines that are toxic to mice can be dialyzed from samples before testing. All samples should be kept refrigerated after collection. The standard laboratory diagnostic test for clinical specimens and foods is the mouse bioassay, in which type-specific antitoxin protects mice against any botulinum toxin present in the sample. The mouse bioassay can detect as little as 0.03 ng of botulinum toxin and usually yields results in 1 to 2 days (range, 6-96 hours). Fecal and gastric specimens also are cultured anaerobically, with results typically available in 7 to 10 days (range, 5-21 days). Toxin production by culture isolates is confirmed by the mouse bioassay.

An electromyogram with repetitive nerve stimulation at 20 to 50 Hz can sometimes distinguish between causes of acute flaccid paralysis. The characteristic electromyographic findings of botulism include normal nerve conduction velocity, normal sensory nerve function, a pattern of brief, small-amplitude motor potentials, and, most distinctively, an incremental response (facilitation) to repetitive stimulation often seen only at 50 Hz. Immediate access to electrophysiological studies may be difficult to obtain in an outbreak of botulism.

Additional diagnostic procedures may be useful in rapidly excluding botulism as the cause of paralysis. Cerebrospinal fluid (CSF) is unchanged in botulism but is abnormal in many central nervous system diseases. Although the CSF protein level eventually is elevated in Guillain-Barré syndrome, it may be normal early in illness. Imaging of the brain, spine, and chest may reveal hemorrhage, inflammation, or neoplasm. A test dose of edrophonium chloride briefly reverses paralytic symptoms in many patients with myasthenia gravis and, reportedly, in some with botulism. A close inspection of the skin, especially the scalp, may reveal an attached tick that is causing paralysis.

Other tests that require days for results include stool culture for *Campylobacter jejuni* as a precipitant of Guillain-Barré syndrome and assays for the autoantibodies that cause myasthenia gravis, Lambert-Eaton syndrome, and Guillain-Barré syndrome. Foods suspected of being contaminated should be refrigerated until retrieval by public health personnel. The US Food and Drug Administration and the US Department of Agriculture can assist other public health laboratories with testing of suspect foods by using methods similar to those applied to clinical samples.

Therapy

The mortality and sequelae associated with botulism have diminished with contemporary therapy. In the United States, the percentage of persons who died of foodborne botulism decreased from 25% during 1950-1959 to 6% during 1990-1996, with a similar reduction for each botulinum toxin type. Despite this increase in survival, the paralysis of botulism can persist for weeks to months with concurrent requirements for fluid and nutritional support, assisted ventilation, and treatment of complications.

Therapy for botulism consists of supportive care and passive immunization with equine antitoxin. Optimal use of botulinum antitoxin requires early suspicion of botulism. Timely administration of passive neutralizing antibody will minimize subsequent nerve damage and severity of disease but will not reverse existent paralysis. Antitoxin should be given to patients with neurologic signs of botulism as soon as possible after clinical diagnosis. Treatment should not be delayed for microbiological testing. Antitoxin may be withheld at the time of diagnosis if it is certain that the patient is improving from maximal paralysis.

In the United States, botulinum antitoxin is available from the CDC via state and local health departments. The licensed trivalent antitoxin contains neutralizing antibodies against botulinum toxin types A, B, and E, the most common causes of human botulism. If another toxin type was intentionally disseminated, patients could potentially be treated with an investigational heptavalent (ABCDEFG) antitoxin held by the US Army. However, the time required for correct toxin typing and subsequent administration of heptavalent antitoxin would decrease the utility of this product in an outbreak.

The dose and safety precautions for equine botulinum antitoxin have changed over time. Clinicians should review the package insert with public health authorities before using antitoxin. At present, the dose of licensed botulinum antitoxin is a single 10-mL vial per patient, diluted 1:10 in 0.9% saline solutions, administered by slow intravenous infusion. One vial provides between 5500 and 8500 IU of each type-specific antitoxin. The amount of neutralizing antibody in both the licensed and the investigational equine antitoxins far exceeds the highest serum toxin levels found in foodborne botulism patients, and additional doses are usually not required. If a patient has been exposed to an unnaturally large amount of botulinum toxin as a biological weapon, the adequacy of neutralization by antitoxin can be confirmed by retesting serum for toxin after treatment.

There are few published data on the safety of botulinum antitoxins. From 1967 to 1977, when the recommended dose was larger than today, approximately 9% of recipients of equine botulinum antitoxin in the United States displayed urticaria, serum sickness, or other reactions suggestive of hypersensitivity. Anaphylaxis occurred within 10 minutes of receiving antitoxin in 2% of recipients. When the US Army's investigational heptavalent antitoxin was given to 50 individuals in a large Egyptian outbreak of type E foodborne botulism in 1991, 1 recipient (2%) displayed serum sickness, and 9 (18%) had mild reactions. To screen for hypersensitivity, patients are given small challenge doses of equine antitoxin before receiving a full dose. Patients responding to challenge with a substantial wheal and flare may be desensitized over 3 to 4 hours before additional antitoxin is given.

During the infusion of antitoxin, diphenhydramine and epinephrine should be on hand for rapid administration in case of adverse reaction. Although both equine antitoxins have been partially despeciated by enzymatic cleavage of the allogenic F_c region, each contains a small residual of intact antibody that may sensitize recipients to additional doses. Botulism patients require supportive care that often includes feeding by enteral tube or parenteral nutrition, intensive care, mechanical ventilation, and treatment of secondary infections. Patients with suspected botulism should be closely monitored for impending respiratory failure. In nonventilated infants with botulism, a reverse Trendelenburg positioning with cervical vertebral support has been helpful, but applicability of this positioning to adults with botulism remains untested. This tilted, flat-body positioning with neck support may improve ventilation by reducing entry of oral secretions into the airway and by suspending more of the weight of the abdominal viscera from the diaphragm, thereby improving respiratory excursion.

In contrast, placing a botulism patient in a supine or semirecumbent position (trunk flexed 45° at the waist) may impede respiratory excursion and airway clearance, especially if the patient is obese. The desired angle of the reverse Trendelenburg position is 20° to 25°. Botulism patients should be assessed for adequacy of gags and cough reflexes, control of oropharyngeal secretions, oxygen saturation, vital capacity, and inspiratory force. Airway obstruction or aspiration usually precedes hypoventilation in botulism. When respiratory function deteriorates, controlled, anticipatory intubation is indicated. The proportion of patients with botulism who require mechanical ventilation has varied from 20% in a foodborne outbreak to more than 60% in infant botulism. In a large outbreak of botulism, the need for mechanical ventilators, critical care beds, and skilled personnel might quickly exceed local capacity and persist for weeks or months. Development of a reserve stockpile of mechanical ventilators in the United States is under way and will require a complement of staff trained in their use.

Antibiotics have no known direct effect on botulinum toxin. However, secondary infections acquired during botulism often require antibiotic therapy. Aminoglycoside antibiotics and clindamycin are contraindicated because of their ability to exacerbate neuromuscular blockade. Standard treatments for detoxification, such as activated charcoal, may be given before antitoxin becomes available, but there are no data regarding their effectiveness in human botulism.

Special Populations

Based on limited information, there is no indication that treatment of children, pregnant women, and immunocompromised persons with botulism should differ from standard therapy. Despite the risks of immediate hypersensitivity and sensitization to equine proteins, both children and pregnant women have received equine antitoxin without apparent short-term adverse effects. The risks to fetuses of exposure to equine antitoxin are unknown. Treatment with human-derived neutralizing antibody would decrease the risk of allergic reactions posed by equine botulinum antitoxin, but use of the investigational product, Botulism Immune Globulin Intravenous (Human) (California Department of Health Services, Berkeley), is limited to suspected cases of infant botulism.

Prophylaxis

Botulism can be prevented by the presence of neutralizing antibody in the bloodstream. Passive immunity can be provided by equine botulinum antitoxin or by specific human hyperimmune globulin, while endogenous immunity can be induced by immunization with botulinum toxoid. Use of antitoxin for postexposure prophylaxis is limited by its scarcity and its reactogenicity. Because of the risks of equine antitoxin therapy, it is less certain how best to care for persons who may have been exposed to botulinum toxin but who are not yet ill. In a small study of primates exposed to aerosolized toxin in which supportive care was not provided, all 7 monkeys given antitoxin after exposure but before the appearance of neurologic signs survived, while 2 of 4 monkeys treated with antitoxin only after the appearance of neurologic signs died. Moreover, all monkeys infused with neutralizing antibody before exposure to toxin displayed no signs of botulism. In a balance between avoiding the potential adverse effects of equine antitoxin and needing to rapidly neutralize toxin, it is current practice in foodborne botulism outbreaks to closely monitor persons who may have been exposed to botulinum toxin and to treat them promptly with antitoxin at the first signs of illness.

To facilitate distribution of scarce antitoxin following the intentional use of botulinum toxin, asymptomatic persons who are believed to have been exposed should remain under close medical observation and, if feasible, near critical care services. In the United States, an investigational pentavalent (ABCDE) botulinum toxoid is distributed by the CDC for laboratory workers at high risk of exposure to botulinum toxin and by the military for protection of troops against attack. A recombinant vaccine is also in development. The pentavalent toxoid has been used for more than 30 years to immunize more than 3000 laboratory workers in many countries. Immunization of the population with botulinum toxoid could in theory eliminate the hazard posed by botulinum toxins A through E. However, mass immunization is neither feasible nor desirable for reasons that include scarcity of the toxoid, rarity of natural disease, and elimination of the potential therapeutic benefits of medicinal botulinum toxin. Accordingly, preexposure immunization currently is neither recommended for nor available to the general population. Botulinum toxoid induces immunity over several months and, so, is ineffective as postexposure prophylaxis.

Decontamination

Despite its extreme potency, botulinum toxin is easily destroyed. Heating to an internal temperature of 85°C for at least 5 minutes will detoxify contaminated food or drink. All foods suspected of contamination should be promptly removed from potential consumers and submitted to public health authorities for testing. Persistence of aerosolized botulinum toxin at a site of deliberate release is determined by atmospheric conditions and the particle size of the aerosol. Extremes of temperature and humidity will degrade the toxin, while fine aerosols will eventually dissipate into the atmosphere. Depending on the weather, aerosolized toxin has been estimated to decay at less than 1% to 4% per minute.

At a decay rate of 1% per minute, substantial inactivation (13 logs) of toxin occurs by 2 days after aerosolization. Recognition of a covert release of finely aerosolized botulinum toxin would probably occur too late to prevent additional exposures. When exposure is anticipated, some protection may be conferred by covering the mouth and nose with clothing such as an undershirt, shirt, scarf, or handkerchief. In contrast with mucosal surfaces, intact skin is impermeable to botulinum toxin. After exposure to botulinum toxin, clothing and skin should be washed with soap and water. Contaminated objects or surfaces should be cleaned with 0.1% hypochlorite bleach solution if they cannot be avoided for the hours to days required for natural degradation.

Infection Control

Medical personnel caring for patients with suspected botulism should use standard precautions. Patients with suspected botulism do not need to be isolated, but those with flaccid paralysis from suspected meningitis require droplet precautions.

Additional research in diagnosis and treatment of botulism is required to minimize its threat as a weapon. Rapid diagnostic and toxin typing techniques currently under development would be useful for recognizing and responding to a bioterrorist attack. Although polymerase chain reaction assays can detect the botulinum toxin gene, they are unable, as yet, to determine whether the toxin gene is expressed and whether the expressed protein is indeed toxic. Assays that exploit the enzymatic activity of botulinum toxin have the potential to supplant the mouse bioassay as the standard for diagnosis. Detection of botulinum toxin in aerosols by enzyme-linked immunosorbent assay is a component of the US military's Biological Integrated Detection System for rapid recognition of biological agents in the battlefield.

The distribution of botulinum antitoxin to local hospitals from regional depots takes several hours. In contrast, standard detoxification techniques can be applied immediately. Studies are needed to assess whether activated charcoal and osmotic catharsis can prevent gastrointestinal tract absorption or reduce circulating levels of botulinum toxin. Enteral detoxification may be less useful in inhalational botulism than in foodborne disease.

The competing needs for immunity to weaponized botulinum toxin and for susceptibility to medicinal botulinum toxin could be reconciled by supplying human antibody that neutralizes toxin. With a half-life of approximately 1 month, human antibody would provide immunity for long periods and avoid the reactogenicity of equine products. Existing in vitro technologies could produce the stockpiles of fully human antibody necessary both to deter terrorist attacks and to avoid the rationing of antitoxin that currently would be required in a large outbreak of botulism. A single small injection of oligoclonal human antibodies could, in theory, provide protection against toxins A through G for many months. Until such a product becomes available, the possibilities for reducing the population's vulnerability to the intentional misuse of botulinum toxin remain limited.

15

Plague as a Biological Weapon

The working group has identified a limited number of agents that, if used as weapons, could cause disease and death in sufficient numbers to cripple a city or region. These agents also comprise the top of the list of "Critical Biological Agents" recently developed by the Centers for Disease Control and Prevention (CDC). *Yersinia pestis*, the causative agent of plague, is one of the most serious of these. Given the availability of *Y pestis* around the world, capacity for its mass production and aerosol dissemination, difficulty in preventing such activities, high fatality rate of pneumonic plague and potential for secondary spread of cases during an epidemic, the potential use of plague as a biological weapon is of great concern.

The working group comprised 25 representatives from major academic medical centers and research, government, military, public health, and emergency management institutions and agencies. MEDLINE databases were searched from January 1966 to June 1998 using the Medical Subject Headings (MeSH) *plague, Yersinia pestis, biological weapon, biological terrorism, biological warfare,* and *biowarfare*. Review of the bibliographies of the references identified by this search led to subsequent identification of relevant references published prior to 1966. In addition, participants identified other unpublished references and sources in their fields of expertise. Additional MEDLINE searches were conducted through January 2000 during the review and revisions of the statement.

The first draft of the consensus statement was a synthesis of information obtained in the initial formal evidence-gathering process. Members of the working group were asked to make formal written comments on this first draft of the document in September 1998. The document was revised incorporating changes suggested by members of the working group, which was convened to review the second draft of the document on October 30, 1998. Following this meeting and a second meeting of the working group on May 24, 1999, a third draft of the document was completed, reviewed, and revised. Working group members had a final opportunity to review the document and suggest revisions. The final document incorporates all relevant evidence obtained by the literature search in conjunction with consensus recommendations supported by all working group members. The assessment and recommendations provided herein represent the best professional judgment of the working group based on data and expertise currently available. The conclusions and recommendations need to be regularly reassessed as new information becomes available.

Potential as a Bioterrorist Agent

In AD 541, the first recorded plague pandemic began in Egypt and swept across Europe with attributable population losses of between 50% and 60% in North Africa, Europe, and central and southern Asia. The second plague pandemic, also known as the *black death* or *great pestilence*, began in 1346 and eventually killed 20 to 30 million people in Europe, one third of the European population. Plague spread slowly and inexorably from village to village by infected rats and humans or more quickly from country to country by ships. The pandemic lasted more than 130 years and had major political, cultural, and religious ramifications. The third pandemic began in China in 1855, spread to all inhabited continents, and ultimately killed more than 12 million people in India and China alone. Small outbreaks of plague continue to occur throughout the world.

Advances in living conditions, public health, and antibiotic therapy make future pandemics improbable. However, plague outbreaks following use of a biological weapon are a plausible threat. In World War II, a secret branch of the Japanese army, Unit 731, is reported to have dropped plague-infected fleas over populated areas of China, thereby causing outbreaks of plague. In the ensuing years, the biological weapons programs of the United States and the Soviet Union developed techniques to aerosolize plague directly, eliminating dependence on the unpredictable flea vector. In 1970, the World Health Organization (WHO) reported that, in a worst-case scenario, if 50 kg of *Y pestis* were released as an aerosol over a city of 5 million, pneumonic plague could occur in as many as 150,000 persons, 36,000 of whom would be expected to die. The plague bacilli would remain viable as an aerosol for 1 hour for a distance of up to 10 km. Significant numbers of city inhabitants might attempt to flee, further spreading the disease.

While US scientists had not succeeded in making quantities of plague organisms sufficient to use as an effective weapon by the time the US offensive program was terminated in 1970, Soviet scientists were able to manufacture large quantities of the agent suitable for placing into weapons. More than 10 institutes and thousands of scientists were reported to have worked with plague in the former Soviet Union. In contrast, few scientists in the United States study this disease. There is little published information indicating actions of autonomous groups or individuals seeking to develop plague as a weapon.

However, in 1995 in Ohio, a microbiologist with suspect motives was arrested after fraudulently acquiring *Y pestis* by mail. New antiterrorism legislation was introduced in reaction.

Naturally Occurring Plague

Human plague most commonly occurs when plague-infected fleas bite humans who then develop bubonic plague. As a prelude to human epidemics, rats frequently die in large numbers, precipitating the movement of the flea population from its natural rat reservoir to humans. Although most persons infected by this route develop bubonic plague, a small minority will develop sepsis with no bubo, a form of plague termed *primary septicemic plague.* Neither bubonic nor septicemic plague spreads directly from person to person. A small percentage of patients with bubonic or septicemic plague develop secondary pneumonic plague and can then spread the disease by respiratory droplet. Persons contracting the disease by this route develop primary pneumonic plague.

Plague remains an enzootic infection of rats, ground squirrels, prairie dogs, and other rodents on every populated continent except Australia. Worldwide, on average in the last 50 years, 1700 cases have been reported annually. In the United States, 390 cases of plague were reported from 1947 to 1996, 84% of which were bubonic, 13% septicemic and 2% pneumonic. Concomitant case fatality rates were 14%, 22%, and 57%, respectively. Most US cases were in New Mexico, Arizona, Colorado, and California. Of the 15 cases following exposure to domestic cats with plague, 4 were primary pneumonic plague. In the United States, the last case of human-to-human transmission of plague occurred in Los Angeles in 1924.

Although pneumonic plague has rarely been the dominant manifestation of the disease, large outbreaks of pneumonic plague have occurred. In an outbreak in

Manchuria in 1910-1911, as many as 60,000 persons developed pneumonic plague; a second large Manchurian pneumonic plague outbreak occurred in 1920-1921. As would be anticipated in the preantibiotic era, nearly 100% of these cases were reported to be fatal. Reports from the Manchurian outbreaks suggested that indoor contacts of affected patients were at higher risk than outdoor contacts and that cold temperature, increased humidity, and crowding contributed to increased spread. In northern India, there was an epidemic of pneumonic plague with 1400 deaths reported at about the same time. While epidemics of pneumonic plague of this scale have not occurred since, smaller epidemics of pneumonic plague have occurred recently. In 1997 in Madagascar, 1 patient with bubonic plague and secondary pneumonic infection transmitted pneumonic plague to 18 persons, 8 of whom died.

Use of a Biological Weapon

The epidemiology of plague following its use as a biological weapon would differ substantially from that of naturally occurring infection. Intentional dissemination of plague would most probably occur via an aerosol of *Y pestis*, a mechanism that has been shown to produce disease in nonhuman primates.

A pneumonic plague outbreak would result with symptoms initially resembling those of other severe respiratory illnesses. The size of the outbreak would depend on factors including the quantity of biological agent used, characteristics of the strain, environmental conditions, and methods of aerosolization. Symptoms would begin to occur 1 to 6 days following exposure, and people would die quickly following onset of symptoms. Indications that plague had been artificially disseminated would be the occurrence of cases in locations not known to have enzootic infection, in persons without known risk factors, and in the absence of prior rodent deaths.

Microbiology and Virulence Factors

Y pestis is a nonmotile, gram-negative bacillus, sometimes coccobacillus that shows bipolar (also termed *safety pin*) staining with Wright, Giemsa, or Wayson stain. *Y pestis* is a lactose nonfermenter, urease and indole negative, and a member of the Enterobacteriaceae family. It grows optimally at 28°C on blood agar or MacConkey agar, typically requiring 48 hours for observable growth, but colonies are initially much smaller than other Enterobacteriaceae and may be overlooked. *Y pestis* has a number of virulence factors that enable it to survive in humans by facilitating use of host nutrients, causing damage to host cells, and subverting phagocytosis and other host defense mechanisms.

Naturally Occurring Plague

In most cases of naturally occurring plague, the bite by a plague-infected flea leads to the inoculation of up to thousands of organisms into a patient's skin. The bacteria migrate through cutaneous lymphatics to regional lymph nodes where they are phagocytosed but resist destruction. They rapidly multiply, causing destruction and necrosis of lymph node architecture with subsequent bacteremia, septicemia, and endotoxemia that can lead quickly to shock, disseminated intravascular coagulation, and coma.

Patients typically develop symptoms of bubonic plague 2 to 8 days after being bitten by an infected flea. There is sudden onset of fever, chills, and weakness and the development of an acutely swollen tender lymph node, or bubo, up to 1 day later. The bubo most typically develops in the groin, axilla, or cervical region and is often so painful that it prevents patients from moving the affected area of the body. Buboes are 1 to 10 cm in diameter, and the overlying skin is erythematous. They are extremely tender, nonfluctuant, and warm and are often associated with considerable surrounding edema, but seldom lymphangitis.

Rarely, buboes become fluctuant and suppurate. In addition, pustules or skin ulcerations may occur at the site of the flea bite in a minority of patients. A small minority of patients infected by fleas develop *Y pestis* septicemia without a discernable bubo, the form of disease termed *primary septicemic plague.*

Septicemia can also arise secondary to bubonic plague. Septicemic plague may lead to disseminated intravascular coagulation, necrosis of small vessels, and purpuric skin lesions. Gangrene of acral regions such as the digits and nose may also occur in advanced disease, a process believed responsible for the name *black death* in the second plague pandemic. However, the finding of gangrene would not be expected to be helpful in diagnosing the disease in the early stages of illness when early antibiotic treatment could be lifesaving.

Secondary pneumonic plague develops in a minority of patients with bubonic or primary septicemic plague—approximately 12% of total cases in the United States over the last 50 years. This process, termed *secondary pneumonic plague,* develops via hematogenous spread of plague bacilli to the lungs. Patients commonly have symptoms of severe bronchopneumonia, chest pain, dyspnea, cough, and hemoptysis.

Primary pneumonic plague resulting from the inhalation of plague bacilli occurs rarely in the United States. Reports of 2 recent cases of primary pneumonic plague, contracted after handling cats with pneumonic plague, reveal that both patients had pneumonic symptoms as well as prominent gastrointestinal symptoms including nausea, vomiting, abdominal pain, and diarrhea. Diagnosis and treatment were delayed more than 24 hours after symptom onset in both patients, both of whom died.

Less common plague syndromes include plague meningitis and plague pharyngitis. Plague meningitis follows the hematogenous seeding of bacilli into the meninges and is associated with fever and meningismus. Plague pharyngitis follows inhalation or ingestion of plague bacilli and is associated with cervical lymphadenopathy.

The pathogenesis and clinical manifestations of plague following a biological attack would be notably different than naturally occurring plague. Inhaled aerosolized *Y pestis* bacilli would cause primary pneumonic plague. The time from exposure to aerosolized plague bacilli until development of first symptoms in humans and nonhuman primates has been found to be 1 to 6 days and most often, 2 to 4 days. The first sign of illness would be expected to be fever with cough and dyspnea, sometimes with the production of bloody, watery, or less commonly, purulent sputum. Prominent gastrointestinal symptoms, including nausea, vomiting, abdominal pain, and diarrhea, might be present.

The ensuing clinical findings of primary pneumonic plague are similar to those of any severe rapidly progressive pneumonia and are quite similar to those of secondary pneumonic plague. Clinicopathological features may help distinguish primary from secondary pneumonic plague. In contrast to secondary pneumonic plague, features of primary pneumonic plague would include absence of buboes (except, rarely, cervical buboes) and, on pathologic examination, pulmonary disease with areas of profound lobular exudation and bacillary aggregation. Chest radiographic findings are variable but bilateral infiltrates or consolidations are common.

Laboratory studies may reveal leukocytosis with toxic granulations, coagulation abnormalities, aminotransferase elevations, azotemia, and other evidence of multiorgan failure. All are nonspecific findings associated with sepsis and systemic inflammatory response syndrome. The time from respiratory exposure to death in humans is reported to have been between 2 to 6 days in epidemics during the preantibiotic era, with a mean of 2 to 4 days in most epidemics.

Given the rarity of plague infection and the possibility that early cases are a harbinger of a larger epidemic, the first clinical or laboratory suspicion of plague must lead to immediate notification of the hospital epidemiologist or infection control practitioner, health department, and the local or state health laboratory. Definitive tests can thereby be arranged rapidly through a state reference laboratory or, as necessary, the Diagnostic and Reference Laboratory of the CDC and early interventions instituted.

The early diagnosis of plague requires a high index of suspicion in naturally occurring cases and even more so following the use of a biological weapon. There are no effective environmental warning systems to detect an aerosol of plague bacilli.

The first indication of a clandestine terrorist attack with plague would most likely be a sudden outbreak of illness presenting as severe pneumonia and sepsis. If there are only small numbers of cases, the possibility of them being plague may be at first overlooked given the clinical similarity to other bacterial or viral pneumonias and that few Western physicians have ever seen a case of pneumonic plague. However, the sudden appearance of a large number of previously healthy patients with fever, cough, shortness of breath, chest pain, and a fulminant course leading to death should immediately suggest the possibility of pneumonic plague or inhalational anthrax. The presence of hemoptysis in this setting would strongly suggest plague.

There are no widely available rapid diagnostic tests for plague. Tests that would be used to confirm a suspected diagnosis—antigen detection, IgM enzyme immunoassay, immunostaining, and polymerase chain reaction—are available only at some state health departments, the CDC, and military laboratories. The routinely used passive hemagglutination antibody detection assay is typically only of retrospective value since several days to weeks usually passed after disease onset before antibodies develop.

Microbiologic studies are important in the diagnosis of pneumonic plague. A Gram stain of sputum or blood may reveal gram-negative bacilli or coccobacilli.

A Wright, Giemsa, or Wayson stain will often show bipolar staining, and direct fluorescent antibody testing, if available, may be positive. In the unlikely event that a cervical bubo is present in pneumonic plague, an aspirate (obtained with a 20-gauge needle and a 10-mL syringe containing 1-2 mL of sterile saline for infusing the node) may be cultured and similarly stained. Cultures of sputum, blood, or lymph node aspirate should demonstrate growth approximately 24 to 48 hours after inoculation. Most microbiology laboratories use either automated or semiautomated bacterial identification systems. Some of these systems may misidentify *Y pestis*.

In laboratories without automated bacterial identification, as many as 6 days may be required for identification, and there is some chance that the diagnosis may be missed entirely. Approaches for biochemical characterization of *Y pestis* are described in detail elsewhere.

If a laboratory using automated or nonautomated techniques is notified that plague is suspected, it should split the culture: 1 culture incubated at 28°C for rapid growth and the second culture incubated at 37°C for identification of the diagnostic capsular (F_1) antigen. Using these methods, up to 72 hours may be required following specimen procurement to make the identification (May Chu, PhD, CDC, Fort Collins, Colo, written communication, April 9, 1999). Antibiotic susceptibility testing should be performed at a reference laboratory because of the lack of standardized susceptibility testing procedures for *Y pestis*. A process establishing criteria and training measures for laboratory diagnosis of this disease is being undertaken jointly by the Association of Public Health Laboratories and the CDC.

Vaccination

The US-licensed formaldehyde-killed whole bacilli vaccine was discontinued by its manufacturers in 1999 and is no longer available. Plans for future licensure and production are unclear. This killed vaccine demonstrated efficacy in preventing or ameliorating bubonic disease, but it does not prevent or ameliorate the development of primary pneumonic plague. It was used in special circumstances for individuals deemed to be at high risk of developing plague, such as military personnel working in plague endemic areas, microbiologists working with *Y pestis* in the laboratory, or researchers working with plague-infected rats or fleas. Research is ongoing in the pursuit of a vaccine that protects against primary pneumonic plague.

Recommendations for the use of antibiotics following a plague biological weapon exposure are conditioned by the lack of published trials in treating plague in humans, limited number of studies in animals, and possible requirement to treat large numbers of persons. A number of possible therapeutic regimens for treating plague have yet to be adequately studied or submitted for approval to the Food and Drug Administration (FDA). For these reasons, the working group offers consensus recommendations based on the best available evidence. The recommendations do not necessarily represent uses currently approved by the FDA or an official position on the part of any of the federal agencies whose scientists participated in these discussions. Recommendations will need to be revised as further relevant information becomes available.

In the United States during the last 50 years, 4 of the 7 reported primary pneumonic plague patients died. Fatality rates depend on various factors including time to initiation of antibiotics, access to advanced supportive care, and the dose of inhaled bacilli. The fatality rate of patients with pneumonic plague when treatment is delayed more than 24 hours after symptom onset is extremely high.

Historically, the preferred treatment for plague infection has been streptomycin, an FDA-approved treatment for plague. Administered early during the disease, streptomycin has reduced overall plague mortality to the 5% to 14% range. However, streptomycin is infrequently used in the United States and only modest supplies are available. Gentamicin is not FDA approved for the treatment of plague but has been used successfully and is recommended as an acceptable alternative by experts. In 1 case series, 8 patients with plague were treated with gentamicin with morbidity or mortality equivalent to that of patients treated with streptomycin. In vitro studies and an in vivo study in mice show equal or improved activity of gentamicin against many strains of *Y pestis* when compared with streptomycin. In addition, gentamicin is widely available, inexpensive, and can be given once daily.

Tetracycline and doxycycline also have been used in the treatment and prophylaxis of plague; both are FDA approved for these purposes. In vitro studies have shown that *Y pestis* susceptibility to tetracycline and doxycycline is equivalent to that of the aminoglycosides. In another investigation, 13% of *Y pestis* strains in Madagascar were found to have some in vitro resistance to tetracycline. Experimental murine models of *Y pestis* infection have yielded data that are difficult to extrapolate to humans. Some mouse studies have shown doxycycline to be a highly efficacious treatment of infection or prophylaxis against naturally occurring plague strains. Experimental murine infection with F_1-deficient variants of *Y pestis* have shown decreased efficacy of doxycycline, but only 1 human case of F_1-deficient plague infection has been reported.

Russell and colleagues reported poor efficacy of doxycycline against plague-infected mice, but the dosing schedules used in this experiment would have failed to maintain drug levels above the minimum inhibitory concentration due to the short half-life of doxycycline in mice. In another study, doxycycline failed to prevent death in mice intraperitoneally infected with 29 to 290,000 times the median lethal inocula of *Y pestis*.

There are no controlled clinical trials comparing either tetracycline or doxycycline to aminoglycoside in the treatment of plague, but anecdotal case series and a number of medical authorities support use of this class of antimicrobials for prophylaxis and for therapy in the event that streptomycin or gentamicin cannot be administered. Based on evidence from in vitro studies, animal studies, and uncontrolled human data, the working group recommends that the tetracycline class of antibiotics be used to treat pneumonic plague if aminoglycoside therapy cannot be administered. This might be the case in a mass casualty scenario when parenteral therapy was either unavailable or impractical. Doxycycline would be considered pharmacologically superior to other antibiotics in the tetracycline class for this indication, because it is well absorbed without food interactions, is well distributed with good tissue penetration, and has a long half-life.

The fluoroquinolone family of antimicrobials has demonstrated efficacy in animal studies. Ciprofloxacin has been demonstrated to be at least as efficacious as aminoglycosides and tetracyclines in studies of mice with experimentally induced pneumonic plague.

In vitro studies also suggest equivalent or greater activity of ciprofloxacin, levofloxacin, and ofloxacin against *Y pestis* when compared with aminoglycosides or tetracyclines. However, there have been no trials of fluoroquinolones in human plague, and they are not FDA approved for this indication.

Chloramphenicol has been used to treat plague infection and has been recommended for treatment of plague meningitis because of its ability to cross the blood-brain barrier. However, human clinical trials demonstrating the superiority of chloramphenicol in the therapy of classic plague infection or plague meningitis have not been performed. It has been associated with dose dependent hematologic abnormalities and with rare idiosyncratic fatal aplastic anemia.

A number of different sulfonamides have been used successfully in the treatment of human plague infection: sulfathiazole, sulfadiazine, sulfamerazine, and trimethoprim-sulfamethoxazole. The 1970 WHO analysis reported that sulfadiazine reduced mortality for bubonic plague but was ineffective against pneumonic plague and was less effective than tetracycline overall. In a study comparing trimethoprim-sulfamethoxazole with streptomycin, patients treated with trimethoprim-sulfamethoxazole had a longer median duration of fever and a higher incidence of complications. Authorities have generally considered trimethoprim-sulfamethoxazole a second-tier choice. Some have recommended sulfonamides only in the setting of pediatric prophylaxis. No sulfonamides have been FDA approved for the treatment of plague.

Antimicrobials that have been shown to have poor or only modest efficacy in animal studies have included rifampin, aztreonam, ceftazidime, cefotetan, and cefazolin; these antibiotics should not be used. Antibiotic resistance patterns must also be considered in making treatment recommendations.

Naturally occurring antibiotic resistance to the tetracycline class of drugs has occurred rarely. Recently, a plasmid-mediated multidrug-resistant strain was isolated in Madagascar. A report published by Russian scientists cited quinolone-resistant *Y pestis*. There have been assertions that Russian scientists have engineered multidrug-resistant strains of *Y pestis*, although there is as yet no scientific publication confirming this.

Antibiotic Therapy

The working group treatment recommendations are based on literature reports on treatment of human disease, reports of studies in animal models, reports on in vitro susceptibility testing, and antibiotic safety. Should antibiotic susceptibility testing reveal resistance, proper antibiotic substitution would need to be made.

In a contained casualty setting, a situation in which a modest number of patients require treatment, the working group recommends parenteral antibiotic therapy. Preferred parenteral forms of the antimicrobials streptomycin or gentamicin are recommended. However, in a mass casualty setting, intravenous or intramuscular therapy may not be possible for reasons of patient care logistics and/or exhaustion of equipment and antibiotic supplies, and parenteral therapy will need to be supplanted by oral therapy. In a mass casualty setting, the working group recommends oral therapy, preferably with doxycycline (or tetracycline) or ciprofloxacin.

Patients with pneumonic plague will require substantial advanced medical supportive care in addition to antimicrobial therapy. Complications of gram-negative sepsis would be expected, including adult respiratory distress syndrome, disseminated intravascular coagulation, shock, and multiorgan failure.

Once it was known or strongly suspected that pneumonic plague cases were occurring, anyone with fever or cough in the presumed area of exposure should be immediately treated with antimicrobials for presumptive pneumonic plague. Delaying therapy until confirmatory testing is performed would greatly decrease survival. Clinical deterioration of patients despite early initiation of empiric therapy could signal antimicrobial resistance and should be promptly evaluated.

Management of Special Groups

Consensus recommendations for special groups as set forth in the following reflect the clinical and evidence-based judgments of the working group and do not necessarily correspond to FDA approved use, indications, or labeling.

Children

The treatment of choice for plague in children has been streptomycin or gentamicin. If aminoglycosides are not available or cannot be used, recommendations for alternative antimicrobial treatment with efficacy against plague are conditioned by balancing risks associated with treatment against those posed by pneumonic plague. Children aged 8 years and older can be treated with tetracycline antibiotics safely.

However, in children younger than 8 years, tetracycline antibiotics may cause discolored teeth, and rare instances of retarded skeletal growth have been reported in infants.

Chloramphenicol is considered safe in children except for children younger than 2 years who are at risk of "gray baby syndrome." Some concern exists that fluoroquinolone use in children may cause arthropathy, although fluoroquinolones have been used to treat serious infections in children. No comparative studies assessing efficacy or safety of alternative treatment strategies for plague in children has or can be performed.

Given these considerations, the working group recommends that children in the contained casualty setting receive streptomycin or gentamicin. In a mass casualty setting or for postexposure prophylaxis, we recommend that doxycycline be used. Alternatives are listed for both settings. The working group assessment is that the potential benefits of these antimicrobials in the treating of pneumonic plague infection substantially outweigh the risks.

Pregnant Women

It has been recommended that aminoglycosides be avoided in pregnancy unless severe illness warrants, but there is no more efficacious treatment for pneumonic plague. Therefore, the working group recommends that pregnant women in the contained casualty setting receive gentamicin. Since streptomycin has been associated with rare reports of irreversible deafness in children following fetal exposure, this medication should be avoided if possible. The tetracycline class of antibiotics has been associated with fetal toxicity including retarded skeletal growth, although a large case-control study of doxycycline use in pregnancy showed no significant increase in teratogenic risk to the fetus.

Liver toxicity has been reported in pregnant women following large doses of intravenous tetracycline (no longer sold in the United States), but it has also been reported following oral administration of tetracycline to nonpregnant individuals. Balancing the risks of pneumonic plague infection with those associated with doxycycline use in pregnancy, the working group recommends that doxycycline be used to treat pregnant women with pneumonic plague if gentamicin is not available.

Of the oral antibiotics historically used to treat plague, only trimethoprim-sulfamethoxazole has a category C pregnancy classification; however, many experts do not recommend trimethoprim-sulfamethoxazole for treatment of pneumonic plague. Therefore, the working group recommends that pregnant women receive oral doxycycline for mass casualty treatment or postexposure prophylaxis. If the patient is unable to take doxycycline or the medication is unavailable, ciprofloxacin or other fluoroquinolones would be recommended in the mass casualty setting.

The working group recommendation for treatment of breastfeeding women is to provide the mother and infant with the same antibiotic based on what is most safe and effective for the infant: gentamicin in the contained casualty setting and doxycycline in the mass casualty setting. Fluoroquinolones would be the recommended alternative.

Immunosuppressed Persons

The antibiotic treatment or postexposure prophylaxis for pneumonic plague among those who are immunosuppressed has not been studied in human or animal models of pneumonic plague infection. Therefore, the consensus recommendation is to administer antibiotics according to the guidelines developed for immunocompetent adults and children.

Postexposure Prophylaxis Recommendations

The working group recommends that in a community experiencing a pneumonic plague epidemic, all persons developing a temperature of 38.5°C or higher or new cough should promptly begin parenteral antibiotic treatment. If the resources required to administer parenteral antibiotics are unavailable, oral antibiotics should be used according to the mass casualty recommendations. For infants in this setting, tachypnea would also be an additional indication for immediate treatment. Special measures would need to be initiated for treatment or prophylaxis of those who are either unaware of the outbreak or require special assistance, such as the homeless or mentally handicapped persons. Continuing surveillance of patients would be needed to identify individuals and communities at risk requiring postexposure prophylaxis.

Asymptomatic persons having household, hospital, or other close contact with persons with untreated pneumonic plague should receive postexposure antibiotic prophylaxis for 7 days and watch for fever and cough. Close contact is defined as contact with a patient at less than 2 meters. Tetracycline, doxycycline, sulfonamides, and chloramphenicol have each been used or recommended as postexposure prophylaxis in this setting. Fluoroquinolones could also be used based on studies in mice.

The working group recommends the use of doxycycline as the first choice antibiotic for postexposure prophylaxis; other recommended antibiotics are noted. Contacts who develop fever or cough while receiving prophylaxis should seek prompt medical attention and begin antibiotic treatment.

Infection Control

Previous public health guidelines have advised strict isolation for all close contacts of patients with pneumonic plague who refuse prophylaxis. In the modern setting, however, pneumonic plague has not spread widely or rapidly in a community, and therefore isolation of close contacts refusing antibiotic prophylaxis is not recommended by the working group. Instead, persons refusing prophylaxis should be carefully watched for the development of fever or cough during the first 7 days after exposure and treated immediately should either occur.

Modern experience with person-to-person spread of pneumonic plague is limited; few data are available to make specific recommendations regarding appropriate infection control measures. The available evidence indicates that person-to-person transmission of pneumonic plague occurs via respiratory droplets; transmission by droplet nuclei has not been demonstrated. In large pneumonic plague epidemics earlier this century, pneumonic plague transmission was prevented in close contacts by wearing masks.

Commensurate with this, existing national infection control guidelines recommend the use of disposable surgical masks to prevent the transmission of pneumonic plague.

Given the available evidence, the working group recommends that, in addition to beginning antibiotic prophylaxis, persons living or working in close contact with patients with confirmed or suspect pneumonic plague that have had less than 48 hours of antimicrobial treatment should follow respiratory droplet precautions and wear a surgical mask. Further, the working group recommends avoidance of unnecessary close contact with patients with pneumonic plague until at least 48 hours of antibiotic therapy and clinical improvement has taken place. Other standard respiratory droplet precautions (gown, gloves, and eye protection) should be used as well.

The patient should remain isolated during the first 48 hours of antibiotic therapy and until clinical improvement occurs. If large numbers of patients make individual isolation impossible, patients with pneumonic plague may be cohorted while undergoing antibiotic therapy. Patients being transported should also wear surgical masks. Hospital rooms of patients with pneumonic plague should receive terminal cleaning in a manner consistent with standard precautions, and clothing or linens contaminated with body fluids of patients infected with plague should be disinfected as per hospital protocol.

Microbiology laboratory personnel should be alerted when *Y pestis* is suspected. Four laboratory-acquired cases of plague have been reported in the United States. Simple clinical materials and cultures should be processed in biosafety level 2 conditions. Only during activities involving high potential for aerosol or droplet production (eg, centrifuging, grinding, vigorous shaking, and animal studies) are biosafety level 3 conditions necessary.

Bodies of patients who have died following infection with plague should be handled with routine strict precautions. Contact with the remains should be limited to trained personnel, and the safety precautions for transporting corpses for burial should be the same as those when transporting ill patients. Aerosol-generating procedures, such as bone-sawing associated with surgery or postmortem examinations, would be associated with special risks of transmission and are not recommended. If such aerosol-generating procedures are necessary, then high-efficiency particulate air filtered masks and negative-pressure rooms should be used as would be customary in cases in which contagious biological aerosols, such as *Mycobacterium tuberculosis*, are deemed a possible risk.

Environmental Decontamination

There is no evidence to suggest that residual plague bacilli pose an environmental threat to the population following the dissolution of the primary aerosol. There is no spore form in the *Y pestis* life cycle, so it is far more susceptible to environmental conditions than sporulating bacteria such as *Bacillus anthracis*. Moreover, *Y pestis* is very sensitive to the action of sunlight and heating and does not survive long outside the host. Although some reports suggest that the bacterium may survive in the soil for some time, there is no evidence to suggest environmental risk to humans in this setting and thus no need for environmental decontamination of an area exposed to an aerosol of plague. In the WHO analysis, in a worst case scenario, a plague aerosol was estimated to be effective and infectious for as long as 1 hour. In the setting of a clandestine release of plague bacilli, the aerosol would have dissipated long before the first case of pneumonic plague occurred.

16

Smallpox as a Biological Weapon

Smallpox is one of the most serious of these diseases. If used as a biological weapon, smallpox represents a serious threat to civilian populations because of its case-fatality rate of 30% or more among unvaccinated persons and the absence of specific therapy.

Although smallpox has long been feared as the most devastating of all infectious diseases, its potential for devastation today is far greater than at any previous time. Routine vaccination throughout the United States ceased more than 25 years ago. In a now highly susceptible, mobile population, smallpox would be able to spread widely and rapidly throughout this country and the world.

Members of the working group were selected by the chairman in consultation with principal agency heads in the Department of Health and Human Services (DHHS) and the US Army Medical Research Institute of Infectious Diseases (USAMRIID). The first author (D.A.H.) conducted a literature search in conjunction with the preparation of another publication on smallpox as well as this article. The literature was reviewed and opinions were sought from experts in the diagnosis and management of smallpox, including members of the working group.

The first draft of the working group's consensus statement was the result of synthesis of information obtained in the evidence-gathering process. Members of the working group were asked to make written comments on the first draft of the document in September 1998. Suggested revisions were incorporated into the second draft of the statement. The working group was convened to review the second draft of the statement on October 30, 1998. Consensus recommendations were made and no significant disagreements existed at the conclusion of this meeting. The third draft incorporated changes suggested at the conference and working group members had an additional opportunity to suggest final revisions. The final statement incorporates all relevant evidence obtained by the literature search in conjunction with final consensus recommendations supported by all working group members.

This article is intended to provide the scientific foundation and initial framework for the detailed planning that would follow a bioterrorist attack with smallpox. This planning must encompass coordinated systems approaches to bioterrorism, including public policies and consequence management by local and regional public and private institutions. The assessment and recommendations provided herein represent the best professional judgment of the working group at this time based on data and expertise currently available. The conclusions and recommendations need to be regularly reassessed as new information becomes available.

Potential as a Bioweapon

Smallpox probably was first used as a biological weapon during the French and Indian Wars (1754-1767) by British forces in North America. Soldiers distributed blankets that had been used by smallpox patients with the intent of initiating outbreaks among American Indians.

Epidemics occurred, killing more than 50% of many affected tribes. With Edward Jenner's demonstration in 1796 that an infection caused by cowpox protected against smallpox and the rapid diffusion worldwide of the practice of cowpox inoculation (i.e., vaccination), the potential threat of smallpox as a bioweapon was greatly diminished.

A global campaign, begun in 1967 under the aegis of the World Health Organization (WHO), succeeded in eradicating smallpox in 1977. In 1980, the World Health Assembly recommended that all countries cease vaccination. A WHO expert committee recommended that all laboratories destroy their stocks of variola virus or transfer them to 1 of 2 WHO reference laboratories—the Institute of Virus Preparations in Moscow, Russia, or the Centers for Disease Control and Prevention (CDC) in Atlanta, Ga. All countries reported compliance. The WHO committee later recommended that all virus stocks be destroyed in June 1999, and the 1996 World Health Assembly concurred. In 1998, possible research uses for variola virus were reviewed by a committee of the Institute of Medicine (IOM). The IOM committee concluded, as did the preceding WHO committee, that there were research questions that might be addressed if the virus were to be retained. However, the IOM committee did not explore the costs or relative priority to be assigned to such an effort, and that committee was not asked to weigh the possible benefits resulting from such research activities contrasted with the possible benefits resulting from an international decision to destroy all virus stocks. These considerations will be weighed and decided by the 1999 World Health Assembly.

Recent allegations from Ken Alibek, a former deputy director of the Soviet Union's civilian bioweapons program, have heightened concern that smallpox might be used as a bioweapon. Alibek reported that beginning in 1980, the Soviet government embarked on a successful program to produce the smallpox virus in large quantities and adapt it for use in bombs and intercontinental ballistic missiles; the program had an industrial capacity capable of producing many tons of smallpox viruses annually. Furthermore, Alibek reports that Russia even now has a research program that seeks to produce more virulent and contagious recombinant strains. Because financial support for laboratories in Russia has sharply declined in recent years, there are increasing concerns that existing expertise and equipment might fall into non-Russian hands.

The deliberate reintroduction of smallpox as an epidemic disease would be an international crime of unprecedented proportions, but it is now regarded as a possibility. An aerosol release of variola virus would disseminate widely, given the considerable stability of the orthopoxviruses in aerosol form and the likelihood that the infectious dose is very small. Moreover, during the 1960s and 1970s in Europe, when smallpox was imported during the December to April period of high transmission, as many as 10 to 20 second-generation cases were often infected from a single case. Widespread concern and, sometimes, panic occurred, even with outbreaks of fewer than 100 cases, resulting in extensive emergency control measures.

Epidemiology

Smallpox was once worldwide in scope, and before vaccination was practiced, almost everyone eventually contracted the disease. There were 2 principal forms of the disease, variola major and a much milder form, variola minor (or alastrim). Before eradication took place, these forms could be differentiated clinically only when occurring in outbreaks; virological differentiation is now possible. Through the end of the 19th century, variola major predominated throughout the world. However, at the turn of the century, variola minor was first detected in South Africa and later in Florida, from whence it spread across the United States and into Latin America and Europe.

Typical variola major epidemics such as those occurred in Asia resulted in case-fatality rates of 30% or higher among the unvaccinated, whereas variola minor case-fatality rates were customarily 1% or less.

Smallpox spreads from person to person, primarily by droplet nuclei or aerosols expelled from the oropharynx of infected persons and by direct contact. Contaminated clothing or bed linens can also spread the virus. There are no known animal or insect reservoirs or vectors.

Historically, the rapidity of smallpox transmission throughout the population was generally slower than for such diseases as measles or chickenpox. Patients spread smallpox primarily to household members and friends; large outbreaks in schools, for example, were uncommon. This finding was accounted for in part by the fact that transmission of smallpox virus did not occur until onset of rash. By then, many patients had been confined to bed because of the high fever and malaise of the prodromal illness. Secondary cases were thus usually restricted to those who came into contact with patients, usually in the household or hospital.

The seasonal occurrence of smallpox was similar to that of chickenpox and measles—its incidence was highest during winter and early spring. This pattern was consonant with the observation that the duration of survival of orthopoxviruses in the aerosolized form was inversely proportional to both temperature and humidity. Likewise, when imported cases occurred in Europe, large outbreaks sometimes developed during the winter months and rarely in the summer.

The patient was most infectious from onset of rash through the first 7 to 10 days of rash. As scabs formed, infectivity waned rapidly. Although the scabs contained large amounts of viable virus, epidemiological and laboratory studies indicate that they were not especially infectious, presumably because the virions were bound tightly in the fibrin matrix.

The age distribution of cases depended primarily on the degree of smallpox susceptibility in the population. In most areas, cases predominated among children because adults were protected by immunity induced by vaccination or previous smallpox infection. In rural areas that had seen little vaccination or smallpox, the age distribution of cases was similar to the age distribution of the population. The age distribution pattern of cases in the United States presumably would be such if smallpox were to occur now because vaccination immunity in the population has waned so substantially.

Microbiology

Smallpox, a DNA virus, is a member of the genus orthopoxvirus. The orthopoxviruses are among the largest and most complex of all viruses. The virion is characteristically a brick-shaped structure with a diameter of about 200 nm. Three other members of this genus (monkeypox, vaccinia, and cowpox) can also infect humans, causing cutaneous lesions, but only smallpox is readily transmitted from person to person. Monkeypox, a zoonotic disease, presently is found only in tropical rain forest areas of central and western Africa and is not readily transmitted among humans. Vaccinia and cowpox seldom spread from person to person.

Pathogenesis and Clinical Presentation

Natural infection occurs following implantation of the virus on the oropharyngeal or respiratory mucosa. The infectious dose is unknown but is believed to be only a few virions. After the migration of virus to and multiplication in regional lymph nodes, an asymptomatic viremia develops on about the third or fourth day, followed by multiplication of virus in the spleen, bone marrow, and lymph nodes. A secondary viremia begins on about the eighth day and is followed by fever and toxemia. The virus, contained in leukocytes, then localizes in small blood vessels of the dermis and beneath the oral and pharyngeal mucosa and subsequently infects adjacent cells.

At the end of the 12- to 14-day incubation period (range, 7-17 days), the patient typically experiences high fever, malaise, and prostration with headache and backache and severe abdominal pain and delirium are sometimes present. A maculopapular rash then appears on the mucosa of the mouth and pharynx, face, and forearms, and spreads to the trunk and legs. Within 1 to 2 days, the rash becomes vesicular and, later, pustular. The pustules are characteristically round, tense, and deeply embedded in the dermis; crusts begin to form on about the eighth or ninth day of rash. As the patient recovers, the scabs separate and characteristic pitted scarring gradually develops. The scars are most evident on the face and result from the destruction of sebaceous glands followed by shrinking of granulation tissue and fibrosis.

The lesions that first appear in the mouth and pharynx ulcerate quickly because of the absence of a stratum corneum, releasing large amounts of virus into the saliva. Virus titers in saliva are highest during the first week of illness, corresponding with the period during which patients are most infectious. Although the virus in some instances can be detected in swabs taken from the oropharynx as many as 5 to 6 days before the rash develops, transmission does not occur during this period.

Except for the lesions in the skin and mucous membranes and reticulum cell hyperplasia, other organs are seldom involved. Secondary bacterial infection is not common, and death, which usually occurs during the second week of illness, most likely results from the toxemia associated with circulating immune complexes and soluble variola antigens. Encephalitis sometimes ensues that is indistinguishable from the acute perivascular demyelination observed as a complication of infection due to vaccinia, measles, or varicella.

Neutralizing antibodies can be detected by the sixth day of rash and remain at high titers for many years. Hemagglutinin-inhibiting antibodies can be detected on about the sixth day of rash, or about 21 days after infection, and complement-fixing antibodies appear approximately 2 days later. Within 5 years, hemagglutinin-inhibiting antibodies decline to low levels and complement-fixing antibodies rarely persist for longer than 6 months.

Although at least 90% of smallpox cases are clinically characteristic and readily diagnosed in endemic areas, 2 other forms of smallpox are difficult to recognize—hemorrhagic and malignant. Hemorrhagic cases are uniformly fatal and occur among all ages and in both sexes, but pregnant women appear to be unusually susceptible. Illness usually begins with a somewhat shorter incubation period and is characterized by a severely prostrating prodromal illness with high fever and head, back, and abdominal pain. Soon thereafter, a dusky erythema develops, followed by petechiae and frank hemorrhages into the skin and mucous membranes. Death usually occurs by the fifth or sixth day after onset of rash.

In the frequently fatal malignant form, the abrupt onset and prostrating constitutional symptoms are similar. The confluent lesions develop slowly, never progressing to the pustular stage but remaining soft, flattened, and velvety to the touch. The skin has the appearance of a fine-grained, reddish-colored crepe rubber, sometimes with hemorrhages. If the patient survives, the lesions gradually disappear without forming scabs or, in severe cases, large amounts of epidermis might peel away.

The illness associated with variola minor is generally less severe, with fewer constitutional symptoms and a sparser rash. A milder form of disease is also seen among those who have residual immunity from previous vaccination. In partially immune persons, the rash tends to be atypical and more scant and the evolution of the lesions more rapid.

There is little information about how individuals with different types of immune deficiency responded to natural smallpox infection. Smallpox was eradicated before human immunodeficiency virus (HIV) was identified and before suitable techniques became available for measuring cell-mediated immunity. However, it is probable that the underlying cause of some cases of malignant and hemorrhagic smallpox resulted from defective immune responses. Vaccination of immune-deficient persons sometimes resulted in a continually spreading primary lesion, persistent viremia, and secondary viral infection of many organs. One such case is documented to have occurred in a vaccinated soldier who had HIV infection.

Diagnosis

The discovery of a single suspected case of smallpox must be treated as an international health emergency and be brought immediately to the attention of national officials through local and state health authorities.

The majority of smallpox cases present with a characteristic rash that is centrifugal in distribution, i.e., most dense on the face and extremities. The lesions appear during a 1- to 2-day period and evolve at the same rate. On any given part of the body, they are generally at the same stage of development. In varicella (chickenpox), the disease most frequently confused with smallpox, new lesions appear in crops every few days and lesions at very different stages of maturation (ie, vesicles, pustules, and scabs) are found in adjacent areas of skin. Varicella lesions are much more superficial and are almost never found on the palms and soles. The distribution of varicella lesions is centripetal, with a greater concentration of lesions on the trunk than on the face and extremities.

The signs and symptoms of both hemorrhagic and malignant smallpox were such that smallpox was seldom suspected until more typical cases were seen and it was recognized that a smallpox outbreak was in progress. Hemorrhagic cases were most often initially identified as meningococcemia or severe acute leukemia. Malignant cases likewise posed diagnostic problems, most often being mistaken for hemorrhagic chickenpox or prompting surgery because of severe abdominal pain.

Laboratory confirmation of the diagnosis in a smallpox outbreak is important. Specimens should be collected by someone who has recently been vaccinated (or is vaccinated that day) and who wears gloves and a mask. To obtain vesicular or pustular fluid, it is often necessary to open lesions with the blunt edge of a scalpel. The fluid can then be harvested on a cotton swab. Scabs can be picked off with forceps. Specimens should be deposited in a vacutainer tube that should be sealed with adhesive tape at the juncture of stopper and tube. This tube, in turn, should be enclosed in a second durable, watertight container. State or local health department laboratories should immediately be contacted regarding the shipping of specimens. Laboratory examination requires high-containment (BL-4) facilities and should be undertaken only in designated laboratories with the appropriate training and equipment. Once it is established that the epidemic is caused by smallpox virus, clinically typical cases would not require further laboratory confirmation.

Smallpox infection can be rapidly confirmed in the laboratory by electron microscopic examination of vesicular or pustular fluid or scabs. Although all orthopoxviruses exhibit identically appearing brick-shaped virions, history taking and clinical picture readily identify cowpox and vaccinia. Although smallpox and monkeypox virions may be indistinguishable, naturally occurring monkeypox is found only in tropical rain forest areas of Africa. Definitive laboratory identification and characterization of the virus involves growth of the virus in cell culture or on chorioallantoic egg membrane and characterization of strains by use of various biologic assays, including polymerase chain reaction techniques and restriction fragment-length polymorphisms. The latter studies can be completed within a few hours.

Pre-exposure Preventive Vaccination

Before 1972, smallpox vaccination was recommended for all US children at age 1 year. Most states required that each child be vaccinated before school entry. The only other requirement for vaccination was for military recruits and tourists visiting foreign countries. Most countries required that the individual be successfully vaccinated within a 3-year period prior to entering the country. Routine vaccination in the United States stopped in 1972 and since then, few persons younger than 27 years have been vaccinated. The US Census Bureau reported that in 1998, approximately 114 million persons, or 42% of the US population, were aged 29 years or younger.

In addition, the immune status of those who were vaccinated more than 27 years ago is not clear. The duration of immunity, based on the experience of naturally exposed susceptible persons, has never been satisfactorily measured. Neutralizing antibodies are reported to reflect levels of protection, although this has not been validated in the field. These antibodies have been shown to decline substantially during a 5- to 10-year period. Thus, even those who received the recommended single-dose vaccination as children do not have lifelong immunity. However, among a group who had been vaccinated at birth and at ages 8 and 18 years as part of a study, neutralizing antibody levels remained stable during a 30-year period. Because comparatively few persons today have been successfully vaccinated on more than 1 occasion, it must be assumed that the population at large is highly susceptible to infection.

In the United States, a limited reserve supply of vaccine that was produced by Wyeth Laboratories, Lancaster, Pa, in the 1970s is in storage. This supply is believed to be sufficient to vaccinate between 6 and 7 million persons. This vaccine, now under the control of the CDC, consists of vaccine virus grown on scarified calves. After purification, it was freeze-dried in rubber-stoppered vials that contain sufficient vaccine for at least 50 doses when a bifurcated needle is used. It is stored at -20°C (James LeDuc, PhD, oral communication, 1998). Although quantities of vaccine have also been retained by a number of other countries, none have reserves large enough to meet more than their own potential emergency needs. WHO has 500,000 doses.

There are no manufacturers now equipped to produce smallpox vaccine in large quantities. The development and licensure of a tissue cell culture vaccine and the establishment of a new vaccine production facility is estimated to require at least 36 months. Because of the small amounts of vaccine available, a preventive vaccination program to protect individuals such as emergency and health care personnel is not an option at this time. When additional supplies of vaccine are procured, a decision to undertake preventive vaccination of some portion of the population will have to weigh the relative risk of vaccination complications against the threat of contracting smallpox.

A further deterrent to extensive vaccination is the fact that presently available supplies of vaccinia immune globulin (VIG), also maintained by the CDC, are very limited in quantity. The working group recommends VIG for the treatment of severe cutaneous reactions occurring as a complication of vaccination. Vaccinia immune globulin has also been given along with vaccination to protect those who needed vaccination but who were at risk of experiencing vaccine-related complications. It has been estimated that if 1 million persons were vaccinated, as many as 250 persons would experience adverse reactions of a type that would require administration of VIG (James LeDuc, PhD, oral communication, 1998). How much VIG would be needed to administer with vaccine to those at risk is unknown.

Post-exposure Therapy

At this time, the best that can be offered to the patient infected with smallpox is supportive therapy plus antibiotics as indicated for treatment of occasional secondary bacterial infections. No antiviral substances have yet proved effective for the treatment of smallpox, and the working group is not aware of any reports that suggest any antiviral product is therapeutic.

Encouraging initial reports in the 1960s describing the therapeutic benefits of the thiosemicarbazones, cytosine arabinoside, and adenine arabinoside proved questionable on further study.

Recent studies on tissue culture, mice, and a small number of monkeys have suggested the possibility that cidofovir, a nucleoside analog DNA polymerase inhibitor, might prove useful in preventing smallpox infection if administered within 1 or 2 days after exposure (John Huggins, PhD, oral communication, 1998). At this time, there is no evidence that cidofovir is more effective than vaccination in this early period. Moreover, the potential utility of this drug is limited, given the fact that it must be administered intravenously and its use is often accompanied by serious renal toxicity.

Post-exposure Infection Control

A smallpox outbreak poses difficult public health problems because of the ability of the virus to continue to spread throughout the population unless checked by vaccination and/or isolation of patients and their close contacts.

A clandestine aerosol release of smallpox, even if it infected only 50 to 100 persons to produce the first generation of cases, would rapidly spread in a now highly susceptible population, expanding by a factor of 10 to 20 times or more with each generation of cases." Between the time of an aerosol release of smallpox virus and diagnosis of the first cases, an interval as long as 2 weeks or more is apt to occur because of the average incubation period of 12 to 14 days and the lapse of several additional days before a rash was sufficiently distinct to suggest the diagnosis of smallpox. By that time, there would be no risk of further environmental exposure from the original aerosol release because the virus is fully inactivated within 2 days.

As soon as the diagnosis of smallpox is made, all individuals in whom smallpox is suspected should be isolated immediately and all household and other face-to-face contacts should be vaccinated and placed under surveillance. Because the widespread dissemination of smallpox virus by aerosol poses a serious threat in hospitals, patients should be isolated in the home or other nonhospital facility whenever possible. Home care for most patients is a reasonable approach, given the fact that little can be done for a patient other than to offer supportive therapy.

In the event of an aerosol release of smallpox and a subsequent outbreak, the rationale for vaccinating patients suspected to have smallpox at this time is to ensure that some with a mistaken diagnosis are not placed at risk of acquiring smallpox. Vaccination administered within the first few days after exposure and perhaps as late as 4 days may prevent or significantly ameliorate subsequent illness. An emergency vaccination program is also indicated that would include all health care workers at clinics or hospitals that might receive patients; all other essential disaster response personnel, such as police, firefighters, transit workers, public health staff, and emergency management staff; and mortuary staff who might have to handle bodies. The working group recommends that all such personnel for whom vaccination is not contraindicated should be vaccinated immediately irrespective of prior vaccination status.

Vaccination administered within 4 days of first exposure has been shown to offer some protection against acquiring infection and significant protection against a fatal outcome. Those who have been vaccinated at some time in the past will normally exhibit an accelerated immune response. Thus, it would be prudent, when possible, to assign those who had been previously vaccinated to duties involving close patient contact.

It is important that discretion be used in identifying contacts of patients to ensure, to the extent that is possible, that vaccination and adequate surveillance measures are focused on those at greatest risk. Specifically, it is recommended that *contacts* be defined as persons who have been in the same household as the infected individual or who have been in face-to-face contact with the patient after the onset of fever. Experience during the smallpox global eradication program showed that patients did not transmit infection until after the prodromal fever had given way to the rash stage of illness.

Isolation of all contacts of exposed patients would be logistically difficult and, in practice, should not be necessary. Because contacts, even if infected, are not contagious until onset of rash, a practical strategy calls for all contacts to have temperatures checked at least once each day, preferably in the evening. Any increase in temperature higher than 38°C (101°F) during the 17-day period following last exposure to the case would suggest the possible development of smallpox and be cause for isolating the patient immediately, preferably at home, until it could be determined clinically and/or by laboratory examination whether the contact had smallpox. All close contacts of the patients should be promptly vaccinated.

Although cooperation by most patients and contacts in observing isolation could be ensured through counseling and persuasion, there may be some for whom forcible quarantine required. Some states and cities in the United States, but not all, confer broad discretionary powers on health authorities to ensure the safety of the public's health and, at one time, this included powers to quarantine. Under epidemic circumstances, this could be an important power to have. Thus, each state and city should review its statutes as part of its preparedness activities.

During the smallpox epidemics in the 1960s and 1970s in Europe, there was considerable public alarm whenever outbreaks occurred and, often, a demand for mass vaccination throughout a very widespread area, even when the vaccination coverage of the population was high. In the United States, where few people now have protective levels of immunity, such levels of concern must be anticipated. However, the US vaccine supply is limited at present; thus, vaccine would have to be carefully conserved and used in conjunction with measures to implement rapid isolation of smallpox patients.

Hospital Epidemiology and Infection Control

Smallpox transmission within hospitals has long been recognized as a serious problem. For this reason, separate hospitals for smallpox patients were used for more than 200 years. Throughout the 1970s, both England and Germany had fully equipped standby hospitals in case smallpox should be imported. Infections acquired in hospitals may occur as the result of droplets spread from patients to staff and visitors in reasonably close contact or by a fine particle aerosol. In 1 such occurrence in Germany, a smallpox patient with a cough, although isolated in a single room, infected persons on 3 floors of a hospital. Persons with the usually fatal hemorrhagic or malignant forms of the disease pose a special problem because they often remain undiagnosed until they are near death and extremely contagious. A number of outbreaks have occurred in laundry workers who handled linens and blankets used by patients. The working group recommends that in an outbreak setting, all hospital employees as well as patients in the hospital be vaccinated. For individuals who are immunocompromised or for whom vaccination is otherwise contraindicated, VIG should be provided, if available. If it is not available, a judgment will have to be made regarding the relative risks of acquiring the disease in contrast with the risks associated with vaccination.

In the event of a limited outbreak with few cases, patients should be admitted to the hospital and confined to rooms that are under negative pressure and equipped with high-efficiency particulate air filtration. In larger outbreaks, home isolation and care should be the objective for most patients. However, not all will be able to be so accommodated and, to limit nosocomial infections; authorities should consider the possibility of designating a specific hospital or hospitals for smallpox care. All persons isolated as such and those caring for them should be immediately vaccinated. Employees for whom vaccination is contraindicated should be furloughed.

Standard precautions using gloves, gowns, and masks should be observed. All laundry and waste should be placed in biohazard bags and autoclaved before being laundered or incinerated. A special protocol should be developed for decontaminating rooms after they are vacated by patients. Laboratory examination requires high-containment (BL-4) facilities and should be undertaken only in designated laboratories with the appropriate trained personnel and equipment. Specific recommendations for safe specimen transport are described in the section on "Differential Diagnosis and Diagnostic Tests."

Protecting against the explosive spread of virus from the hemorrhagic or malignant case is difficult. Such cases occurring during the course of an outbreak may be detected if staff is alert to the possibility that any severe, acute, prostrating illness must be considered smallpox until proven otherwise. Patients who die of smallpox should be cremated whenever possible and mortuary workers should be vaccinated.

Vaccine Administration and Complications

Smallpox vaccine is currently approved by the US Food and Drug Administration (FDA) for use only in persons in special-risk categories, including laboratory workers directly involved with smallpox or closely related orthopoxviruses. Under epidemic circumstances, widespread vaccination would be indicated, as recommended by the working group.

Vaccination has been successfully and safely administered to persons of all ages, from birth onward. However, there are certain groups for whom elective vaccination has not been recommended because of the risk of complications. Under epidemic circumstances, however, such contraindications will have to be weighed against the grave risks posed by smallpox. If available, VIG can be administered concomitantly with vaccination to minimize the risk of complications in these persons.

Vaccination is normally performed using the bifurcated needle. A sterile needle is inserted into an ampoule of reconstituted vaccine and, on withdrawal, a droplet of vaccine sufficient for vaccination is held by capillarity between the 2 tines. The needle is held at right angles to the skin; the wrist of the vaccinator rests against the arm. Fifteen perpendicular strokes of the needle are rapidly made in an area of about 5 mm in diameter. The strokes should be sufficiently vigorous so that a trace of blood appears at the vaccination site after 15 to 30 seconds. After vaccination, excess vaccine should be wiped from the site with gauze that should be discarded in a hazardous waste receptacle. The site should be covered with a loose, nonocclusive bandage to deter the individual from touching the site and perhaps transferring virus to other parts of the body.

After about 3 days, a red papule appears at the vaccination site and becomes vesicular on about the fifth day. By the seventh day, it becomes the typical Jennerian pustule—whitish, umbilicated, multilocular, containing turbid lymph and surrounded by an erythematous areola that may continue to expand for 3 more days. Regional lymphadenopathy and fever is not uncommon. As many as 70% of children have 1 or more days of temperature higher than 39°C (100°F) between days 4 and 14. The pustule gradually dries, leaving a dark crust, which normally falls off after about 3 weeks.

A successful vaccination for those with partial immunity may manifest a gradient of responses. These range from what appears to be a primary take (as described herein) to an accelerated reaction in which there may be little more than a papule surrounded by erythema that reaches a peak between 3 and 7 days. A response that reaches a peak in erythema within 48 hours represents a hypersensitivity reaction and does not signify that growth of the vaccinia virus has occurred. Persons exhibiting such a reaction should be revaccinated.

Complications

The frequency of complications associated with use of the New York Board of Health strain (the strain used throughout the United States and Canada for vaccine) is the lowest for any established vaccinia virus strain, but the risks are not inconsequential.

Post-vaccinial Encephalitis

Post-vaccinial encephalitis occurred at a rate of 1 case per 300,000 vaccinations and was observed only in primary vaccinees; one fourth of these cases were fatal and several had permanent neurological residua. Between 8 and 15 days after vaccination, encephalitic symptoms developed—fever, headache, vomiting, drowsiness, and, sometimes, spastic paralysis, meningitic signs, coma, and convulsions. Cerebrospinal fluid usually showed a pleocytosis. Recovery was either complete or associated with residual paralysis and other central nervous system symptoms and, sometimes, death. There was no treatment.

Progressive Vaccinia (Vaccinia Gangrenosa)

Cases of progressive vaccinia occurred both among primary vaccinees and revaccinees. It was a frequently fatal complication among those with immune deficiency disorders. The vaccinial lesion failed to heal and progressed to involve adjacent skin with necrosis of tissue, spreading to other parts of the skin, to bones, and to viscera. Vaccinia immune globulin was used for this problem. One case in a soldier with acquired immunodeficiency syndrome was successfully treated with VIG and ribavirin. These treatment strategies were off-label and would be considered experimental.

Eczema Vaccinatum

A sometimes serious complication, eczema vaccinatum occurred in some vaccinees and contacts with either active or healed eczema. Vaccinial skin lesions extended to cover all or most of the area once or currently afflicted with eczema. Vaccinia immune globulin was therapeutic.

Generalized Vaccinia

A secondary eruption almost always following primary vaccination, generalized vaccinia resulted from blood-borne dissemination of virus. Lesions emerged between 6 and 9 days after vaccination and were either few in numbers or generalized. This complication was usually self-limited. In severe cases, VIG was indicated.

Inadvertent Inoculation

Transmission to close contacts or autoinoculation to sites such as face, eyelid, mouth, and genitalia sometimes occurred. Most lesions healed without incident, although VIG was useful in some cases of periocular implantation.

Miscellaneous

Many different rashes have been associated with vaccination. Most common are erythema multiforme and variously distributed urticarial, maculopapular, and blotchy erythematous eruptions, which normally clear without therapy.

Groups at Special Risk for Complications

Consensus recommendations for special-risk groups as set forth herein reflect the best clinical and science-based judgment of the working group and do not necessarily correspond to FDA-approved uses.

Five groups of persons are ordinarily considered at special risk of smallpox vaccine complications:

- Persons with eczema or other significant exfoliative skin conditions;
- Patients with leukemia, lymphoma, or generalized malignancy who are receiving therapy with alkylating agents, antimetabolites, radiation, or large doses of corticosteroids;
- Patients with HIV infection;
- Persons with hereditary immune deficiency disorders; and
- Pregnant women.

If persons with contraindications have been in close contact with a smallpox patient or the individual is at risk for occupational reasons, VIG, if available, may be given simultaneously with vaccination in a dose of 0.3 mL/kg of body weight to prevent complications. This does not alter vaccine efficacy. If VIG is not available, vaccine administration may still be warranted, given the far higher risk of an adverse outcome from smallpox infection than from vaccination.

VIG Therapy for Complications

Vaccinia immune globulin is valuable in treating patients with progressive vaccinia, eczema vaccinatum, severe generalized vaccinia, and periocular infections resulting from inadvertent inoculation. It is administered intramuscularly in a dose of 0.6 mL/kg of body weight. Because the dose is large (eg, 42 mL for a person weighing 70 kg), the product is given intramuscularly in divided doses over a 24- to 36-hour period and may be repeated, if necessary, after 2 to 3 days if improvement is not occurring. Because the availability of VIG is so limited, its use should be reserved for the most serious cases. Vaccinia immune globulin, as well as vaccinia vaccine, is made available by the CDC through state health departments. Consultative assistance in the diagnosis and management of patients with complications can be obtained through state health departments.

Decontamination

Vaccinia virus, if released as an aerosol and not exposed to UV light, may persist for as long as 24 hours or somewhat longer under favorable conditions. It is believed that variola virus would exhibit similar properties. However, by the time patients had become ill and it had been determined that an aerosol release of smallpox virus had occurred; there would be no viable smallpox virus in the environment. Vaccinia virus, if released as an aerosol, is almost completely destroyed within 6 hours in an atmosphere of high temperature (31°C-33°C) and humidity (80%). In cooler temperatures (10°C-11°C) and lower humidity (20%), nearly two thirds of a vaccinia aerosol survives for as long as 24 hours. It is believed that variola would behave similarly.

The occurrence of smallpox infection among personnel who handled laundry from infected patients is well documented and it is believed that virus in such material remains viable for extended periods. Thus, special precautions need to be taken to ensure that all bedding and clothing of smallpox patients is autoclaved or laundered in hot water to which bleach has been added. Disinfectants that are used for standard hospital infection control, such as hypochlorite and quaternary ammonia, are effective for cleaning surfaces possibly contaminated with virus.

Virus in scabs is more durable. At a temperature of 35°C and 65% relative humidity, the virus has persisted for 3 weeks. At cooler temperatures (26°C), the virus has survived for 8 weeks at high relative humidity and 12 weeks at a relative humidity less than 10%. Dutch investigators demonstrated that it was possible to isolate variola virus from scabs that had been sitting on a shelf for 13 years. It is unlikely, however, that the smallpox virus, bound in the fibrin matrix of a scab, is infectious in humans. This is borne out by studies conducted during the eradication program and by surveillance for cases in newly smallpox-free areas. It was reasoned that if the virus were able to persist in nature and infect humans, there would be cases occurring for which no source could be identified. Cases of this type were not observed. Rather, when cases were found, there were antecedent human cases with which they had direct contact.

Priority should be directed to 3 areas of smallpox research: vaccines, immunotherapy and drugs, and diagnostics. The working group recommends that an emergency stockpile of at least 40 million doses of vaccine and a standby manufacturing capacity to produce more is a critical need. At a minimum, this quantity of vaccine would be needed in the control of an epidemic during the first 4 to 8 weeks after an attack. Smallpox vaccine, contained in glass-sealed ampoules and stored at -20°C, retains its potency almost indefinitely. However, several steps are necessary before manufacturing can begin. The traditional method for producing vaccine on the scarified flank of a calf is no longer acceptable because the product inevitably contains some microbial contaminants, however stringent the purification measures. Contemporary vaccines require the use of tissue cell cultures. Thus, as a first step, the traditional New York Board of Health strain needs to be grown in a suitable tissue cell culture and comparative studies performed of the reactogenicity and immunogenicity of calf-derived and tissue cell culture vaccines. This should be a comparatively straightforward exercise. The cost of such a stockpile should be comparatively modest because the vaccine would be packaged in 50-dose rather than costly single-dose containers. In the mid-1970s, 40 million doses would have cost less than $5 million (D.A.H., unpublished data, 1975).

The frequency of vaccine complications is sufficiently great to recommend development, if possible, of a more attenuated strain that, hopefully, would retain full efficacy. Development of an entirely new, genetically engineered strain would be both costly and time consuming. Moreover, it would be difficult at this time to justify its use in large numbers of human subjects to evaluate safety. There is, however, a candidate attenuated strain that was developed and field tested in Japan in the mid-1970s (a Lister strain–derived vaccine that has been produced in volume in rabbit kidney cell culture and has been given to more than 100,000 persons in Japan). Research showed no severe complications among the first 30,000 vaccinees. The cutaneous responses to vaccination were much less severe and far fewer vaccinees developed fever. More than 95% developed a Jennerian pustule; immunogenicity, as measured by neutralizing antibody, was slightly lower than for nonattenuated strains.

Vaccinia immune globulin has been used for the treatment of vaccine complications and for administration with vaccine to those for whom vaccine is otherwise contraindicated. Production of VIG should be a high priority for research. An alternative to VIG is also needed because VIG is difficult to produce and cumbersome to administer. Immunotherapy using humanized monoclonal antibodies is an alternative that should be explored. Studies of antiviral agents or drugs already approved or near approval for marketing for use in other viral diseases, have suggested that 1 or more such products might prove useful.

Finally, a simple, rapid diagnostic test to identify variola virus in the oropharynx during the prodrome or early in the exanthematous phase of illness would be of considerable help in triage of suspected patients during the course of an outbreak.

The specter of resurgent smallpox is ominous, especially given the enormous efforts that have been made to eradicate what has been characterized as the most devastating of all the pestilential diseases. Unfortunately, the threat of an aerosol release of smallpox is real and the potential for a catastrophic scenario is great unless effective control measures can quickly be brought to bear.

Early detection, isolation of infected individuals, surveillance of contacts, and a focused selective vaccination program are the essential items of a control program. Educating health care professionals about the diagnostic features of smallpox should permit early detection; advance regionwide planning for isolation and care of infected individuals in their homes as appropriate and in hospitals when home care is not an option will be critical to deter spread. Ultimately, success in controlling a burgeoning epidemic will depend on the availability of adequate supplies of vaccine and VIG. An adequate stockpile of those commodities would offer a relatively inexpensive safeguard against tragedy.

Bibliography

Abuza, Zachary. *Militant Islam in Southeast Asia*. Boulder, CO: Lynne Rienner, 2003.

Acquaviva, Mike. *Terrorism: Special Studies*. Bethesda, MD: University Publications of America, 1989.

Adams, James. *Next World War: Computers Are the Weapons and the Front Line is Everywhere*. New York: Simon & Schuster, 1998.

Adams, James. *Secret Armies: Inside the American, Soviet and European Special Forces*. New York: Atlantic Monthly Press, 1987.

Adams, Neal. *Terrorism & Oil*. Tulsa, OK: PennWell, 2003.

Adams, Simon. *All the Troubles: Terrorism, War and the World After 9/11*. North Fremantle, Australia: Fremantle Arts Centre Press, 2004.

Addison, Michael. *Violent Politics: Strategies of Internal Conflict*. Basingstoke: Palgrave, 2002.

Akhahenda, Elijah F. *When Blood and Tears United a Country: The Bombing of the American Embassy in Kenya*. Lanham, MD: University Press of America, 2002.

Akhavan, Jacqueline. *Chemistry of Explosives*. Cambridge, MA: Royal Society of Chemistry Information Service, 1998.

Alexander, Yonah. *Aerial Piracy and Aviation Security*. International Studies on Terrorism; Boston, MA: M. Nijhoff, 1990.

Alexander, Yonah. *Cyber Terrorism and Information Warfare: Threats and Responses*. Terrorism Documents of International Local Control. Ardsley, NY: Transnational Publishers, 2001.

Alexander, Yonah. *Middle East Terrorism: Current Threats and Future Prospects*. International Library of Terrorism; 5. New York: G.K. Hall & Co., 1994.

Alexander, Yonah. *Middle East Terrorism: Selected Group Profiles*. Washington, DC: Jewish Institute for National Security Affairs, 1994.

Alexander, Yonah. *Super Terrorism: Biological Chemical and Nuclear*. Ardsley, NY: Transnational Publishers, 2001.

Alexander, Yonah. *Terrorism and Medical Responses: U.S. Lessons and Policy Implications*. Ardsley, NY: Transnational, 2001.

Alexander, Yonah; Latter, Richard, editors, *Terrorism and the Media: Dilemmas for Government, Journalists and the Public*. Washington, DC: Brassey's, 1990.

Allison, Graham. *Avoiding Nuclear Anarchy: Containing the Threat of Loose Russian Nuclear and Fissile Material*. Cambridge, MA: MIT Press, 1996.

Anti-Defamation League, *Beyond the Bombing: The Militia Menace Grows*. New York: Anti-Defamation League, 1995.

Anti-Defamation League, *High-Tech Hate: Extremist Use of the Internet*. New York: Anti-Defamation League, 1997.

Arquilla, John. *Networks and Netwars: The Future of Terror, Crime, and Militancy*. Santa Monica, CA: RAND, 2001.

Arterburn, Stephen. *130 Questions Children Ask About War and Terrorists*. Wheaton, IL: Tyndale House, 2002.

As'ad, AbuKhalil. *Osama bin Laden & the Taliban:*

Consequences of U.S. Foreign Policy. New York: Seven Stories Press, 2002.

Ascher, Michael S. *Countering Agricultural Bioterrorism*. "Committee on Biological Threats to Agricultural Plants and Animals". Washington, DC: National Academies Press, 2003.

Austin, Linda S. *Responding to Disaster: A Guide for Mental Health Professionals*. Washington, DC: American Psychiatric Press, 1992.

Australian Government, *Transnational Terrorism: The Threat to Australia*. Australia: Commonwealth of Australia, 2004.

Baker, David. *Biological, Nuclear, and Chemical Weapons*. Vero Beach, FL: Rourke, 2006. Juvenile Audience.

Ballard, James David. *Terrorism, Media and Public Policy: The Oklahoma City Bombing*. Hampton Press communication series. Cresskill, NJ: Hampton Press, 2005.

Balmer, Brian. *Britain and Biological Warfare: Expert Advice and Science Policy, 1930-65*. New York: Palgrave, 2001.

Barnaby, Frank. *How Nuclear Weapons Spread: Nuclear-Weapon Proliferation in the 1990s*. New York: Routledge, 1993.

Barnaby, Wendy. *The Plague Makers: The Secret World of Biological Warfare*. 3rd edition. New York: Continuum, 2002.

Bastin, John P. *Brady Pocket Reference for Chemical, Biological, and Radiologic Agents*. Upper Saddle River, NJ: Pearson Prentice Hall, 2005.

Bell, J. Bowyer. *The Gun in Politics: An Analysis of Irish Political Conflict, 1916-1986*. New Brunswick, NJ: Transaction Publishers, 1987.

Carr, Caleb. *Lessons of Terror: A History of Warfare Against Civilians: Why it Has Always Failed and Why it Will Fail Again*. New York: Random House, 2002.

Carus, W. Seth. *Threat of Bioterrorism*. Washington, DC:

National Defense University, Institute for National Strategic Studies, 1997.

Cashman, John R. *Emergency Response to Chemical and Biological Agents*. New York: Lewis, 2000.

Casil, Amy Sterling. *Coping With Terrorism*. New York: Rosen Publishing, 2004. Juvenile Audience.

Dando, Malcolm. *Preventing Biological Warfare: The Failure of American Leadership*. New York: Palgrave, 2002.

Dando, Malcolm. *The New Biological Weapons: Threat, Proliferation, and Control*. Boulder, CO: Lynne Rienner Publishers, 2001. Davids, Douglas J. *Narco-Terrorism: A Unified Strategy to Fight a Growing Terrorist Menace*. Ardsley, NY: Transnational Publishers, 2002.

Davis, Jim A. *The Gathering Biological Warfare Storm*. Westport, CT: Praeger, 2004.

Davis, Lee. *Man-made Catastrophes: From the Burning of Rome to the Lockerbie Crash*. New York: Facts on File, 1993.

Davis, Lynn E. *Individual Preparedness and Response to Chemical, Radiological, Nuclear, and Biological Terrorist Attacks*. Santa Monica, CA: RAND, 2003.

Dewar, Michael. *Weapons and Equipment of Counter-Terrorism*. 2nd ed. New York: Sterling, 1995.

Dobson, Christopher. *Terrorists: Their Weapons, Leaders and Tactics*. Rev. ed. New York: Facts on File, 1982.

Ellis, John. *Police Analysis and Planning for Chemical Biological and Radiological Attacks*. Springfield, IL: C.C. Thomas, 1999.

Ellison, D. Hank. *Handbook of Chemical and Biological Warfare Agents*. Boca Raton, FL: CRC Press LLC, 1999.

Epstein, Joshua M. *Toward a Containment Strategy For Smallpox Bioterror: An Individual-Based Computational Approach*. Washington, DC: Brookings Institution Press, 2004.

Geissler, Erhard. *Biological and Toxin Weapons: Research, Development, and Use From the Middle Ages to 1945*. New York: Oxford University Press, 1999.

Gerberding, Julie. *CDC Responds: Bioterrorism & the Healthcare Epidemiology/Infection Control Team*. Videocassette (VHS) 90 minutes. Atlanta, GA: Centers for Disease Control and Prevention, 2001.

Ghosh, Tushar K. *Science and Technology of Terrorism and Counterterrorism*. New York: Dekker, 2002.

Hippchen, Leonard J. *Terrorism, International Crime, and Arms Control*. Springfield, IL: C.C. Thomas, 1982.

Hoenig, Steven. *Handbook of Chemical Warfare and Terrorism*. Westport, CT: Greenwood Press, 2002.

Jalazai, Musa Khan, editor. *Terrorism and Ethnic Violence in South Asia*. Lahore: Publishers Emporium, 1995.

Jenkins, Brian M. *High Technology Terrorism and Surrogate War: The Impact of New Technology on Low-Level Violence*. Santa Monica, CA: RAND, 1975.

Jenkins, Brian M. *International Terrorism: A New Kind of Warfare*. Santa Monica, CA: RAND, 1974.

Kallen, Stuart A. *Biological and Chemical Weapons*. At Issue, National Security. Detroit, MI: Greenhaven Press, 2006.

Karasik, Theodore. *Toxic Warfare*. Santa Monica, CA: RAND, 2002.

Karl, Jonathan. *Right to Bear Arms: The Rise of America's New Militias*. New York: Harper Paperbacks, 1995.

Lakos, Amos. *Nuclear Terrorism Threat: A Bibliography*. Monticello, IL: Vance Bibliographies, 1985.

LaPierre, Wayne. *Guns, Freedom and Terrorism*. Nashville, TN: WND Books, 2003.

Lutz, James M. and Lutz, Brenda J. *Terrorism: Origins and Evolution*. New York: Palgrave MacMillian, 2005.

Malllin, Jay. *Terror and Urban Guerillas: A Study of Tactics and Documents*. Coral Gables, FL: University of Miami Press, 1971.

Norris, John. *NBC: Nuclear, Biological and Chemical Warfare on the Modern Battlefield*. London: Brassey's, 1997.

Norton, Augustus R. *Studies in Nuclear Terrorism*. Boston, MA: G.K. Hall & Co., 1979.

Norton, Augustus R. *Understanding the Nuclear Terrorism Problem*. Gaithersburg, MD: International Association of Chiefs of Police, 1979.

O'Day, Alan. *Weapons of Mass Destruction and Terrorism*. The international library of essays in terrorism. Burlington, VT: Ashgate, 2005.

Paletz, David L. *Terrorism and the Media*. Newbury Park, CA: Sage, 1992.

Poolos, J. *The Nerve Gas Attack on the Tokyo Subway*. New York: Rosen Pub, 2002. Juvenile Audience.

Rattray, Gregory J. *Strategic Warfare in Cyberspace*. Cambridge, MA: MIT Press, 2001.

Schamis, Gerardo Jorge. *War and Terrorism in International Affairs*. New Brunswick, NJ: Transaction Books, 1980.

Schlagheck, Donna. *International Terrorism: An Introduction to the Concepts and Actors*. Lexington, MA: Lexington Books, 1988.

Schmid, Alex. *Violence as Communication: Insurgent Terrorism and the Western News Media*. Beverly Hills, CA: Sage, 1982.

Stewart, Charles. *Weapons of Mass Casualties and Terrorism Response Handbook*. Sudbury, MA: Jones and Bartlett, 2005.

U. S. Office of Technology Assessment, *Technology Against Terrorism: Structuring Security*. Irvine, CA: Global Professional Publications, 1993.

Van Der Veer, Peter. *Media, War, and Terrorism: Responses from the Middle East and Asia*. New York: Curzon, 2004.

Van Krieken, Peter J. *Terrorism and the International Legal Order: With Special Reference to the UN, the EU and Cross-Order Aspects*. The Hague: TMC Asser, 2002.

Venkatraman, S. *Media in a Terrorized World: Reflections in the Wake of 9/11*. New York: Eastern Universities Press, 2004.

Venske, Ben. *First Responder Chem-Bio Handbook: Practical Manual for On-Scene Responders*. Alexandria, VA: Tempest, 1999.

Verton, Dan. *Black Ice: The Invisible Threat of Cyber-Terrorism*. New York: McGraw-Hill, 2003.

Ward, Richard H. *Terrorism and the New World Disorder*. Chicago, IL: Office of International Criminal Justice, University of Illinois at Chicago, 1998.

Waugh, William L. *International Terrorism: How Nations Respond to Terrorists*. Salisbury, NC: Documentary Publications, 1982.

Waugh, William L. *Living With Hazards, Dealing with Disasters: An Introduction to Emergency Management*. Armonk, NY: M.E. Sharpe, 2000.

Webster, William H. *Wild Atom: Nuclear Terrorism*. Washington, DC: Center for Strategic and International Studies, 1998.

Wecht, Cyril H. *Forensic Aspects of Chemical and Biological Terrorism*. Tucson, AZ: Lawyers and Judges Pub, 2004.

Weider, Michael. *Hazardous Materials for First Responders*. second edition. Stillwater, OK: Fire Protection Publications, Oklahoma State University, 1994.

Weimann, Gabriel. *Terror on the Internet: The New Arena, the New Challenges*. Washington, DC: United States Institute of Peace, 2006.

Index